EUGENE CARSON BLAKE

EUGENE CARSON BLAKE

PROPHET WITH PORTFOLIO

R. Douglas Brackenridge

A Crossroad Book
THE SEABURY PRESS • NEW YORK

92

B5795

7810139

1978. The Seabury Press. 815 Second Avenue. New York, N.Y. 10017

Library of Congress Cataloging in Publication Data

Brackenridge, R. Douglas.
Eugene Carson Blake, prophet with portfolio.
"A Crossroad book."
Bibliography: p.
Includes index.
1. Blake, Eugene Carson, 1906–   2. Presbyterian Church—Clergy—Biography. 3. Clergy—United States—Biography. I. Title.
BX9225.B5475B73   285'.131 [B]   77-25281   ISBN 0-8164-0383-X

To
Duncan and Anne Boss
"Catholic, Reformed, and Evangelical"

Presbyterian Historical Society Publications

This volume has been chosen to be listed in this distinguished series of books:

1. *The Presbyterian Enterprise* by M. W. Armstrong, L. A. Loetscher and C. A. Anderson (Westminster Press, 1956; Paperback reprinted for P.H.S., 1963 & 1976)
*2. *Presbyterian Ministry in American Culture* by E. A. Smith (Westminster Press, 1962)
3. *Journals of Charles Beatty, 1762–1769*, edited by Guy S. Klett (Pennsylvania State University Press, 1962)
*4. *Hoosier Zion, The Presbyterians in Early Indiana* by L. C. Rudolph (Yale University Press, 1963)
*5. *Presbyterianism in New York State* by Robert Hastings Nichols, edited and completed by James Hastings Nichols (Westminster Press, 1963)
6. *Scots Breed and Susquehanna* by Hubertis M. Cummings (University of Pittsburgh Press, 1964)
7. *Presbyterians and the Negro—A History* by Andrew E. Murray (Presbyterian Historical Society, 1966)
8. *A Bibliography of American Presbyterianism During the Colonial Period* by Leonard J. Trinterud (Presbyterian Historical Society, 1968)
9. *George Bourne and "The Book and Slavery Irreconcilable"* by John W. Christie and Dwight L. Dumond (Historical Society of Delaware and Presbyterian Historical Society, 1969)
10. *The Skyline Synod: Presbyterianism in Colorado and Utah* by Andrew E. Murray (Synod of Colorado/Utah, 1977)
11. *The Life and Writings of Francis Makemie*, edited by Boyd S. Schlenther (Presbyterian Historical Society, 1971)
12. *A Younger Church in Search of Maturity: Presbyterianism in Brazil from 1910 to 1959* by Paul Pierson (Trinity University Press, 1974)
13. *Presbyterians in the South*, Vols. II and III, by Ernest Trice Thompson (John Knox Press, 1973)
14. *Ecumenical Testimony* by John T. McNeill and James H. Nichols (Westminster Press, 1974)
15. *Iglesia Presbiteriana: A History of Presbyterians and Mexican Americans in the Southwest* by R. Douglas Brackenridge and Francisco O. Garcia-Treto (Trinity University Press, 1974)
16. *The Rise and Decline of Education for Black Presbyterians* by Inez M. Parker (Trinity University Press, 1977)
17. *Minutes of the Presbyterian Church in America, 1706–1788* edited by Guy S. Klett (Presbyterian Historical Society, 1977)
18. *Eugene Carson Blake: Prophet With Portfolio* by R. Douglas Brackenridge (The Seabury Press 1978)

* Out of Print

ACKNOWLEDGMENTS

My first personal contact with Eugene Carson Blake came in the fall of 1975. As chairman of the Oral History Committee of the Presbyterian Historical Society, I had asked Blake if he would be willing to do some interviews for the Society's new oral history collection. He agreed to meet me in New York when I came east for a board meeting of the Presbyterian Historical Society in Philadelphia.

Our initial conversation convinced me that Blake was a man of substance and personal integrity whose influence on religious history should be examined. To my surprise, I discovered that no one was engaged in serious research on his career. After returning to San Antonio, I decided to undertake writing his biography, and he indicated his willingness to cooperate in the research process by granting me extended interview time.

In fairness both to myself and to Eugene Carson Blake, however, I must emphasize that this is not an "authorized" biography. It has not been controlled by Blake or supported by the United Presbyterian Church or the World Council of Churches. Although I have been extended research courtesies by the Presbyterian Historical Society and the World Council of Churches and have received detailed and candid information from Blake himself, the structure and conclusions of the biography are my own. Blake has never asked for nor received any right of approval or rejection of my manuscript. In a few instances, he has requested confidentiality, and I have honored this trust. In my opinion, the information withheld does not affect the substance of the biography.

My analysis of Eugene Carson Blake's career unquestionably is influenced by my background and educational training, which includes a Presbyterian upbringing, study at a denominational college and seminary, and doctoral work at the University of Glasgow in Scotland. Nevertheless, I have tried to maintain a standard

En EUGENE CARSON BLAKE

of objectivity and honesty based on careful historical investigation. Even though I did not observe Blake's public career firsthand, I have during the course of my research talked both to friendly and to hostile witnesses, and I have examined Blake's vast collection of papers in Philadelphia, Pennsylvania, and Geneva, Switzerland. I also visited Blake's former pastorates in Albany, New York, and Pasadena, California. Throughout the book, I have documented the source of my information so that readers can evaluate its reliability.

Biographers foolish enough to claim that they have unlocked the door of human personality and motivation are, unfortunately, also often foolish enough to believe that what they write is always correct. I make no such claim, nor do I consider that all the ramifications of Eugene Carson Blake's career have been covered in this biography. More research should be done, for example, to evaluate his impact on the history of the United Presbyterian Church and on the World Council of Churches.

During the preparation of this biography many people have been extremely helpful to me. At the risk of omitting someone, I would like to mention the following: William B. Miller and Gerald Gillette of the Presbyterian Historical Society, Mr. Ans Van Der Bent and the staff of the World Council of Churches Library in Geneva, the friends of Dr. Blake at the First Presbyterian Church, Albany, New York, and at the Pasadena Presbyterian Church, Pasadena, California, and all those who contributed personal reminiscences of Dr. Blake in letters or on tape. To this list I would add Duncan Boss and William Gentz, who have given me encouragement and support throughout the project, and Virginia Olmo and Marcie Norman, who did the typing and checking of references. Most of all I want to thank Lois Boyd, editor of Trinity University Press, for her professional assistance and personal interest in this biography. Her criticisms, probing questions, and practical advice have helped me to identify and to articulate the major results of my research on Eugene Carson Blake.

Trinity University   R. Douglas Brackenridge
San Antonio, Texas   Department of Religion
September 1977

CONTENTS

PREFACE

"Ministers must risk being wrong rather than to be silent and safe."

In an interview with a young Roman Catholic priest in 1967, Eugene Carson Blake concluded his observations on the fundamental authority of Scripture by saying, "I consider myself conservative in many ways." The priest responded, "Doctor Blake, there are a lot of people who will find that hard to believe!"[1]

Observers of Eugene Carson Blake have tended to label him during his long career, but they have rarely called him conservative. Admirers saw him as a prophetic figure who spoke and acted boldly for social justice and human rights and as a charismatic leader of ecumenical Christianity who dedicated his life to try to unite a divided Christendom. Opponents pejoratively called him a liberal and an "ecumaniac" who was determined to create a super church based on the lowest common denominator of theological truth. While many applauded Blake's outspoken views on race, poverty, and church-state relations, detractors described him as "an ultra-liberal, soft-on-Communism, socialistic propagandist."[2] According to one religious news editor, some disgruntled church people looked out their windows on rainy, dismal days, meditated on the unsalubrious climate, and muttered, "That Blake again!"[3] At the same time, a Presbyterian elder echoed the sentiments of many of his peers when he said, "Eugene Carson Blake is always on the humane side of every issue."[4]

xi

Eugene Carson Blake cannot be described in any such positive or negative terms, for he is a complex individual. During his career, one could see the consistent interplay between his traditional theology and his institutional loyalties and his more independent qualities of individualism and involvement in controversial causes. Despite these contrasts, both friend and foe agree that one word describes Blake's public ministry and his impact on society. That word is "prophetic."

The term "prophetic" when applied to Eugene Carson Blake must be qualified. Blake did not wish to take the position of an Amos or a Jeremiah who stood apart from the hierarchy and community in order to criticize the religious establishment. Few people have been able to work so effectively within the system as Blake and simultaneously function as a critic of the status quo. Blake saw his prophetic role as one whereby he would stay within existing structures to help institutional Christianity turn theoretical ideals into actual practice. When Blake asked Presbyterians to abandon racist policies, he was calling the church to work out the practical implications of its repeated affirmation of a "non-segregated church and a non-segregated society." Blake's call for major denominations to take concrete steps toward the reunion of Christ's church was a challenge to implement decades of ecumenical rhetoric about the sin of sectarianism. In each instance Blake attempted to actualize rather than to transform community values.

Blake never knowingly tried to take the church further than it was prepared to go. "In terms of the great majority," he said, "I think I was in the middle of the road and pressing forward. I never meant to be foolhardy. I'm sure of that."[5] Although Blake experienced considerable criticism for his convictions, especially concerning social issues and ecumenism, his actions were always ratified by the highest representative body of the church as being in harmony with long-standing principles and procedures. Blake once described his blending of prophetic challenge and priestly caution in an address on how ministers should preach on controversial topics.

> It's like a football game. There are two ways for
> the man carrying the ball to be thrown for a loss.

One is for him to let his interference get too far ahead of him. The other, just as bad, is to run ahead of his interference. So in preaching on controversial areas . . . I am urging you to use a little commonsense with your convictions. Yes, I am saying that you must take account of the prejudices of your listeners. Don't run ahead of your interference. But don't drag your feet either. A consistent calm pressure for a Christian society based upon the Christian faith is what you are bound to try to exert from your pulpit. But don't be a whole loaf man. Three half loafs that you can get are more than a whole loaf anyway, especially if you can't get it.[6]

Blake's actions also should be set within the framework of his confidence in the wisdom of corporate decisions. By his own admission he is an "organization man" who has more faith in notoriously cumbersome church procedures than in independent freelance activities. In the long run, Blake thought that institutional actions were more effective than solitary dissent. He said, "The spirit speaks to a group of people gathered in faith and prayer ready to hear Him speak. The word is the final authority but the interpretation of that word is given in our Church not to a single person but to a group of Christians bound together by faith and love!"[7]

Underlying Blake's administrative and social involvement was his desire to be in the mainstream of the Protestant thought of his era. "I was an ex-fundamentalist who became neo-orthodox," he said, "and I knew what I had done."[8] Although sensitive to the need of finding new ways to restate traditional doctrines, Blake affirmed an "ecumenical consensus theology," basic truths accepted by Protestants, Orthodox, and Roman Catholics. He summarized this theology as a belief in a transcendent God who revealed Himself in Jesus Christ, knowledge of God by reading the Bible and understanding it in its historical context, and belief that God, Creator and Redeemer, is fulfilling His purposes in history. To these he added the need to review radically what

Christian action demands today in contrast to what was required in a previous generation.[9]

This consensus theology, rather than humanistic or pragmatic considerations, undergirded Blake's social concern. Blake always contended that *only because* he took traditional, orthodox Christianity seriously could he be deeply involved in and committed to social causes. He declared, "Only a theological 'conservative,' meaning one who takes seriously the good news of the transcendent God who entered into human history in Jesus Christ, His Son, can be a Christian radical in social questions. It is because the Christian is in the process of becoming a new man in Christ under the Cross, that he is able to be critical of the conservative assumptions of most men in most ordinary situations."[10] Throughout his career Blake preached the great themes of evangelical Christianity and refused to support such avant-garde movements as the death-of-God theology or Christian secularism.

Blake's adherence to ethical application of traditional theology never excluded the possibility of compromise. Compromise was a logical corollary of his belief in the efficacy of corporate decision-making processes, and Blake perfected the art of compromise during his career as a way in which the church could move forward without abandoning the basic principles of individual members. Blake was particularly skillful in explicating fundamental issues and enabling a group to reach a reasonable and honorable consensus that recognized essential values on both sides of a question.

Despite Blake's ability to accommodate to different views, he remained a fierce competitor who relished a physical, intellectual, or political contest. He also liked to win. Just as he struggled to attain a football letter at Princeton University, he later fought hard to achieve his goals and to implement his ideas. At a staff session of the World Council of Churches where most of the reports were negative and discouraging, Blake asked for some specific signs of ecumenical progress. When the response was very limited, Blake complained: "I feel like the football coach who told his team, 'I'm tired of all these moral victories. I want to go out and win a game.' "[11]

Out of self-esteem and confidence, Eugene Carson Blake was a blunt, forthright person who has always spoken his mind. A friend said that Blake "knew who he was, knew what he could do well, and was not ashamed to admit it."[12] In his work Blake could often be impatient with those who did not grasp his argument or were unable to articulate their own viewpoints. Although he rarely displayed public anger, Blake did lose his temper in private, particularly when carelessness or indifference in another person had caused some problem. He could, and still does, dominate a group discussion. Being in a group with Eugene Carson Blake, said one church executive, was "like playing Ping-pong, except Gene is the only one who has a paddle. You have to bounce the balls off his paddle."[13]

In his administrative preparation Blake was painstaking and meticulous, not casual and impromptu. Yet he was also capable of impulsive, intuitive actions. Of necessity, some of Blake's most significant decisions had to be made quickly, in tense situations with little time for examining and weighing alternatives. Inevitably Blake could supply sound theological and rational arguments in defense of his earlier spontaneous response.

Blake's confident assertiveness disguised his sensitivity and modesty. He realized when he had pushed too hard and when he needed to soften a criticism or to offer encouragement. With all his brashness, Blake has never considered himself infallible; in fact, part of his self-esteem has derived from his ability to recognize his limitations and to accept them in others. "He's a bad man to pick a fight with," commented a friend, "but I don't know anyone I'd rather turn to if I were in deep personal trouble."[14]

Blake was also not so impervious to criticism, especially attacks on his racial and ecumenical views, as he appeared to be. At times, only the prudent warnings of his close advisers kept him from responding. When church people and responsible critics opposed his positions or misunderstood his actions, Blake felt personal pain. The months after his arrest in 1963 for attempting to integrate a Baltimore amusement park were emotionally draining and stressful even though he managed to maintain a sense of perspective. "If you are to have any influence in this world," he wrote to a friend, "you must be ready to be criticized by people who don't like the direction of your influence. This I have learned to live with without letting it upset me too much. I try to listen to criticism but not worry about it."[15]

Because of his intensity and sensitivity, Blake took himself, his position, and his work extremely seriously. At the same time, however, he possessed a keen sense of humor. He enjoyed a good story and could tell one with great effectiveness. Yet Blake never had the latest joke to tell because he was always too busy to have had time to hear the latest joke. Blake's humor came more in the form of a witty remark or in his ability to see humor in a situation even when the laugh was on himself. Before his departure from the United States to assume the leadership of the World Council of Churches, Presbyterians arranged an elaborate farewell dinner for Blake at the Americana Hotel in New York. They wanted it to be a surprise but that was not really possible since they needed to be sure that the honoree would be present. Some days beforehand Blake confessed to an acquaintance that he found himself worrying about the occasion. When asked why, he said, "I guess I just can't imagine their organizing a thing of this magnitude without me."[16]

Despite Blake's affability and gregariousness, he has known loneliness. In his career he experienced the isolation which comes with making difficult decisions when only one person could be responsible for the consequences. Moreover, although Blake has listened sympathetically to his friends' problems, he has rarely ever shared his own with them. Many people know a great deal about Eugene Carson Blake's career but very few know him personally. Because of his desire to be a "private person," Blake will probably remain an enigma, even to those who know him well. Opinions about Blake as a person and his accomplishments as a pastor, stated clerk of the General Assembly, and general secretary of the World Council of Churches, vary according to individual and ideological views. Few people, however, could charge that Eugene Carson Blake failed to live by his professional credo: "Ministers must risk being wrong rather than to be silent and safe."[17]

·I·
CHILD OF A
CHRISTIAN HOME

"It is generally true that you are able to trace the genesis of a Christian man or woman back to those early influences of home and family."

November 7, 1906 was the day after an important election, when Missourians had gone to the polls to elect both local and national leaders. Many races were so close that morning newspapers could not decide if citizens had maintained the state's traditional Democratic support or had endorsed the progressive Republicanism of incumbent President Theodore Roosevelt. Under normal circumstances, Orville Prescott Blake, St. Louis steel salesman and stanch Republican, would have been deeply engrossed in election statistics. Something more significant and personal than elections, however, claimed his attention. On that particular postelection morning his wife, Lulu, gave birth to their second son, Eugene Carson Blake.

Eugene Carson Blake joined his sister, Rhea, and his brother, Howard, in what was a typical middle-class, urban family where people took both their work and their religion very seriously. O. P. Blake worked for the Inland Steel Company and at the age of thirty-six was already an executive with a promising future. Lulu Blake was a mother and housewife and also devoted time to Sunday school and missionary society responsibilities. Both O. P. and Lulu Blake were devout Christians whose spiritual life in St. Louis

1

centered around West Presbyterian Church, which they and their family faithfully attended. Eugene Carson Blake's earliest memory of his home was its distinct religious orientation.

> . . . From the earliest childhood my parents confronted me by precept and example with Jesus and the Father. I was presented at the altar for Christian baptism. One of the first things that I remember reading was that old motto which hung in the dining room: "Christ is the head of this house, the unseen guest at every meal, the silent listener to every conversation."[1]

The first decades of the twentieth century, in which Eugene Carson Blake grew up, have been called "the Progressive Era," a pivotal period of American history when political, social, economic, and religious reform captured public imagination. Theodore Roosevelt, who came to the presidency in 1901, embodied a political Progressivism which sought to regulate big business and to prevent exploitation of unwary citizens and natural resources. Religious leaders like Washington Gladden and Walter Rauschenbusch preached a "social gospel" dedicated to alleviating social ills in the context of Christian idealism and morality. Despite deep-rooted opposition to Progressivism from many quarters of society, and despite enormous and complex problems facing earnest reformers, an unshakable optimism prevailed until World War I confronted Americans with apocalyptic nightmares.[2]

In St. Louis, the very week in which Eugene Carson Blake was born, federal officials instituted action to dissolve the Standard Oil Company controlled by John D. Rockefeller. In the same week, local newspapers headlined a race riot in Atlanta, Georgia, where "Whites began to beat and kill Negroes indiscriminately" despite efforts by police to maintain law and order. A clergyman bemoaned to the press that America was suffering from "motorphobic fever," weekend touring in new-fangled automobiles, instead of going to church. His warnings of immanent moral and spiritual degradation, however, could hardly compete with an advertisement on the following page extolling the virtues of a beautiful new four-cylinder Cadillac available for immediate delivery at only $2,500. America's dominant Protestant religious ethos also surfaced in a statement from Secretary of War William Howard Taft prohibiting Sunday baseball in army camps. Taft issued the proclamation in response to an irate Arkansas minister who complained about "sabbath desecration" and threatened Taft with a moral crusade if he did not immediately suppress Sunday sports.[3]

Long before Progressivism dominated society, and Cadillacs and baseball disrupted the Sabbath calm, Eugene Carson Blake's ancestors had been part of the American scene. Early in the eighteenth century the Carsons emigrated via Scotland and Northern Ireland (Ulster) and settled in various parts of Pennsylvania. Details are sketchy but there is a family tradition that three brothers arrived about the same time and formed the nucleus of the Carson clan. Ephraim Chidester Carson, grandfather of Eugene Carson Blake, was born in Beaver County, Pennsylvania in 1832 but his family moved soon afterward to Meigs County in southern Ohio. In 1857 Ephraim Carson married Elizabeth Ewing. They had seven children, the third of whom was Lulu Carson, born on May 30, 1869 in Pomeroy, Ohio.[4]

Ephraim Carson apparently never stayed too long at any one occupation. At one time or another he worked as a carpenter, agent, machinist, mechanic, and postal clerk. During the Civil War he enlisted in the 4th Regiment of the Virginia Volunteers and was discharged in 1863 because of tuberculosis. He later mustered in 1864 as captain of the 174th Ohio Volunteers and served until the cessation of hostilities. Carson never fully recovered from his physical disability and died on October 29, 1880, only forty-eight years old. He left behind his wife, Elizabeth, and a large family of young children. Elizabeth later followed her eldest son, Winifield Scott Carson, to Kansas City, Missouri, where he and some of his brothers became railroad employees.[5]

No one in the Blake family knows exactly when their ancestors first came to America from England. Eugene Carson Blake's grandfather, Elzy Blake, was born on March 4, 1836. He later married Emma Pearson, a native of Maine who was one of the few women in the era to have studied Greek and classics at Bath Female Seminary in Maine. Elzy Blake served as a captain of a

3

Union company during the Civil War and afterward became an agent for McGuffey's Readers. He traversed the country west of the Mississippi influencing legislatures and school boards to adopt the Readers, which were written by a Presbyterian clergyman, William H. McGuffey. When Elzy Blake died in 1882 from injuries incurred in a carriage accident, a local newspaper described him as "the well-known, highly successful representative of the McGuffey Publishing House."[6]

Elzy Blake's premature death left his wife Emma with one daughter and three sons. The youngest boy, Orville Prescott Blake, was born in 1870 in the country village of Kirkwood, Missouri just outside St. Louis. Orville was just twelve years old when his father died. Even at that young age he dropped out of school and worked to help support the family.[7] After four or five years Orville Blake decided that he wanted to obtain a college education. Somehow he prepared himself to be accepted, probably with the help of his mother, Emma, who had a strong educational background.

Blake matriculated at Marietta College in southern Ohio as a candidate for a bachelor's degree. He had hoped to attend Princeton University but lack of financial resources and educational background left that dream to be fulfilled only later in the lives of his two sons, Howard and Eugene. O. P. (as he preferred to be called) worked his way through college by selling typewriters and serving as a night nurse for invalids. When he ran out of funds, he would sit out a term and work fulltime in order to build up his financial reserves. During one Christmas vacation he was a floorwalker in Kauffman's Department Store in Pittsburgh. When the manager kept postponing Blake's lunch hour because of heavy business, the independent young college student simply walked out and never went back. He graduated from Marietta College in 1892 with a fine record as a popular and active student, captain of the baseball team, and leader in the Phi Gamma Delta fraternity.[8]

Upon graduation from Marietta College, Blake signed on the crew of a cargo ship to England to visit his ancestral homeland. By selling American-made Remington typewriters he earned enough money for room and board, for travel, and for literary research in the British Museum. After about a year he returned to the United

States and became a salesman for the Kingman Implement Company in Kansas City, Missouri. At one of the local Presbyterian churches Blake met tall, dark, and strikingly attractive Lulu Carson, who was keeping house for her older brother Cassius, a recent widower with three young children. After a customary period of courtship they were married in 1896.

Shortly after the wedding Blake's supervisor called him into the office and informed him that his salary ($85 a month) was being reduced considerably. Apparently the supervisor surmised that since Blake was recently married and thus was dependent on his job, he would accept a salary cut. Blake did not accept the reduction, resigned, and returned to St. Louis. Industrious, responsible, and knowledgeable, O. P. Blake worked for several large firms until he finally established himself as a successful sales executive for the Inland Steel Company.[9]

Blake was never a stereotypical salesman who traveled around the country carrying a big canvas bag of samples. "My theory," he told his young sons, "is always sell something that is too big to carry in a sample case." Moreover, unlike many of his contemporaries who promoted sales with gifts and alcohol, Blake operated under ethical standards based on a sense of fairness and responsibility both to his company and to his customers. Whenever he learned of an impending steel rise, for instance, he immediately contacted his regular customers so that they could buy at the lower price.[10]

Blake was a family man who preferred to be at home with his wife and children in the evening. Blake enjoyed playing tiddlywinks, Parcheesi, and checkers with his children until, as the boys described it, "we got good enough to beat him." When Blake's sales responsibilities took him on the road, he frequently was accompanied by his wife and two sons even if the boys had to miss school. For Howie and Gene it meant the excitement of riding trains, collecting railroad maps and schedules, and becoming acquainted with different parts of the midwest. On one trip to Fremont, Nebraska, Gene had a memorable experience. In his haste to get the best seat in the carriage that was to take them from the depot to the hotel, he barged in first, pushed against the opposite door, and fell out onto the dusty street. Before he knew what had

5

happened, the carriage started off without him. His frantic shouts brought the carriage to a halt, however, and he was rescued, somewhat disheveled but still full of enthusiasm and energy.[11]

O. P. Blake accepted the scholastic fundamentalism that characterized much of the Presbyterian church in his day. He was a ruling elder, a Sunday school teacher, superintendent of Sunday school, president of the Men's Club, leader in Boy Scouts, and treasurer of the Synod of Missouri. Blake was asked to address the Synod of Missouri in 1916, a time when his country faced the questions of military involvement overseas and burgeoning social unrest at home. Reading from a prepared text, he spoke plainly about his Christian convictions in such confusing times.

He spoke for peace.

> We deceive ourselves with the idea that this is a Christian nation. Witness the feverish haste in which the "preparedness" program is being carried out today. More money is being expended on our Army and Navy at this time than ever before in our history. Party leaders tell us these measures are purely defensive. In defense of what? Surely we do not fear for our lives, no, but our property!

He spoke for patriotism.

> We should yield to no one in devotion to our Country when she is in the right, but NEVER in the wrong. There are sufficient Christians in America to wield the balance of power on any political question, state, national or international. Almighty God grant that we shall be led by His Spirit and not be dominated by the almighty dollar.

He spoke for the poor.

> The Master came "to seek and to save that which was lost," but we are too much inclined, in our cities, to neglect the hungry and thirsty, the stranger and the naked, the sick and those in prison. We turn the hungry and thirsty over to the Rescue Mission, the strangers and the naked to Welfare Societies, and the sick and imprisoned to the deaconesses and

6

chaplains. How much greater consideration is given to those in comfortable and affluent circumstances than to the poor and outcast?[12]

In addition to his church activities, O. P. Blake served on the Council of Municipal Voters League of St. Louis and represented the Republican Party at a number of regional conventions. Despite his Republican commitments, however, Blake crossed party lines when the party was in conflict with his principles. After reading Woodrow Wilson's State Papers in the St. Louis *Post-Dispatch*, for example, Blake twice voted for the Democratic candidate because he believed in Wilson's moral idealism.[13]

As an avocation, Blake studied Greek and classics and kept the family library stocked with a variety of works of poetry and fiction. Discussion and debate interested the father, and his appreciation of the intellectual and the literary was picked up by his children. For both Howard and Eugene, their father Orville was the primary adult model during their childhood and adolescence.[14]

Lulu Carson Blake complemented and contrasted her husband in personality traits. Like O. P., she was deeply religious and committed to traditional fundamentalist piety. Unlike O. P., her responses were often short and emotional. For example, when Eugene was a college student at Princeton, he announced to his family that he was going to vote for Al Smith. O. P. asked for some literature about Smith so that he could intelligently discuss the issues. Lulu, on the other hand, responded by saying, "Eugene, you're just plain contrary!" With that remark she ended the discussion about politics for the evening.[15]

Because her husband was frequently away from home, Lulu Blake was the disciplinarian and manager of household routines and chores. However, the Blakes did not run a very strict home. Apart from rules about Sunday observance, unquestioned by religious families, there were few regulations. And apparently there was little need for many rules. Neither Howard nor Gene Blake ever caused their parents many anxious moments with rebellious or mischievous behavior. Gene Blake recalled once as a child walking in downtown St. Louis with his mother. Ahead of them a young boy suddenly broke loose from his mother's grasp and ran off, with the mother frantically trying to catch up with him. Holding his own mother's hand, Gene looked up at her and said quizzically, "What would happen to me if I did that?" It was a rhetorical question, for the occasion for such discipline in the Blake household never arose.[16]

In a number of ways Lulu Blake made contributions to the developing character of her children. Some of Eugene Carson Blake's drive to unite a divided Christendom might well be traced to his hearing his mother relate eyewitness accounts of the tragedy and heartbreak that emerged during the Civil War when families divided, one son off to wear the Blue and another to wear the Gray.[17] In St. Louis, a city which was neither northern nor southern, Blake experienced on the playground something of the ambivalence of what an earlier generation had experienced on the battlefield.

> I well remember snowy mornings in the boys yard of the public school, the cry would go up, "Here's North!" to be echoed by other small boys, "Here's South!" and at once a snow ball battle would be engaged. The battle would be hard fought until the nine o'clock bell summoned us all obediently to class, marching two by two in formal lines, ex-Yank and ex-Rebel marching mates and friends again.[18]

Lulu Blake's attitudes also reinforced some of her son's earliest misgivings about the anti-Semitism that he saw in society, even as a child. Later he would tell one of his congregations:

> I find myself prejudiced in favor of the Jewish people, their kindness, their loyalty, their friendliness. . . . As I have wondered why, I remember that there was a Jewish neighbor in my earliest days who was exceptionally kind to my mother. I absorbed my mother's thankfulness almost before I knew what a Jew was. It is these earliest influences that have made us what we are.[19]

Their mother's interest in foreign missions also made an impression on her two sons. As a leader in the Southwest Foreign Missions Board, Lulu Blake often provided hospitality for visiting missionaries and teachers. A frequent guest was Dr. Samuel Higginbottom, founder of the Allahabad Agricultural Institute in India, who captivated the Blake boys with exciting adventure stories of a land beyond the seas. So strong was the emphasis on foreign missions in the Blake household that young Gene had the distinct impression that his mother thought that people who worked in local or national missions were not fully Christian! Both he and Howard entertained ideas of becoming foreign missionaries and following in the steps of David Livingstone or Mary Slessor.[20]

In addition to his parents, Eugene Carson Blake also had a close and lasting relationship with his brother Howard and his sister Rhea. Rhea was only three months old when her mother died. She was cared for by her Aunt Lulu, who was then still single. After Lulu and Orville Blake married in 1896, they adopted Rhea. Because she was thirteen years older than Gene, Rhea was away at college or working during his childhood and adolescent years. Nevertheless, Gene remembers his sister tutoring him in French and trying unsuccessfully to teach him to sing on tune. She was a great storyteller and fascinated the boys with tales both true and fanciful. After she left home for college, Howard and Gene looked forward to her vacations, especially because they enjoyed meeting her many friends and acquaintances who came to the Blake household when she was in residence. With her artistic skills and competence in the classics, Rhea set a high standard of scholarship for her brothers. After graduation she became one of the first occupational therapists in the country, with the Veterans Administration in Oteen, North Carolina and West Haven, Connecticut.

Howard was nearly three years older than Eugene and was a brilliant, serious-minded student who also set high standards for his brother. From an early age Howard considered the possibility of full-time Christian service, and he shared his thoughts and hopes with Eugene, who naturally applied much of the discussion to his own life. Howard's decision to enter Princeton Seminary in preparation for the Presbyterian ministry was a major factor in Gene's decision to follow the same vocation.[21]

Beyond these influences was a good-natured sibling rivalry, with the younger brother always trying to catch up with his older brother and his friends. From bicycling to baseball, from Bible to biology, from geometry to Greek, Gene always seemed to come in second to Howard. His brother's superior intellectual achievements even followed him to Princeton University. Gene's Greek professor at Princeton once called him up after class and said, "I will give you an 'A,' Mr. Blake. You are a very good Greek scholar." However, he added, "But not as good as your brother."[22] Even though Blake graduated *cum laude* from Princeton, he could not match Howard's Phi Beta Kappa key and valedictorian standing in the class of 1924; nevertheless, he tried to excel in all that he did.

While home and family influences were major factors in molding Eugene Carson Blake's character, the local Presbyterian church was important, too. Going to church was a normal routine for the Blakes, and prayer, Bible study, and catechizing were part of their everyday life. "Even now," said Howard Blake, "I still know what 'effectual calling' is." And as Gene Blake once commented, "Although you modify some of the ideas and practices as you mature, it's the basic commitment that stays with you."[23]

While the Blakes lived in St. Louis, their home church was West Presbyterian Church, a U.S.A. Presbyterian congregation at the corner of Maple and Maryville Avenue. The boys passed it every day on their way to school and were on friendly terms with the pastor, Dr. Francis W. Russell, and his family. Largely through Russell's influence, the Blakes also attended fundamentalist summer conferences where well-known speakers clarified doctrines taught in the local church. One of Eugene Carson Blake's childhood memories was the trip east in 1916 to Stony Brook, New York, when they covered over 1,200 miles of unimproved roads in their new Hudson Super-Six.[24]

Both Howard and Eugene Blake joined West Presbyterian Church at an early age and were among the growing number of young people from the congregation who pursued full-time ministries.[25] Two brief letters, tucked away in a family scrapbook, testify to the seriousness with which both Howard and Eugene took their obligations to West Presbyterian Church. Both boys asked their father for money to give to the church.

10

Dear Pop,

> I want to ask you for some money.
> You owe me 90¢ on July's allowance
> and $1.55 on August's which makes
> $2.45, besides my church dues
> which are $2.00 to Mrs. Jackes,
> and my envelopes. I wish you
> would pay the church and send
> $2.45 to me.

> Lovingly,
>
> Howard

In the same envelope Eugene penned his own note to father, not quite so sophisticated as Howard's but equally effective.

Dear Pop,

> I hope it is not hot in old St.
> Louis today. It has been cool here
> every day since you left except
> today.

> Lovingly,
>
> Eugene

P.S.   Pop, Please send me $2.50 for the same reason of Howard's.[26]

Both Howard and Eugene joined an informal Bible study group consisting of the Blake brothers and three other children who cycled every Friday afternoon after school to the home of Miss Madeleine Bushman. There they memorized Scripture and developed a familiarity with the contents of the Bible that remained with them permanently. "I learned much of what I know about the Bible from Miss Bushman," said Gene Blake in recalling the congenial group of avid biblical scholars.[27]

In Blake's home, religious belief and practice were part of the daily routine, but none of the three children felt any direct

11

pressure from their parents concerning religion. Rhea Blake said, "We were raised to be Christians—not really Presbyterians— because there was no attempt made to drum particular doctrines into our heads."[28] Nevertheless, it was obvious to the children that O. P. and Lulu had found the meaning of life in the church. Eugene Carson Blake said, "We wanted to be part of that context."[29]

· II ·
STUDENT WITH
RELIGIOUS PRIORITIES

"I decided that I was going to trust God and that religion was not going to be a problem for me anymore. . . . From that time forward, God has not been a problem for me, though the intellectual questions never stop."

Eugene Carson Blake celebrated his twelfth birthday less than a week before the Armistice was signed ending World War I. Most of his formative years, therefore, were spent in a revolutionary new America where traditional manners and morals were rapidly changing. The "roaring twenties" brought jazz, speakeasies, gang wars, and a booming prosperity that multiplied material goods and weakened religious and moral sanctions. Popular appropriations of insights derived from John Dewey and Sigmund Freud made "self-expression" and "self-realization" watchwords of the day. Literary figures like Sinclair Lewis, H. L. Mencken, and Scott Fitzgerald made a frontal attack on America's "puritanism" and dismissed religion as antiquated, false, and absurd, a blend of prudery, cant, and sanctimoniousness. People seemed to be less sin-ridden and more self-indulgent, and many agreed, privately at least, with what Mencken so effectively insisted: "Doing good" was either a dull business or "in bad taste."[1]

Churches were not untouched by this shift in the mood of the American people. The Social Gospel movement declined rapidly after World War I and mainline Protestant denominations found themselves caught up in a modernist-fundamentalist controversy that threatened to destroy the witness and integrity of American Christianity. The obscurantism, violent language, and "smear" tactics that characterized so much of the religious struggle received national attention in the famous "monkey trial" at Dayton, Tennessee in 1925 when Clarence Darrow and William Jennings Bryan fought an inconclusive battle over biblical literalism and evolution. Another world war would come along before schismatic controversy died down and denominations turned to face an entirely different set of problems.[2]

Blake's varied early education reflected the change and uncertainty of the times. In St. Louis he attended Dozier Elementary and Ben Blewett Junior High schools. When World War I broke out, his father was called to Washington, D.C. as a dollar-a-year man to stimulate steel production for defense purposes. Eugene attended school there one year. Following the war the Blakes moved to Bronxville, New York, where O. P. Blake served the Presbyterian Board of Church Extension for a short time. The elder Blake then returned to Inland Steel and accepted an executive position in the company's Chicago headquarters. From 1919 to 1921 the Blakes resided in the suburb of Winnetka, Illinois and Blake attended the progressive New Trier School, modeled after the parent institution in Germany. The curriculum at New Trier was unstructured, with students encouraged to explore and to develop new interests. Blake took specialized courses in South American and Latin American history and learned French in a class where the teacher never spoke a word of English. He flourished in the openness and individuality of New Trier but admitted in retrospect that it made it difficult for him when he had to adjust to more traditional educational methods at prep school and the university.[3]

Blake completed his formal education prior to college by attending the Lawrenceville School in Lawrenceville, New Jersey (1921–24), an interdenominational prep school that specialized in preparing young men for entrance into nearby Princeton and other Ivy League universities. Initially Blake had intended to stay at Lawrenceville only two years and then enroll at Princeton University. His brother Howard had followed the same procedure, however, and had discovered that he was not socially or physically mature enough to benefit fully from university life. Howard persuaded his parents to let Eugene spend an extra year at Lawrenceville and enter Princeton in the fall of 1924. His brother's suggestion provided an extra year of intellectual, social, and physical maturation for Blake, which proved to be valuable for his classroom and athletic activities at Princeton.[4]

At Lawrenceville two teachers in particular helped Blake consider his values and vocational goals. One was Thornton Wilder, at that time a French teacher and literary club adviser, later to become an eminent playwright and novelist; and the other was Leslie Glenn, housemaster and mathematics professor. Wilder came to Lawrenceville in 1921 from an extended stay in Europe where he had studied archeology at the American Academy in Rome. He was unenthusiastic about his role as French teacher ("absurd French exercises corrected and indignantly marked with red crayon") but did enjoy his assignment as adviser to the literary club.[5] Wilder's writing career was ahead of him, but even in these early days he wrote short plays and queried his students about their intellectual, social, and religious backgrounds. Blake saw in Wilder's novel, *Heaven's My Destination*, a reflection of impressions of midwest religious fundamentalism that Wilder had gleaned from his Lawrenceville students. The central figure of the novel is George Brush, a pious schoolbook salesman who traverses the midwest dispensing theological clichés and platitudes and simultaneously reveals a simple admirable moral integrity and spiritual consciousness.[6]

Wilder pushed Blake to look beyond the limited horizons of his childhood world, to ask questions, to enlarge his literary and esthetic interests, and to take a critical look at his religious presuppositions. Perhaps because Wilder himself came from a devout Christian family (his mother was the daughter of a prominent Presbyterian clergyman), he could communicate to his students a sincere religious faith that, however, went beyond denominational labels and theological postulates. Although Wilder disclaimed any didactic purposes in his writing, he was very conscious that his era resisted writings of "religious" tendencies and openly declared that it was precisely in this vein that he "would most like to do well."[7] From Wilder, Blake began to appreciate something that he would understand even better when he became acquainted with the writing of William Temple: "God is interested in more things than religion."[8]

Leslie Glenn, a graduate engineer, influenced Blake more by his example than by his ideas. Glenn remembered the algebra class where Gene Blake was a "bright, eager child sitting in the front row who was always first to answer questions."[9] But it was outside class that Glenn made his greatest impact on Blake. During Blake's years at Lawrenceville, Glenn wrestled with the personal decision of entering the Episcopal ministry or continuing his career as a teacher. As Glenn debated his vocational future he shared some of his thoughts with Blake and other students. Blake still remembers Glenn's counsel that the most important element in any personal decision is to be honest with yourself and do what you really want to do. Otherwise you will always be unhappy no matter how successful you eventually become. Glenn finally resigned his post at Lawrenceville and studied for the ministry. His example was a positive factor later when Blake faced a similar choice between academic and pastoral careers.[10]

By the time that Blake had completed prep school in the spring of 1924 he had already in orderly fashion outlined the major goals he hoped to attain during his career at Princeton University. First of all, he aspired toward continued academic excellence and scholarly achievement. His brother Howard had earned a Phi Beta Kappa key in his junior year, so Blake intended to settle for nothing less than that. Second, he decided that he would be active in campus religious activities because of his inclinations toward the ministry and because it would perhaps help clarify some of his religious questions. Finally, he determined to excel in athletics. Tall, broad-shouldered, and muscular, Blake had already demonstrated proficiency in a number of sports in high school and prep school. He lacked the speed necessary to become a superstar but he had enough confidence in his abilities to think that he could become a solid performer, especially on the gridiron.[11]

Blake's interest in athletics began in childhood when his parents took him to see the St. Louis Browns and Cardinals play baseball.

Whenever possible he was outdoors playing baseball, football, and tennis. He also enjoyed cycling, swimming, and running, although in the latter he soon found that his mind worked faster than his feet. Although his playmates in St. Louis used to call him "Spider" because of his size and build, by the time he reached his teens he had become a robust six-footer. At New Trier High School in Chicago, he joined the swimming team and specialized in the "plunge for distance." With hard practice he could go almost sixty feet in one minute. Recounting events some fifty years later it still seemed to bother him that he never quite made the entire sixty feet. He played football and baseball at Lawrenceville but gave up baseball after suffering a broken collarbone.[12]

In the fall of 1924 Blake was one of the most enthusiastic candidates for the freshman football squad who ever set foot on the practice field. It was a discouragement, therefore, when the coach dropped him from the squad because he lacked the speed or size needed by an interior lineman. But Blake wasn't ready to admit defeat. He joined the intramural squad, worked hard, and managed later on in the season to get back on the frosh roster. His position on the squad was so precarious, however, that in order to participate in the traditional game with Yale he had to pay his own railfare to New Haven.[13]

His athletic fortunes did not improve much during the next two years. In his sophomore year Blake established himself as a steady performer at guard whenever he broke into the lineup. At the end of the season five guards received varsity letters. Blake was number six. In his junior year he improved to where he was number three guard on the team and played in most varsity games. However, he did not participate in the Yale or Harvard games, which in those days was an essential criterion in earning a varsity letter. In those games that year the coach substituted only in the case of injury, and, unfortunately for Blake, the number one and two guards played without a scratch.[14]

Finally, in his senior year, Eugene Carson Blake became a starting guard on the varsity squad, played in every game and won the elusive "P" that had been his goal. In addition, he received honorable mention on several All-Eastern teams and won the coveted Poe Cup awarded annually for sportsmanship and "good moral

17

character." The only discouraging note of the year was that Princeton missed an undefeated season by losing its last game when Yale scored in the closing moments of the contest. Ironically, it was the only game that Orville Blake, who had come all the way from Kansas City, ever saw his son play. Looking back on his athletic career, Blake reminisced, "I have never been an instant success anywhere, but I am competitive and persistent."[15]

While Blake always derived satisfaction from his athletic accomplishments, he was reluctant to use his athletic prowess as a means of furthering his academic or ecclesiastical career. He refused to be exhibited or exploited as a "Christian" athlete but did maintain his interest in sports by part-time and volunteer coaching and a regular regime of exercise including badminton, tennis, and golf. Later in life when he spoke at athletic banquets Blake always emphasized the benefits of hard, intercollegiate competition and frequently concluded with his own personal philosophy:

> Football after all is a game. But it is a good game. MY PRIN-
> CIPLE IS: "If you choose to play, contend to the uttermost."
> And that lesson, if you learn it, is perhaps the best thing
> football can teach you.[16]

Despite the same persistence and determination that he displayed on the athletic field, Blake's goal of achieving a Phi Beta Kappa key at Princeton eluded him. He almost attained the necessary qualifications but a low grade in an elective architecture class and several marginal examination scores eliminated him from consideration. Possibly the effort given to athletics limited his time and energy but Blake never offered this as an excuse. Nevertheless, Blake received an excellent education at Princeton University as an undergraduate student and found that it prepared him well for graduate work and an ecclesiastical career.[17]

Blake recalls several Princeton professors who influenced him. From history professor Dana Carlton Monroe, Sr., he learned to examine primary sources before consulting secondary materials. Monroe once told his medieval history class: "Gentlemen, you have read every contemporary document about the medieval university; everything else you will ever read is based upon these sources."[18] Blake applied Monroe's advice as an administrator, a pastor, and a newspaper reader. Whenever possible he tried to get his information directly from the source rather than listening to what someone else interpreted or surmised the information to be. For instance, he read the New York *Times* from back to front, that is, direct accounts first, then the interpretive reporting. From Professor George Priest, Blake had his political presuppositions challenged. Priest's liberal, Democratic viewpoint was in contrast to Blake's more conservative, Republican upbringing and caused Blake to look more carefully at both sides of any political question. It was Priest's influence that caused Blake to announce his support of Al Smith in the 1928 election much to the surprise of his Republican parents.[19]

However, if any one Princeton professor can be singled out as having changed the direction of Blake's life, it would be Theodore Meyer Greene, a young assistant philosophy professor who later had a distinguished career at Yale and Stanford. Through Greene's influence Blake changed his major from classics to philosophy and expanded his studies to include esthetics, art, and art criticism. Philosophy with its emphasis on ideas and logic stimulated and sharpened Blake's naturally keen sense of analysis and evaluation.[20]

In a broader sense Greene gave Blake an understanding liberal education. Blake frequently quoted Greene:

> He [Greene] said a liberal education should enable a man or a woman to distinguish a stone, a statue, a dog, a man, and God and to know the proper or requisite response to each. A man who used a fine bit of sculpture for a doorstop (instead of a stone) is not well educated. A woman who treats her dog better than her neighbor down the street is uneducated. But most important of all, an education which does not teach men how to know God and properly to respond to Him is no education.[21]

In addition to his academic and athletic endeavors, Blake devoted considerable time and energy to constructing a personal religious philosophy and participating in campus religious activities.

19

Since traditional religion was not fashionable in the twenties, especially on a college campus, Blake found little support. Many of his fellow students and some of his professors were either hostile or indifferent to Christian theology and ethics. For example, Blake attended an ethics course taught by Professor Warner Fite, who let students know that they would have to "fight" to defend any Christian values in discussions or examinations. Because Blake was not willing to abandon his basic Christian commitments, he realized that he would have to look beyond formal educational structures to seek answers to some of his religious questions and to experience a sense of Christian fellowship.[22]

Outside the classroom Blake found the services at the First Presbyterian Church, where Dr. Charles R. Erdman was interim pastor, spiritually enlightening and stimulating. He also attended the university chapel when someone interesting was scheduled to preach. It was there he first heard Reinhold Niebuhr. Most of Blake's religious activity, however, centered on the Philadelphian Society, a vigorous Student Christian Movement group. One of the graduate staff members of this group was Howard Blake. Under the auspices of the Student Christian Movement, Blake frequently went on preaching missions to nearby churches, missions, and correctional schools. Although officially nondenominational, the Philadelphian Society on Princeton's campus was strongly influenced by Dr. Frank Buchman and his First Century Christian Fellowship, later known as Moral Rearmament.[23]

Buchman was a Lutheran clergyman who had become discouraged with the inability of traditional churches to be genuine agents of personal renewal. He was influenced by a personal religious experience in which he recognized pride as the major stumbling block in his religious growth. He then set out to share his life-changing discovery with others. His movement stressed personal discipline—prayer, Bible study, quiet time and witness, communicating to others what conversion to Christ really means.[24] The First Century Christian Fellowship gained momentum in the early 1920s by featuring "houseparties," usually held at a country inn, hotel, or private residence where young people came together to confess their sins and to deepen their religious insights. Many collegians of that era participated in Buchman's programs and found them to be life-changing experiences. One Princeton student wrote:

> First Century Christian Fellowship is no new sect of Religion, but simply a group of people who believe in the Bible, and believe in the possibility of a fully surrendered Christian life such as the early church taught. . . . It was not until someone cut like a knife and laid bare the unsurrendered sin of my own life and made me face life on Christ's absolute standards—not the relative standards of convention—that I began in any sense to live the *maximum* Christian life.[25]

Initially Blake had no qualms about the movement and participated enthusiastically in its activities. He attended houseparties where he was challenged by Sam Shoemaker, Ray Purdy, and others to verbalize and internalize his commitment to Christ which formerly he had taken for granted. But gradually Buchman's theory of "guidance" began to bother Blake. He attended several meetings where group members sat in a large circle and sought direction from the Holy Spirit for the day's agenda. From Blake's perspective, it appeared that everyone was a little vague about what should be done until it came to Buchman. Then he always appeared to have very specific "guidance," which the others readily followed. Blake critically questioned if Buchman's wishes were being identified with the leading of the Holy Spirit.[26]

Blake's final break with Buchman was triggered by his disagreement with the leader over a specific issue of "guidance." Buchman sent Blake a telegram announcing that he had "guidance" that Blake should bring his clubmate, John D. Rockefeller III, to meet Queen Marie of Romania in New York. Blake wired Buchman back a sharp negative reply that it might be Buchman's "guidance" to do this but that it was not Eugene Carson Blake's. "From then on," Blake recalled, "I decided to be an organization man—that is to work through the regular machinery of the organized church. I recognized the importance of voluntary groups but decided to concentrate on supporting and changing existing ecclesiastical structures."[27]

This decision led to an even more difficult one for the Princeton junior who was president-elect of the Philadelphian Society. President John G. Hibben of Princeton University, who was disturbed about Buchman's influence on campus religious activities, issued a directive forbidding the Philadelphian Society to have any dealings with the First Christian Century Fellowship or with Buchman personally. All of the Philadelphian Society's staff members, including Howard Blake who was then studying at Princeton Theological Seminary, resigned their positions in a demonstration of loyalty to Buchman and his principles. Although his friends urged Blake to join them, he remained firm in his decision to stay with the Society and to serve out his term as president.[28]

This decision, which Blake later termed his "first adult decision," meant the rupturing of many close personal friendships. It also marked the first time that he and his brother Howard had differed on any major issue. Although they maintained the bond of affection that had existed between them since childhood, after this they communicated with each other infrequently as their careers developed in different directions. Eugene Carson Blake saw this experience of making a choice in the face of ambiguous evidence and ambivalent feelings as having influenced many of his later judgments as pastor and administrator.[29]

In the midst of the Philadelphian Society controversy, Blake underwent what he later called a "conversion experience," which was a volitional and intellectual decision to serve God. He made this decision during his senior year at a Christian conference held at Northfield where a generation before Blake, Dwight L. Moody once preached and where Robert F. Speer and others received their missionary inspiration. He recounted the event for the readers of *Presbyterian Life* in 1966.

> I decided that I was going to trust God and that religion was not going to be a problem for me anymore; that I was committed by faith to God in Christ. I was not going to let my intellectual doubts throw me out of the church nor was I going to let the dead hand of tradition guide me when I thought it was wrong. If God would use me, I would try to be obedient. . . . From that time forward, God has not been

a problem for me—though the intellectual questions never
stop—but rather He has been the One upon whom my life
has rested.[30]

Having resolved these issues, Blake continued to put together
the pieces of his theological position. However, when he graduated
from Princeton University in the spring of 1928, he still had not
made a final decision about his vocational future. During his senior
year he had committed himself to attend seminary and to enter the
Christian ministry. What form that ministry would take remained
uncertain, and to give him more time to consider possibilities, he
decided to defer his seminary course and go out as a short-term
missionary teacher in one of the many Presbyterian institutions
overseas.[31]

Blake's decision to try mission teaching came about through
Professor Greene's encouragement. Greene himself had taught at
Forman College in India and thought that his protégé needed to
see something of the world and to have first-hand experience with
missionary life. Primarily through Greene's contacts, Blake received a three-year appointment to teach English, philosophy, and
Bible at the Forman Christian College in Lahore, India (now Pakistan), beginning in the fall of 1928. In addition to these assignments
Blake also taught boxing, cross-country, and served as adviser to
the literary society.[32]

The Forman Christian College derived its name from Charles
W. Forman, a Presbyterian missionary who came to Calcutta in
1848 and opened a school the following year at Lahore. After
initial setbacks, the enrollment grew from a modest fifteen students in 1886 to more than one thousand when Blake arrived in
1928. Blake had some of his initial enthusiasm about missionary
teaching dampened even before he arrived on the Forman campus.
On the train from Bombay to Lahore, Blake fell into conversation
with a sophisticated Englishman who freely gave his opinion about
everything from the Sikh rebellions to Mahatma Gandhi. When it
came to religion, he spoke very bluntly: "I can stand Americans,"
he said, "and I can stand missionaries, but when you put the two
together they're very difficult to take."[33]

Nevertheless, Blake entered enthusiastically into the varied responsibilities of mission teaching. He quickly learned that he could not communicate English and philosophy effectively to students who came from totally different backgrounds. After a few weeks he asked one of his brightest students how he thought classes were going. "Very well, sir, very well indeed. Of course, most of the students haven't understood anything yet! He then described how Blake's rapid-fire American accent was unintelligible to students whose ears were tuned to receive a proper refined British accent. Being polite and deferential to their teacher, however, they had not complained. Blake then started his lectures over-slowly.[34]

Colleagues at Forman remembered Blake as an energetic and cooperative teacher who related well to students and did his best to understand and to live within the new cultural milieu. Not long after he started teaching, some Princeton graduates on the faculty wanted to form an unofficial Princeton alumni club. Blake demurred, not wanting to emphasize parochial interests in a context that called for a more catholic outlook.[35] E. D. Lucas, college principal, in whose home Blake lived during his stay at Lahore, said, "Whatever Gene did, whether playing a game, teaching a class, or going on a sightseeing trip, he did it with his whole heart. He did not carry the weight of past achievements, nor worry about future possibilities—he lived life fully at the point he had reached."[36]

The college was some distance from the old city, so students and short-termers used bicycles to get back and forth, but this was too slow for Blake. He shopped around and found a second-hand motorcycle that would provide economical and rapid transportation. He had never ridden a motorcycle before and was not familiar with roads and traffic regulations, but Blake took off with only perfunctory driving instructions. The inevitable accident soon occurred. Swerving to avoid a small cart in front of him, he crashed into a steel guidewire and upended his machine. Fortunately he suffered only minor bruises and cuts. Although friends urged him to sell his motorcycle and join the bicycle riders, Blake refused to be mastered by a machine and he stayed at it until he became an expert rider.[37]

Blake's year at Lahore convinced him that he did not want to make missionary teaching a career. His experiences there were formative, however, for the contact with a different culture illustrated the dangers of making judgments solely on western perspectives. Thus Blake began to develop a more universal concept of religious knowledge, which provided him a basis for dialogue with people of other faiths and traditions.[38]

Blake's decision to leave the Forman Christian College after only one year was motivated by events unrelated to missionary teaching. For some time he had been in love with Valina Gillespie, a petite, attractive native of Stamford, Connecticut, whom he had met while attending summer religious meetings at Stony Brook Conference grounds. Although Valina was a number of years older than Blake, they discovered that they had similar interests and religious backgrounds. Throughout his year in India the couple kept up correspondence and finally decided to marry. Blake secured permission to be released from his teaching contract in the spring of 1929 and met Valina Gillespie and her family in London in late May. After some touring in Britain, they returned to the United States and were married in the chapel of the Stony Brook School by the Reverend Ford C. Ottman on September 12, 1929.[39]

Following their marriage Eugene and Valina sailed for Scotland where Blake planned to do at least one year of theological study at New College, Edinburgh. His original plan was to take a full three-year course at Princeton Theological Seminary. He altered this, however, because Princeton Seminary was then in the midst of a fundamentalist-modernist controversy that had divided both students and faculty and had caused friction and dissent throughout the denomination. Blake reasoned that Princeton would not be a good setting at that time to begin theological training. He chose instead to study abroad at New College, a school rich in Presbyterian theological scholarship and free from fraternal discord.[40]

At Edinburgh the Blakes had an attractive apartment near the castle with a magnificent view across Princes Street Gardens. They entertained frequently and had afternoon tea with faculty, students, and new friends. Blake did exceptionally well in his studies. He and Park Johnson, the only two American undergraduates at New College, walked off with all the class honors much to the chagrin of Scottish students who thought of Americans as activists rather than as scholars. Johnson and Blake also participated in a rugby match against the Auld Kirk Divinity Hall even though they had never played the sport before. New College won and there were complaints from the Auld Kirk side that "those Americans play rough."[41]

Blake's year at Edinburgh was a formative period in his theological career. "At Edinburgh," he said, "I found that you could be a warm evangelical and still have had a decent education and use your mind. This was the first place I'd ever encountered this atmosphere. It gave me real freedom to be myself."[42] Blake found in Hugh Ross Mackintosh, professor of Systematic Theology, a kindrid spirit whose spiritual pilgrimage as a young man paralleled that which the young American was then undergoing. Born in 1870, in the same year as Blake's father, and raised in a traditional Calvinistic context, Mackintosh had his faith severely shaken by exposure to biblical criticism at several German universities where he studied. Faced with the alternatives of fundamentalism or liberalism he rejected both and developed his own synthesis, which combined elements from both positions. He accepted the historical-critical approach to biblical documents without rejecting biblical authority and heralded the return of an intellectually respectable biblical theology that anticipated in some respects the dialectical theology of Karl Barth.[43]

Blake and Mackintosh had a relationship of mutual appreciation and affection. Blake admired Mackintosh's ability to combine critical inquiry, biblical faith, and professorial authority with personal concern. On the other side, Blake impressed Mackintosh as a student who had originality, independence, and the ability to examine theological problems carefully before arriving at any conclusions. He repeatedly encouraged Blake to consider graduate work and become a seminary professor.

A representative example of Blake's work for Mackintosh was a paper entitled, "The Idea of God Underlying *The Westminster Confession:* Is It Christlike?" Blake began by carefully expositing the basic Westminster concepts of God as ultimately good and merciful. As long as the Westminster Divines remained positive and centered on Christian experience, Blake argued, their Confession presented a believable picture of God. However, when they let their metaphysics and logic lure them from experience, they produced an entirely different concept of God, one which Blake personally could not accept because it detracted from the centrality of divine love. Logic led the Westminster theologians to evolve a picture of the deity as implacable and capricious, in Blake's thinking.

> It is hardly necessary to ask if this latter idea of God is Christ-like. Although it may be ever so strongly bulwarked by proof texts, we know that in seeing the mind of Christ in the gospels, and, if you wish, supported by other-proof texts, we may be sure that this idea of God is foreign to Christ.[44]

Yet Blake did not end his treatise on a negative note. Having criticized the Confession for its erroneous deductions from essential truths, Blake felt free to conclude by arguing that the idea of God underlying the Westminster Confession was essentially Christlike and, properly interpreted, a worthy and acceptable symbol of faith. Not surprisingly his analysis of the problem followed guidelines set forth by his mentor, Mackintosh, who commented on Blake's paper: "An admirably clear and strong paper," and gave him an A+.[45]

Blake also saw in Mackintosh not only an exciting, positive teacher but an exemplary churchman and preacher as well. At every possible opportunity he heard Mackintosh preach and found him to be a simple, effective speaker who could take profound theological principles and translate them into language that the average person could understand. He always warned his students never to be abstract preachers and make the mistake of substituting theology, or dogmatics as he called it, for personal faith and commitment to God. "There is only one excuse for dogmatics," he used to say. "Good dogmatics are necessary to drive out bad dogmatics."[46]

Blake reflected his appreciation of Mackintosh's approach in a paper written in the fall of 1929 entitled, "The Bearing of Dogmatics and Preaching on Each Other."

> It is advisable for every preacher to know enough Dogmatics to be sure he is not naively preaching an inconsistent system of doctrine to an already muddled people. Dogmatics is a

> necessary discipline to keep the preacher from teaching the
> incredible and exhorting to that which cannot be performed.
> . . . Entirely too many preachers plead and argue for a faith
> that is not understood either by their people or themselves. It
> would be better, I am sure, to outline quietly a credible and
> understandable systematic statement of the Christian faith
> than to try to argue for a nebulous Christian system as against
> an even more nebulous (in the average preacher's mind)
> mechanistic view of life.[47]

The Blakes ended their year in Scotland and returned to the
United States in time to take up residence in Princeton for the fall
semester, 1930, at Princeton Theological Seminary. After the
freedom and excitement of New College, Blake began to feel
hemmed in by the doctrinal and philosophical rigidity of some of
his professors at Princeton Seminary. Fortunately, from his perspective, he had taken a great many courses in apologetics and
theology at New College and therefore had few such requirements
at Princeton. "It was just as well," he said, "because I would have
been rebelling at what was then being taught at Princeton."[48]

Even so, Blake could not avoid at least one confrontation over
theological presuppositions. Assigned to write a paper on the two
natures of Christ (human and divine), Blake first explained and
concurred with the classical, Chalcedonian understanding of this
christological mystery. But he did not stop there. He argued that it
was the obligation of every theologian to distinguish between the
truth of this doctrine and the philosophical form in which the
doctrine was cast.

> I think even the most orthodox believer in the inspiration of
> the scripture would be bound to admit that of necessity the
> truth of the fact of Jesus' being truly God would have to have
> been expressed by the Holy Spirit through men in terms of
> First Century conceptions. There is a long road of philo-
> sophical and metaphysical development between that day and
> this. . . . My position might be stated: It is evident that the
> New Testament represents Christ as God in the most ulti-
> mate terms that could be used in the First Century; but I also,
> with my new philosophical terms which are to me and my

day most ultimate, endeavor to express the same truth. If I do less, I would run the serious risk of presenting to the present age a picture of the Person of Christ far less adequate than the First Century terminology gave to the believer of the First Century.[49]

In developing his thesis Blake illustrated historically how other great theologians had moved on from earlier philosophies to express theological concepts in new terms. Much to the professor's chagrin, Blake noted that such famous Princeton luminaries as James McCosh and Benjamin B. Warfield had done the same thing. After grading the paper in "Group 2 on its merits," Blake's professor appended a note which read in part:

> I thoroughly disagree with you in your idea that the form and content of truth can thus be separated. . . . If what we hold true today must be changed in form some centuries hence—it is not truth today. . . . In short, the logic of your position to me would lead to absolute scepticism.[50]

For Blake this encounter symbolized his frustration at a seminary where his ideas frequently were at loggerheads with some of the men he most respected. They deemed him heading for "absolute scepticism" and he saw them as advocating an a priori philosophical straitjacket which ultimately impugned human reason and made effective communication of the gospel impossible. Writing in *The Christian Scholar*, Blake recalled the incident.

> The extreme to which this went is illustrated by a teacher for whom I once wrote an essay on the two natures of Christ. He gave me more than a passing grade upon it but was horrified at the thesis I had developed in trying to express the truth of the church's doctrine in the metaphysics of our own time— which I had been studying in college. When I pressed him for an answer to my real question as to what philosophy I should have used, he finally indicated that it was his opinion that the metaphysics taught by James McCosh at Princeton University in the late 19th century was the metaphysics that really was implied in the inspired scriptures. It is no wonder that

ministers trained under this kind of theology have not distinguished themselves intellectually in the world church.[51]

Blake acknowledged that Princeton Seminary did instruct him
well in what the Presbyterian church historically taught and gave
him a good grasp of his denomination's prevailing theological temperament. Moreover, he appreciated the keen minds and supporting spirits of his professors: Armstrong, Blackwood, Erdman,
Loetscher, Donnelly, and Stevenson. At Princeton Seminary also
he sharpened his skills in pulpit oratory. Public-speaking instruc-
tor Donald Wheeler was a perfect mimic, and before the days of
tape recorders and video tapes, this was a valuable talent. Many
times he corrected Blake for careless enunciation and improper emphasis and interpretation of literary passages. Years later when
Blake was guest preacher at the Chapel of Pomona College in
Southern California, Wheeler and Theodore Greene attended the
service. At the conclusion, Wheeler complimented Blake on his
message but added, "You were good but you misread your text."
He then proceeded to mimic Blake and point out his mistake.[52]

When Blake graduated from Princeton Theological Seminary in
the spring of 1932, he realized that he could not be comfortable
with either liberalism or fundamentalism as they were then being
defined in scholarly theological circles. The former, he thought,
did not take the Bible seriously enough, and the latter leaned
dangerously toward obscurantism. While Blake understood the
extremes he was rejecting, he still had not been able to formulate
to his own satisfaction an intermediate position. He continued to
search for a theological perspective that would enable him to take
Scripture and doctrine seriously but not necessarily literally and
would provide him with an ethical framework sufficient to cope
with the complexities of modern society.[53]

Blake also had not settled the question of what form his ministry
should take. Many people were urging him in the direction of
university or seminary teaching, yet Blake did not think that he
would be comfortable as an academician. Instead he decided to
test parish life before he made any final decision about his future.[54]

In the system of Presbyterian government, one must have a call
to a specific congregation or ministry before being ordained by

presbytery, although some persons were ordained before receiving such a call under a provision in the book of government that permitted ordination as an "evangelist." Utilizing this provision, Blake was ordained on April 19, 1932 by West Jersey Presbytery of the Presbyterian Church in the United States of America. A few months later Blake accepted an invitation to become assistant minister at the Collegiate Church of St. Nicholas in New York City, thereby beginning what proved to be almost twenty years in the parish ministry.[55]

· III ·
MINISTER IN THE PARISH

"Reinhold Niebuhr's oft reiterated thesis that a man who is the nearest to God is in the greatest danger of the greatest sin, is an almost perfect aid to the preacher who is nearly lost in admiration for his own theology; economics, politics, and sermons. Next to a sense of humor and prayer, a good dose of Niebuhr is the best thing I know to alleviate a preacher's swollen self-esteem."

J ust after Eugene Carson Blake was ordained, a retired minister said to him, "I'm glad it is you who is beginning your ministry. Things are changing so much I couldn't face being a pastor now."[1] Indeed, nearly half of Blake's public career was spent as a minister during fluctuating and often chaotic times of depression, world war, and social change. Blake assumed his first pastorate in 1932 in metropolitan New York at the depth of the Depression, and he concluded his parish work in 1951 on the west coast during a time of rapid growth in the economy and in the population. During this period, Blake served three apprentice years as an assistant pastor, five years at a church of 1,200 members, and eleven years as senior pastor of one of the largest congregations in the Presbyterian U.S.A. denomination.

Blake's first call was to the Collegiate Church of St. Nicholas (Reformed Church in America), which occupied the corner of Fifth Avenue and 48th Street in New York City before it was razed to make way for Rockefeller Center. Part of a cluster of churches organized under one consistory, it dated back to 1628 when Jonas Michaelius came from Holland to serve 270 communicants living in Manhattan, an area he described as "free, somewhat rough and loose."[2] The New York Collegiate, comprising Marble (made famous by the ministry of Norman Vincent Peale), St. Nicholas, Middle, West End, and Fort Washington Churches, is the oldest Protestant church in America with a continuous organization. All the congregations have had distinguished histories of community service and pulpit eloquence.[3]

The senior pastor of St. Nicholas in 1932 was Dr. Malcolm James MacLeod, originally a Presbyterian minister who had come east in 1910 from Pasadena, California, where he had served a rapidly growing congregation and where Blake himself would later become pastor. A native of Prince Edward Island and an 1890 graduate of Princeton Seminary, MacLeod had secured Blake's name through the seminary placement service as a candidate for the assistantship at St. Nicholas. The two men liked each other from the start. MacLeod warned his prospective assistant that he did not accept biblical literalism as it was then being taught at Princeton Seminary and would have difficulties with anyone who followed that line of thought. When Blake described his own position it was evident that the two shared similar theological perspectives and could relate comfortably to each other.[4]

MacLeod was a homiletical taskmaster and provided Blake with an excellent model of preparation and presentation. He always preached from a meticulously prepared manuscript but had the subject matter so well in mind that he did not appear to be chained to the written text. MacLeod insisted that Blake write out his sermons when he preached on Wednesday evenings and once a month on Sunday evenings, and Blake stayed with this method of sermon preparation throughout his career. He did think, however, that MacLeod tended to over-illustrate his sermons with poetry, literary references, and personal stories and anecdotes. Blake himself relied more on logic and concise language in his own pulpit presentations.[5]

During his three years at St. Nicholas, Blake developed homiletical techniques, gained experience in counseling, and experimented with programs for young people. It became apparent to him that he was comfortable when he could translate theology into action. He was able to do this at St. Nicholas because pastoral visitation played such an important part in Blake's responsibilities. He tried to actualize MacLeod's advice about calling: "Be able to call in some of the best homes on Fifth Avenue and also to walk up a five-floor tenement and always to conduct yourself as a minister of Jesus Christ."[6]

Because the country was in the throes of economic depression, people were coming into St. Nicholas every day asking for assistance. Although the church tried to help by providing free meals for the needy at a nearby restaurant, Blake realized that the problems of poverty were more complex than hot-lunch programs. He watched stores go out of business, read of worsening conditions, and had frightening visions of New York shutting down completely. The experience of the Depression permanently affected Blake, and needs of poor people and efforts to overcome poverty would subsequently always be an important part of his professional and personal life.

The assistantship at St. Nicholas ended in 1935 with a call to the First Presbyterian Church of Albany, New York, whose senior minister was retiring. Although Blake had seriously considered working on a Ph. D. at Harvard University, he ultimately decided that he wished to utilize his talents in the parish ministry. His call to Albany came about through a coincidental contact with the brother of a member of the Albany church pulpit committee who happened to be attending a funeral where Blake officiated. Impressed with Blake's presentation and personality, he recommended him to his brother in Albany. Subsequently, after hearing Blake preach and interviewing him, the Albany congregation called him to become pastor. Blake was not confident that he was ready to step up from an assistantship to being senior minister of a church of 1,200 members, but the congregation assured him of their support and cooperation. After visiting Albany, Gene and Valina Blake decided to make the change and accepted the call.[7]

The First Presbyterian Church of Albany was a distinguished congregation with a history dating back to 1760 when the Synod of New York and Philadelphia received "a very pressing application" for pulpit supplies from "the English Presbyterian gentlemen of

Albany." William Tennent, Jr., revolutionary patriot and evangelist, was one of the first men appointed by synod to preach in Albany. By the time that the Revolutionary War began, Albany had a full-time minister, a fine church building, and a growing congregation. The church's commitment to the Revolution is reflected in their donation of seventy pounds of lead stripped from the steeple and window frames to make bullets for patriot firearms. When Blake became pastor in 1935, the congregation had outgrown three buildings, and its fourth edifice, completed in 1883, comfortably housed its membership only a few blocks from the capitol building in downtown Albany.[8]

Blake realized he was undertaking a difficult task in Albany. Only twenty-nine, admittedly inexperienced about church law, administrative procedures, and regular preaching assignments, and with his distinguished predecessor, Dr. William Herman Hopkins, sitting in a front pew, Blake felt under some pressure to make as few mistakes as possible. He cultivated a close relationship with Dr. Hopkins by visiting the pastor emeritus regularly and seeking his advice and counsel on matters of congregational importance. The gentle, quiet Hopkins and the vigorous, outgoing Blake became good friends.[9]

Despite his desire to be congenial with his congregation, he did not hesitate to follow principles even if they were contrary to the opinions of some of his parishioners. The first Sunday before election day in 1935, only two months after becoming pastor, Blake preached a strong sermon on municipal corruption in Albany, in which he said in part that both the community leaders and the citizens seated in the congregation were partly responsible and should do something about the problem. Some people were offended that he seemed to be meddling in politics but many others appreciated this concept of preaching.[10]

The congregation was also shaken when Blake moved to end the pew rental system, an anachronism from the nineteenth century that was still an accepted feature of church life in Albany. When he asked one of his elders about the possibility of open pews and what effect the change would have on the church, the elder replied, "Why ask me? I've only been a member here thirty years!" Blake's main opposition had come from concerned trustees who feared a dramatic drop-off in income if rented pews were discontinued. Blake took a poll of pew renters to ascertain if they would voluntarily pledge an equal sum to the church without the privilege of a reserved seat. Much to the trustees' surprise, a strong majority expressed their willingness to support the church equally well on a strictly voluntary basis. Blake's combination of tact and tenacity won over even his severest critics. The centuries-old pew rental system was quietly dropped in 1938 with virtually no dissension.[11]

Next Blake campaigned for a complete renovation of the sanctuary even though some members thought that restoration work done sixty years earlier was still adequate. The young pastor convinced people that on esthetic and functional grounds changes should be made in the sanctuary's structure. In the process of remodeling, however, it was necessary to remove several rows of pews. Blake fielded objections to the removal by pointing out that they were front pews and that people seldom occupied them anyway. Wood, he said, was very unresponsive. The end result was a tastefully designed divided chancel, which continues to serve as the focal point of worship in First Church.[12]

Most of Blake's time at Albany was spent with the people. During his first year at Albany he made more than five hundred pastoral calls and with his wife, Valina, entertained small groups of church members at home. Frequently the church bulletin contained this announcement: "Mr. and Mrs. Blake will be at home this Friday from four until six for those members of the congregation who wish to be sure to find them home when they come." He also worked and played with young people of the congregation. Blake's easygoing personality and enthusiastic spirit were engaging. One of his most successful programs was called "Minister's chair by the fire," informal discussions of life and religion held in a give-and-take format. Upward of one hundred young people came on Sunday evenings to discuss such topics as "Peace and Pacifism," "Why Be a Missionary?" and "Is Agnosticism Intelligent?" One church member who was a teenager during Blake's ministry later wrote to him: "I still remember our first contact when with some other young people I took you on a sleigh ride way back in the first weeks of your stay in Albany. You sure clicked with that gang from the very beginning."[13]

Noticing Blake's popularity with Williams College students when he came as a guest speaker, President James Baxter invited the young Albany pastor to teach one course each semester on Christian ethics and theology. Blake secured permission from his session to be away from his parish one day a week in order to fulfill his responsibilities at Williams. For two years, 1937–39, he added these duties to his busy schedule of administrative and pastoral work.[14]

In his search for an adequate textbook on Christian ethics, Blake made his first meaningful contact with the thought of Reinhold Niebuhr, ethicist and theologian who was prominent in interpreting neo-orthodoxy to American scholarship. Blake had written John Bennett at Union Theological Seminary, New York, for assistance in selecting a good text. In response, after listing a number of books and then dismissing them because of flaws in methodology or theology, Bennett commented:

> All teaching of Christian ethics now will depend on the attitude one takes to the kind of challenge which Niebuhr brings to us in America but which is a commonplace of European theology. There is no textbook of Christian ethics which would be at all adequate. . . . Niebuhr's *An Interpretation of Christian Ethics* is splendid but forbidding and easily misunderstood.[15]

After reading and considering the book, Blake was not intimidated by Bennett's warning. He adopted the book as a text and began a careful, systematic study of its contents as a basis for class lectures. It was the only book in his entire career that he took the time to outline paragraph by paragraph so that he could understand the subleties of its arguments.

Largely because of his reading of *An Interpretation of Christian Ethics* Blake considered himself a Niebuhrian. Speaking to a group of ministers in 1943, Blake described his intellectual conversion to a new theological position.

Coming as I had from a theologically conservative background, it took some time to orient myself, to assimilate the
college and seminary knowledge into enough of a unity to be
able to preach without the fear that I would say something
that was utterly contradictory to a position I had taken a few
weeks before. Then one morning three or four years ago, I
woke to find that my general philosophical and theological
position had shifted. It was not a radical change. But the front
had shifted. I had found a new set of devils to fight, the old
battle was over. And, as I thought about it, I realized that
two books had done it. One of them was Whitehead's, *Science
and the Modern World,* and the other was Niebuhr's, *An Interpretation of Christian Ethics.* And of the two, the latter book
was the more decisive in that metaphysics is hardly important
to preaching as is theology and ethics.[16]

Niebuhr's critique of the weaknesses of both liberalism and
fundamentalism made a great impression on Blake. Also,
Niebuhr's ability to appropriate the wisdom of Christian orthodoxy without embracing biblical literalism satisfied Blake's desire for a theological system that was sensitive both to traditional
doctrine and to critical thought. Moreover, since Niebuhr was
primarily interested in applying Christianity to political and social
affairs, he provided Blake with some realistic categories for analyzing and applying the Christian gospel in everyday life.[17]

Blake felt that Niebuhr provided him with a number of specific
theological insights that were particularly important to him in the
development of his ministerial career. For one thing, Niebuhr
helped Blake to understand the significance of biblical apocalypti-
cism.

Schweitzer and the eschatologists had made their points only
too well for my intellectual comfort. But somehow they did
not fit these discoveries, for me at least, into any possible
intellectual or spiritual system.

Niebuhr has given me light to see that the category of time,
as well as that of space, needs to be transcended in theology
and life. I have not yet worked out how I want to preach a
sermon on Mark chapter 13, but if my mind keeps working, I
expect perhaps some day I shall.[18]

Niebuhr's emphasis on the basic sin of pride also had an impact on Blake's understanding of a minister's role as a servant of God.

> Reinhold Niebuhr's oft reiterated thesis that a man who is the nearest to God is in the greatest danger of the greatest sin, is an almost perfect aid to the preacher who is nearly lost in admiration for his own theology, economics, politics, and sermons. Next to a sense of humor and prayer, a good dose of Niebuhr is the best thing I know to alleviate a preacher's swollen self-esteem. Furthermore, Niebuhr's position taken seriously, begins to make you able to appreciate the most difficult of your church laymen. . . . A church, local or national, will make progress in social and economic justice only as these men are appreciated and used by the preachers, influenced rather than castigated.[19]

At the same time Niebuhr's social conscience impelled Blake to take seriously the ethical dimensions of the Christian gospel. By circumstance, Eugene Carson Blake could easily have been nothing more than a chaplain to the rich and to the comfortable. His middle-class upbringing and his association with large, wealthy congregations did not provide much contact with poor and laboring-class people.

> I acknowledge a great debt to Reinhold Niebuhr in keeping me at least in tension with respect to the problems of the so-called laboring classes. . . . Some men completely misunderstand that labor is, to say the least, apathetic in the "fight for freedom" as compared with most of the middle class. My God, a laboring man who has been on relief for most of the last ten years would be a fool not to be a little interested in almost any other social and political system than the one we've got. Too many preachers don't even suspect what is the thought and emotion of the common man.[20]

Blake's estimation of Niebuhr's influence should be placed in the perspective that his previous theological education, especially with Mackintosh in Edinburgh, had already inclined him toward neo-orthodox conclusions. However, Niebuhr helped him put it all together in a systematic fashion that enabled him to avoid extreme or radical theological positions. In accepting neo-orthodoxy, however, Blake did not commit himself to all neo-orthodox theologians. With the thought of Karl Barth, for example, Blake had some sharp differences of opinion. "I am neo-orthodox," he said, "only in the sense that I am also catholic. I never could accept even from Karl Barth the tendency to say that you don't know anything about God unless you read the Bible."[21]

Blake's teaching experience at Williams College stimulated his intellectual growth and, equally important, helped him develop new ways to apply his theoretical concepts to life. Always active in civic groups like Rotary, Community Chest, Red Cross, and Youth Council, Blake also served as president of the Foreign Policy Association of the United States (Albany branch), organizer of the Albany Ministerial Association, and one of the leading figures in the movement to start a Federation of Churches in Albany. On one occasion he served as an arbiter in a local building trades' strike. Out of a panel of men suggested by the State Labor Department the disputants selected Blake as the one man who would be fair and objective. He rendered a decision that gave tradesmen less than they requested but more than management had been willing to concede.[22]

Through Blake's energetic leadership First Church grew numerically and expanded its programs of Christian education and service. Blake gradually formulated his own style and produced sermons that both caught people's attention and often influenced their actions. From time to time pulpit committees sought to interest Blake in leaving Albany but they had not enough appeal for him to leave such a challenging field. Then early in 1940 representatives of the prestigious Pasadena Presbyterian Church in California, where Dr. Robert Freeman had just concluded a thirty-year ministry, began to investigate the young Albany pastor as a possible candidate for their congregation.

Blake came highly recommended even though he was only in his early thirties. Dr. James Baxter, president of Williams College, wrote: "He is a fine, vigorous type, with great force of character, a keen mind, with rare abilities as a preacher and a man of impressive spiritual power." Mr. Howard V. Yergin, executive of New York Synod, said: "Blake is an unusual preacher, forceful, thoughtful, and interesting. He is a good administrator and is much beloved by his congregation and is attractive to young people." A most impressive testimony came from Dr. Malcolm MacLeod, Blake's mentor at St. Nicholas Collegiate Church and former pastor of the Pasadena congregation. "Eugene Carson Blake," said MacLeod, "has a fine personality, is a big man—looks like Phillips Brooks, and has a splendid background. He is a scholar and a fine preacher. In fact, I regard Blake as an A-No. 1 man, with a fine future." After meeting Blake personally, members of the Pasadena pulpit committee were convinced that their long search was over.[23]

Pasadena Presbyterian Church was one of the outstanding urban congregations in the Presbyterian Church, U.S.A. Organized in 1875 with seventy members, PPC expanded in proportion to the phenomenal statewide growth as the population moved westward. Under the leadership of Malcolm J. MacLeod (1900–10) and Robert Freeman (1910–40), PPC constructed a magnificent sanctuary and developed an ambitious program of religious education and community outreach. Simultaneously it took an active role in presbytery, synod, and General Assembly causes. With a membership of 3,500 and a budget of more than $150,000, Pasadena Presbyterian Church had a reputation for progressive orthodoxy. At the same time, however, PPC had many extremely wealthy, conservative adherents; thus the church's pastors dealt with a wide spectrum of personal viewpoints and had to develop a complex organizational structure that could meet a variety of needs and furnish leadership in a number of directions. When PPC extended him a unanimous call on August 20, 1940, Blake took the challenge with the hope that "we shall grow together to do God's work."[24]

Blake's ministry at PPC was pivotal in his future development as an ecclesiastical leader. At Pasadena he matured as a public speaker and won recognition as a solid, articulate biblical preacher. Many of his sermons were published and widely distributed. Moreover, through KPPC, the church radio station, Blake reached an audience far beyond his Sunday morning congregation. At the same time, his involvement in Los Angeles Presbytery increased his understanding of the intricacies of church government and provided opportunities to participate in presbytery and synod activities. During the 1940s Blake also became well-known through his work on the denomination's national Board of Christian Education and in various ecumenical organizations.

Under Blake's leadership PPC evidenced growth in membership, giving, physical plant, programs, and staff. When Blake left Pasadena in 1951 there were nearly 4,500 communicants (third largest in the entire denomination), receipts had risen from $150,000 in 1940 to $225,000, ground had been broken for a new chapel, lounge, and fellowship hall, and the weekly church activity sheet listed some fifty organizations providing meaningful involvement for all ages. The staff at PPC had expanded to six ministers, a director of religious education, choir director, youth directors, caretakers, secretaries, radio station technicians, a switchboard operator, and house managers for the summer camp program. A study conducted by the *Presbyterian Tribune* in 1949 gave PPC the number one ranking in the entire Presbyterian denomination based on total points awarded on the basis of membership, accessions, Sunday school roll, ratio of benevolences to congregational expenses, and total giving.[25]

What these statistics do not show, however, is the personal dimension of Blake's ministry. Even with his heavy administrative and preaching load, Blake could relate to people of all ages. Shortly after he came to Pasadena he wrote in the church paper:

> I am available to all of you, day or night, in emergency. As a general rule, it is necessary for me to keep my mornings clear for writing sermons, speeches, articles, and the like, and for reading. But by appointment, I am always glad to see or talk to as many of the members of the church who want to see me, if for no other reason than that they would like to become acquainted. I, too, want to become acquainted. You do me and the church a disservice if you let it be agreed among you that I am too busy to be seen.[26]

Blake also made regular visits to people in hospitals and to shut-ins and had a policy of visiting every person who was nominated for ruling elder so that he could discuss with them the responsibilities of that office.

As a pastor he gave words of advice, encouragement, and comfort to his parishioners. To a young mother who felt guilty about not being able to help with church school work because of small children in the home, Blake said, "Now is the time that the church should be helping you. Your turn to help the church will come later."[27]

In all situations, Blake tried to be both fair and decisive. Two deacons were engaged in a personal feud that threatened to become a disruptive factor in the church. Blake met with them individually and convinced them that the church could not do without either one. Through Blake's mediation they reconciled and served the congregation with distinction for many years. Similarly, on the opening day of a summer camp where Blake was serving as one of the directors, a young girl reported that her money for camp fees and expenses had apparently been stolen. Tension quickly mounted. No one confessed to the theft, and the money could not be found. Realizing that something had to be done before camp morale was completely ruined, Blake gathered campers and counselors together to discuss the problem. It was everybody's problem, he said, and it needed to be solved immediately so that camp activities could proceed normally and everyone could have a good time. Without trying to ascertain guilt or innocence, Blake suggested that if everyone who could afford it would give just a little money, the unfortunate girl could recover her funds and pay her fees. The group agreed to do this and followed Blake's request to forget the incident and enjoy the camp.[28]

Blake related to the young people at Pasadena as well as he had to those in his previous two pastorates. When summer campers sewed lace frills on his swimming trunks, he played along with the joke by wearing the trunks, lace trailing in the breeze. On occasions when anonymous young people washed his convertible with the roof down, he good-naturedly pretended not to notice the wet seats. One boy remembered the day when a paper airplane inexplicably slipped out of his hand and sailed from the balcony during the church service, dipping and soaring until it landed near the chancel. Facing the ordeal of apologizing to Blake, the boy was surprised when Blake seemed unperturbed about the incident and spent most of the time describing how to fold paper in order to maintain maximum flying results.[29]

Blake encouraged a number of programs designed for young people. A strong believer that youth work should never be "hired out" to an assistant, he participated in youth meetings and summer camps. He changed the traditional prayer meeting midweek service to a family night and arranged for teenagers to eat with their families and then have supervised study halls for those who needed help with school work. Blake also conducted a discussion group with nearby Cal Tech students, which often had more than one hundred participants. One year the program consisted of taking Blake's sermon of the previous week and opening it up point by point for discussion. Students came to respect Blake's candor, openness, and willingness to debate issues on a logical rather than on an emotional level.[30]

In 1948 Blake chartered a train, which he dubbed "The Presbyterian Special," and conveyed some one thousand church members to Fullerton, California, twenty-five miles distant, for the annual picnic. After a full day of softball, sack races, pie-eating contests, and sumptuous supper, Blake entertained everyone on the trip home by traversing the aisles in costume passing out peanuts. One young person excitedly described the event in the church paper and concluded: "Blake is terrific—he played baseball all afternoon and still looked as if he could have played another game!"[31]

In addition to developing a youth program, Blake never ignored the smaller children. Every Sunday morning he visited one of the church school classes. In flowing robes he sat on the floor and played with kindergarteners as though he had no other responsibility in the world. Then he dashed off to the sanctuary where the worship service was already underway. One mother recalled that she and her young daughter were walking down Colorado Street in Pasadena when Blake appeared around the corner dressed in informal sports attire. As he recognized them and approached to have a short chat, the little girl squeezed her mother's hand and said, "Mother, here comes God without his coat!"[32]

Blake also had a close working relationship with his staff. Although he took a personal interest in their areas of responsibility, he let them develop their own ideas and projects. Blake expected everyone to do competent work. At the same time, he was always willing to overlook mistakes and failures provided they did not become habitual and lessen the effectiveness of the church's program. When Howard Swan, director of music at PPC, conferred with the new pastor for the first time, he expected a stiff, formal interview. Much to his surprise Blake greeted him with open collar, feet propped up on the desk, and pipe in hand. In an informal, friendly way they discussed possible ways that PPC's music program could be expanded and improved. "The people who work with me ought to be free to do their own job," Blake concluded. And Swan recalled, "Gene Blake really followed through on that promise."[33]

Every aspect of PPC's program bore the mark of Blake's administrative touch and religious concerns. The Women's Society, which had traditionally been a study group, under Blake's encouragement quickly became actively involved in projects of local importance. They sponsored, for example, parties for Mexican Nationals engaged in nearby agricultural work and biracial dinners and panel discussions on racial tensions in the Pasadena area.

Other church groups assisted in the growing program for servicemen, which had been initiated by Blake. Pasadena Presbyterian Church was one of the first in the area to open a serviceman's club. Every weekend Blake visited the club and mixed with the servicemen. One evening as the club was closing, Blake noticed that most of the men were hanging around the street corners with no place to go. He immediately went to work to set up a dormitory where men could stay overnight. Staffed by volunteers from the church and community, the church housed some three hundred servicemen every weekend and provided them with recreational facilities and opportunities for worship if they so desired.[34]

Blake also recognized the untapped possibilities of a radio ministry and expanded the operations of KPPC, a radio station that had been owned and operated by PPC since 1924. In addition to broadcasting services on Sunday and Wednesday, the station also featured religious and classical music, children's programs, topics of local interest produced by Cal Tech students, and a special

United Nations Report, which was considered somewhat daring by some because of the controversial aspects of the newly organized world political body. Blake also experimented with religious "soap operas" by helping to design a series called "Tales from the Tower of St. John's," where story plots came from sermons preached at PPC and thinly disguised situations in the Pasadena community. In 1949 Blake broadened his radio ministry by becoming chairman of the Board of Trustees of a new organization called the Protestant Radio and Television Commission. The group developed interdenominational and nonsectarian religious programs and provided a speaker's bureau, publicity service, and transcribed programs for religious and commercial stations in the western states.[35]

As an administrator and program developer, Eugene Carson Blake never left anything to chance that could possibly be worked out in advance. He planned session meetings down to the last detail, and was known to suggest an appropriate motion to a cooperative elder beforehand. Sometimes his preparation went beyond the bounds of Presbyterian order. If committees needed to be appointed, moderator Blake came with his slate prepared. One parishioner recalled when she was a member of a nominating committee to select some church officers, Blake was unable to attend the meeting but sent a note indicating those whom he thought should be appointed. The committee members decided to nominate a different slate of officers, and Blake accepted their action graciously. By coincidence or otherwise, however, his choices were elected the following year. When he announced his resignation to the Pasadena session in order to accept the position of stated clerk of the denomination, his last formal words were: "I just happen to have a list of people in my pocket who I think would make a good pulpit committee."[36]

Although Eugene Carson Blake acknowledged the importance of administrative acumen and pastoral proficiency, he spent much time preparing his sermons. Foremost in his mind was his responsibility to preach the gospel as he comprehended it from the Scriptures. This meant cultivating a spirit of openness to his own limited perspectives while simultaneously taking seriously the authority of the pulpit.

It is always surprising to me when someone praises me for preaching what he says is a "very courageous sermon." The reason that this surprises me is that beforehand it never occurs to me whether or not I *dare* say anything. I struggle hard to speak the truth as I see it, and to be persuasive. But should I ever think whether I *dare* speak the truth?[37]

At Pasadena, Blake continued preaching on social issues just as he had done in Albany, and he felt no subject was too sensitive or controversial if it had Christian implications. He frequently raised the issue of racial discrimination and prejudice and unequivocally labeled it immoral and unchristian.[38] He repeatedly warned against the dangers of identifying political ideologies and patriotism with religion and the will of God. During the forties and fifties, when so many public figures had adopted a "my country right or wrong" attitude, Blake insisted that ultimate loyalty was to God and not to any human institution or national goals. He condemned the "hysteria of loyalty investigations" such as the Tenney Committee had conducted in nearby Los Angeles. In a sermon entitled "The Vice of Loyalty," he concluded with these words:

People today would say one cannot love their country and be an internationalist. I would say you cannot love your country truly until that loyalty is enlarged to include a world loyalty and a patriotism of mankind. The vice of loyalty is for it to become narrow and selfish and so degenerate into degrading partisanship. And when loyalties conflict, one must seek the broadest loyalty and cleave to that. For nations, states, and families must yield before the supreme loyalty of every person to hear the word of God and to do it.[39]

Blake's prophetic sermons often evoked vehement criticism. When Blake became aware of substandard housing in Pasadena in which poor families lived and paid unreasonably high rent, he charged parishioners, some of whom owned such properties, to awaken their Christian consciences about the situation. Some members actually walked out during the sermon. Others barraged him with telephone calls. One visitor in the congregation, however, was so impressed with Blake's forthrightness and honesty that he unsuccessfully tried to reach Blake by phone to voice his approval. When he finally did get through, he asked Blake, "Well, Doctor, have they been giving you hell?" "That's about right," Blake replied. "I wanted to tell you," the visitor continued, "that I too heard the sermon and I want to join your church." He proved to be a faithful member and active participant in the life of PPC.[40]

When Blake preached on social ills or community problems, he carefully pointed out that his criticisms were not just personal penchants but were supported by biblical and ecclesiastical precedent. In a sermon on "God and Collective Bargaining," Blake wrestled with labor-management problems as he saw them in relationship to Jesus' parable about workers in the vineyard (Matt. 19:27–20:16). He justified his conclusion that the only solution to industrial relations was collective bargaining by appealing to previously issued church pronouncements.

> I am not speaking as an individual here. As far back as 1920, the General Assembly of our church went on record declaring "for the right of wage owners to organize and to deal through their chosen representatives with the management of industries in which they work." And all through the years the church has reaffirmed from Christian principles that both labor and management need to mend their ways and learn in understanding and mutual respect to determine fair wages and working conditions. A good bargain is of benefit to both parties concerned. A Christian bargain is fair to both sides.[41]

Eugene Carson Blake did not as a preacher stun his congregation every Sunday with prophetic thunderbolts. He was no iconoclast. He repeatedly espoused all the traditional American virtues: patriotism, democracy, free enterprise, hard work, honesty, and stewardship. But he also attempted to deal with the spectrum of biblical themes, doctrines, and psychological insights as he saw them relating to contemporary situations. He took history and tradition seriously and saw the major responsibility of the sermon as an attempt to reinterpret essential Christian truths by cutting through difficulties of language, metaphysics, and theological controversy so these truths could be utilized as valuable human guidelines.[42]

Many preachers began sermon preparation with an idea and then sought in the Bible some religious justification for it. Blake's homiletical methodology always involved the interplay of Scripture and sensitivity to human need.

> The beginning of a sermon with me is that moment when a spark is struck by the steel of the Word in the Bible on the flint of human need. The spark is an idea, a fresh insight, a heightened emotional and intellectual response to a verse or passage of scripture, sometimes very familiar; or the flash of the Gospel's answer to some troubling human problem. Some sermons begin with the problem. Some begin with the Word. But it is no sermon unless flint strikes steel.[43]

One of Blake's favorite techniques in developing a sermon was to present a theological or ethical problem, set out arguments on both sides of the issue, and then reach a conclusion incorporating the best of both arguments. In a sermon entitled "How Comes the Spirit of God?" for example, which discussed religious conversion—should it be dramatic, sudden or a gradual process of spiritual maturation—Blake concluded:

> For myself, it seems clear that we do not have to choose between these two. I do not see them as really opposing each other but as complementary. There is a need to celebrate Mother's Day and Pentecost! Christian nurture is vital to full Christian character and something that may be called conversion is very often fully as important. Gradual Christian nurture without a moment of deep spiritual experience often leaves a life quite ineffective. Sudden conversion without the background of Christian education and training is likely to be wild and fanatic.[44]

No matter what technique Blake employed in presenting his message, the theme which dominated his preaching at Albany and Pasadena was the centrality of Jesus Christ as Lord and Savior. Throughout his public ministry he proclaimed a very traditional message: *Christian faith is not intellectual assent to certain propositions or creeds. It is personal commitment to Jesus Christ.* Blake preached for allegiance to a Christ who was both God and man in the fullest sense of each term, and public acceptance of Jesus Christ had priority over any worthwhile Christian concern or humanitarian cause. Blake summed up his theological thrust in one of a number of sermons dealing with salvation.

> The Christian program of salvation is no detailed plan of a better society, important as that is. It is a gospel message that men who are sinners need most of all to be saved, that God loves them, that if they will respond to His love, He will forgive them their sin and make them over into a new creation. This, of course, implies a new society and renewed dedication to all kinds of goodness as it always has whenever people have stopped running away from God and are reconciled to Him. *But the primary task of the church is to bring people to God in Jesus Christ.*[45]

At Pasadena for the first time Blake's concept of the ministry expanded beyond dimensions of administrator, pastor, and preacher to include responsibilities as a presbyter whose duties extended to the church at large. "At Albany," said Blake, "I would have to confess that I was pretty much a Congregationalist. I became a Presbyterian in Los Angeles through the work of Los Angeles Presbytery."[46] Under the leadership of Tom Holden, presbytery clerk, and Glenn Moore, presbytery executive, Los Angeles Presbytery had become one of the largest and most influential presbyteries in the entire denomination. During World War II, California Presbyterianism had begun to grow rapidly. In the 1940s thirty new churches were organized with a membership of more than five thousand. By 1948 the southern area of the Synod of California alone had 175 churches and faced what one writer called a "boom psychosis" unparalleled in American history. Before 1950 more than 40 percent of the total Presbyterian membership lived west of the Mississippi and the concentration of people and resources on the west coast made Los Angeles Presbytery the center of power and influence for a significant number of constituents.[47]

Primarily through the encouragement of Holden and Moore, Blake assumed a leadership role in the judicatory. The three often met on Sunday evenings to talk about Presbyterian government and how it should function at the local and national level. Because of Blake's position on the National Board of Christian Education, he was selected chairman of the presbytery's Christian Education Committee. At one time or another Blake also served Los Angeles Presbytery as chairman of the Department of Ecclesiastical Procedure, Committee on Candidates for the Ministry, and Committee on Social Education and Action. Unlike many of the ministers of large congregations who appeared at presbytery, made their reports, and then departed, Blake acquired the reputation of being a "bitter-ender." Glenn Moore often teased Blake by saying that the only reason he stayed so long was that he wanted to be certain that nothing slipped by in the last few minutes. Fellow ministers appreciated his willingness to see things to a conclusion even though he had a large church and could easily have pleaded that he was "too busy" to give so much time to judicatory matters.[48]

Much of Blake's knowledge about Presbyterian government was developed in his experience with Los Angeles Presbytery's meticulous ecclesiastical procedures. Committees reprimanded local sessions for flaws in record-keeping procedures and followed up until they made necessary corrections. When one minister married movie actress Lana Turner and millionaire sportsman Henry J. Topping, without waiting the prescribed one year after divorce as then required by Presbyterian law, Los Angeles Presbytery formed a judicial commission (of which Blake was a member) and formally "rebuked" the clergyman for his violation of Presbyterian government. The minister would have received a stronger penalty if he had not publicly confessed his mistake and promised not to repeat it.[49]

Blake's leadership on the Committee on Examination and Oversight of Candidates involved him in a case of judicatorial discipline where presbytery's rights were asserted over against individual freedom. In 1947 Fuller Theological Seminary (nondenominational) was organized and located just up the street from Pasadena Presbyterian Church. Its president, Dr. Harold John Ockenga, a Presbyterian minister and a member of Pittsburgh Presbytery, publicly declared that most denominational seminaries had been vitiated by "modernism" and that the demand for a nondenominational theological school with a "positive, orthodox" emphasis could not be ignored. Blake and other leaders of Los Angeles Presbytery believed that Ockenga's support of Fuller was not in the best interests of the Presbyterian church, which had already committed itself to strengthen nearby San Francisco Seminary rather than create new institutions. A special committee appointed by Los Angeles Presbytery to study the Fuller situation concluded: "For Los Angeles Presbytery to appear to encourage, explicitly or implicitly, any other Seminary, would smack very much of disloyalty to the program of our Church in general, and to the cause of our local seminary in particular."[50]

Los Angeles Presbytery took two steps to restrict the influence of Fuller Seminary on California Presbyterianism. First, it ruled that students who attended Fuller would not be accepted for ordination by Los Angeles Presbytery. Second, presbytery challenged the right of Ockenga and other Presbyterian ministers on Fuller's staff to work within the bounds of Los Angeles Presbytery without approval of that judicatory. After several years of judicatorial debate at the presbytery and General Assembly level, Ockenga and others left the Presbyterian church and united with other denominations rather than relinquish their association with Fuller Seminary.[51]

For many years there was open tension between Fuller and Los Angeles Presbytery. Those at Fuller denied being a divisive influence and Los Angeles Presbytery insisted that only denominationally approved institutions deserved support and recognition. Time, however, had a healing effect. In 1964 Ockenga and Blake (then stated clerk of the General Assembly) had breakfast together and cordially discussed the relationship between Fuller and the United Presbyterian Church. Blake then wrote to the presbytery's general council and asked them to give the whole problem some serious consideration. "Please understand," Blake wrote, "that I am not in any position to suggest what Presbytery should do, but I am anxious, as I was ten years ago, for the Presbytery to take its proper responsibility with regard to the theological education of candidates for our ministry."[52] Today Fuller Seminary uses the facilities of nearby Pasadena Presbyterian Church, Blake's former pastorate, for classrooms and convocations. When questioned about his new attitude toward Fuller, Blake simply said, "We've both changed over the years."[53]

Beyond presbytery circles, Blake became known in the 1940s as a hard-working, articulate leader by his participation in denominational boards and committees. In 1939, while he was still in Albany, Blake was appointed to fill a vacancy in the Board of Christian Education. He subsequently served as chairman of the Subcommittee on Educational Policies and Programs which planned and promoted the innovative Faith and Life Curriculum. In 1942 Blake became a member of the Committee of Camp and Church Activities and two years later the General Assembly appointed him a member of the Committee to Revise and Rewrite the Intermediate Catechism. In addition to these assignments, Blake spoke frequently at seminars, religious emphasis weeks, and Young Adult National Council convocations.[54]

Particularly significant was his work on the Board of Christian Education. As chairman of the Subcommittee on Educational Policies and Programs, Blake required its members to read certain books on religious education and to come prepared to relate them to the denomination's own educational policies. He ended a long-standing practice of having the committee approve manuscripts and authors without first examining the material. Blake made it clear that if his committee was to recommend anything to the board, it would be done only after careful consideration and study. He warned the staff that they were responsible for their own choices and recommendations.[55]

Blake played a key role in the formation of the new Presbyterian Faith and Life Curriculum, which replaced the "uniform lessons" of the International Council of Religious Education. Although Blake was reluctant to abandon an ecumenical project for a denominational enterprise, he realized that intellectual honesty and theological integrity were at stake. The interdenominational lesson writers refused to deal directly with the findings of modern biblical studies. For example, the Uniform Lessons Committee agreed to devote a quarter of one year's lessons to the book of Isaiah. Although most biblical scholars agreed that the book of Isaiah was composed of at least three sources written by different people at different periods of Israel's history, the interdenominational committee dodged the critical question by having study outlines based upon the contents of the book as it stood and not upon the prophets represented in it.[56]

Paul Calvin Payne, general secretary of the Board of Christian Education, decided that the time had come when the Presbyterians must produce a curriculum that took historical criticism and contemporary theology seriously. With the support of Blake's committee, Payne and his staff began a project that took almost ten years to complete and required an investment of several million dollars. Even as the new curriculum was being designed, however, some committee members feared that the Presbyterian church was not ready for an "honest curriculum." They suggested that the Board of Christian Education approve two curricula—one for conservatives and one for progressives. At a crucial committee meeting, Payne placed his position on the line. Unless the committee endorsed one new curriculum, he said, he would resign as general secretary of the Board of Christian Education. Blake supported Payne and asked the committee to move ahead with the innovative curriculum. In a decisive ballot, only two members voted negatively. In 1947 Blake presented the exemplary and pioneering curriculum to the General Assembly of the Presbyterian church.[57]

One other event brought Blake denominational recognition. Dr. Jesse Baird asked Blake to nominate him as moderator of the General Assembly at the 1948 meeting in Seattle, Washington. The young Pasadena pastor gave a dramatic address in which he portrayed Baird as an "incurable pioneer, tall, lank and Lincolnesque . . . with iron gray hair and iron in his soul." He further described Baird as one who responded to the "insistent call to leave easily cultivated places for the challenge of the new frontier which needs men and builders."[58] In a race that was decided only after a record-breaking five ballots, Baird won and rewarded his nominator with appointment to the General Assembly's Committee on Bills and Overtures. This provided Blake with an opportunity to appear prominently before the assembly, and he made the most of it with his well-organized presentations and judicious handling of controversial issues, such as separation of church and state, and ecumenism.[59]

At forty-five years of age, Eugene Carson Blake was in mid-career. He had a secure position in one of the most prestigious churches in the entire denomination. But, in one of the rare passages in his sermons where he became openly autobiographical, Blake described his awareness of inexorable change in life despite longings for permanence and stability. "To Live Is to Change," his sermon topic declared.

> I personally find myself standing a little beyond the middle year of life. I stand in the place of the heat of the day when often the defeats of youth and the approaching twilight of age make men lose their sense of direction in life and a feeling of its importance and begin to look for the easy adjustment to the flux of things. Yet I stand where perhaps best of all one can be objective about the great hopes of youth and the weariness of age. Between beginnings and ends, birth and death.[60]

The very change of which Blake philosophized soon presented him with a personal option that radically altered the thrust of his career. A tragic accident on a Wyoming highway, which took the life of the top permanent official in the Presbyterian Church, U.S.A., presented Blake with both the opportunity and the responsibility of assuming a position in which his leadership would help to shape the history of the denomination.

· IV ·

SERVANT OF
THE GENERAL ASSEMBLY

*"Unless with courage, we are willing in
our time and place to restate the faith in a
language that can be understood, the witness of our church is obscured."*

I am convined that the causes I have supported and the positions I have taken are a part of the Church's life and
thought and will survive without my personal attention."[1] Spoken
in conviction and not arrogance, these words summarize Eugene
Carson Blake's own personal evaluation of his work as stated clerk
of the Presbyterian Church in the United States of America
(United Presbyterian Church in the U.S.A. after a union in 1958)
between 1951 and 1966. Blake was the top executive officer of the
nation's fourth largest Protestant denomination during fifteen of
some of the most challenging years in American history. From the
tensions of the "McCarthy era" through the euphoria of religious
revival to the dramatic struggle for civil rights and antiwar protests
of the 1960s, Blake's commitments to personal freedom, social
justice, and world peace and his courage to speak out on these
issues made him one of the best-known and highly respected Protestant leaders in the United States. During this same time the
Presbyterian church was setting priorities, devising programs, and
making pronouncements, all of far-reaching impact on the church.
Blake gave forceful leadership, which was much broader and
deeper than the title "stated clerk" might seem to imply.[2]

The events leading up to Blake's election as stated clerk of the Presbyterian Church in the U.S.A. began on a rain-slickened, fog-shrouded highway near Windriver Canyon in Wyoming where a car in which Dr. William Barrow Pugh, the stated clerk, was riding, slammed into a skidding semitrailer, and Dr. Pugh was killed instantly. Returning from a meeting of the Synod of Wyoming where he had been a guest speaker, Pugh was on his way to Cheyenne to catch a plane back to his office in Philadelphia. His death on September 14, 1950 left the church without a chief executive until the General Assembly could meet in May 1951 to elect a new stated clerk.[3]

During the interim members of the General Council of the General Assembly guided the continuing work of the two-million-member denomination and appointed several committees to make preparations for the forthcoming General Assembly. One committee was charged to make a careful study of the duties and functions of the stated clerk and the secretary of the General Council. Another Special Committee of Nine was appointed to canvass the church for nominations for the stated clerk's position. The committee was directed to submit not more than three names to a Standing Committee on Nominations of a Stated Clerk, which in turn would present not more than two names to the General Assembly in May 1951. After considering hundreds of candidates, the Special Committee of Nine pared its list down to two names. One was James W. Laurie, pastor of the Central Presbyterian Church in Buffalo, New York, a successful churchman whose work in the local parish and denominational structures had won him recognition by his peers. The other finalist was Eugene Carson Blake, pastor of the Pasadena Presbyterian Church and a leader in both denominational and ecumenical circles.[4]

Although both committee members and nominees were sworn to secrecy, it was common knowledge that Blake and Laurie were prime candidates for the position of stated clerk. When the General Assembly convened in May 1951 in Cincinnati, Ohio, a sealed report was given to the Standing Committee on Nominations of a Stated Clerk for its consideration. In theory, the committee could consider any number of names. In fact, it focused on Laurie and Blake. After considerable discussion, the nominating committee decided to place only one name before the General Assembly. That name was Eugene Carson Blake.[5]

When Blake was announced as the sole nominee on May 29, 1951, some commissioners were disappointed that they had not been given the opportunity to make a choice between at least two candidates. A movement from the floor to nominate Dr. Henry Barraclough, a layman who had served the assembly as an assistant to previous stated clerks, was quashed by Barraclough himself. James W. Laurie stopped any further floor struggle for the stated clerk's position by endorsing Blake and moving that nominations be closed. "I am supporting Gene Blake," Laurie said, "because he is the man called by the Church to this position of great responsibility. And were the situations reversed, he would be doing the same for me."[6] Blake was elected unanimously to the position. His acceptance speech the following day was brief. After thanking the assembly for deeming him worthy of the office, Blake concluded: "I believe one of the first things a Stated Clerk is responsible for is to keep the General Assembly up to the docket. For which reason I thank you and now sit down." He sat down to a prolonged standing ovation.[7]

The same General Assembly that elected Blake stated clerk also approved a full-time secretary of the General Council in a "distinct but complementary" office to that of stated clerk. Previously the stated clerk had served as secretary of the General Council and of all the major General Assembly committees. Under the new structure, Blake was a member of the General Council (not secretary) and participated on other committees only in an ex-officio capacity. Elected to the new position of secretary of the General Council was Glenn Warner Moore, Southern California Synod executive and a close friend of Blake's during his Pasadena ministry. Despite the newness of the organizational structure, Blake and Moore had a good understanding of their relative responsibilities. As Moore frequently expressed it: "I am the chief hired man of the church and you are the chief permanent officer of the church."[8]

Blake's election to the highest position in his denomination was an indication that the Presbyterian Church in the U.S.A. wanted to be known as a national rather than a regional denomination. Blake's predecessor had represented the traditional eastern establishment leadership that had dominated the church throughout most of its history. In fact, every stated clerk prior to Blake had been a member of the Synod of Pennsylvania. Blake's cosmopolitan background, midwestern upbringing, Princeton education, overseas missionary experience, and pastorates on both east and west coasts projected a denominational image of ecumenical Christianity and regional inclusiveness.[9]

At first glance, the title "stated clerk of the General Assembly" might seem puzzling and signify a limitation of the office. However, the title "clerk" is appropriate, because one of the important functions of the office is to keep the minutes of the annual meetings of the General Assembly and to maintain the official correspondence of the church. The adjective "stated" is apt because the clerk is elected to a specific or stated term of office, five years.[10]

The office of stated clerk was created by the first General Assembly in 1789 and initially occupied by the famous revolutionary-war patriot Dr. George Duffield. Until the long-term tenure (1884–1921) of Dr. William H. Roberts, it was a part-time position. From that period, however, the position became increasingly influential in determining the direction and pace of change within the denomination, especially during the tenures of Blake's immediate predecessors, Louis Seymour Mudge (1921–38) and William Barrow Pugh (1938–50). Partly because of a growing fear of concentration of power in the office of stated clerk, the General Assembly decided after Pugh's sudden death in 1950 to reexamine the duties and functions of the office and to create the full-time position of secretary of the General Council.[11]

Many of Blake's friends and associates were surprised that he was willing to leave such a successful and influential pastorate as Pasadena Presbyterian Church to become stated clerk. Every five years Blake would have to face re-election by the General Assembly, a body which changes its composition from year to year; there would be no guarantee of continuing support. Nor did the office bring with it the power and *sui generis* authority of a bishop, metropolitan, or pope. As stated clerk—like the Secretary-General of the United Nations—Blake had limited authority, subject to the General Assembly. Anything else, however, would have to be self-generating by utilizing personal persuasion and close working relationships with committees, judicatories, and boards and agencies of the church.

Blake was aware of this when he became a candidate for stated clerk. Behind his decision were some well-thought-out considerations. First, because of his involvement in judicatories and boards, Blake had come to realize that the Presbyterian church was much more than "prima-donna big-steeple churches and a group of struggling small-steeple churches gathered in some sort of vague association. It was the Church of Jesus Christ and it ought to act like it." Blake had the confidence that he could exert responsible leadership to help his denomination "come of age" in a tremendously challenging period of history.[12] Second, Blake did not let the unpretentious title "stated clerk" keep him from recognizing the position's influence and inherent authority. In addition to interpreting church law and arranging agendas for General Assemblies, Blake noted that his job description said that the stated clerk "shall carry on the general correspondence of the Church." To Blake that meant, "If you want to talk to Presbyterians, you have to talk to the Stated Clerk. You don't talk to the Moderator or the Secretary of the General Council or anybody else who is not the Stated Clerk. In other words, it's the top job."[13] Blake reminded his colleagues on the General Council that they were all subject to the General Assembly. "Look," he would say, "it only takes one resolution of this General Assembly and you are out of business. Now just take care!"[14]

Furthermore, Blake viewed the office of stated clerk as a means of expanding his pastoral ministry. He would continue to counsel, teach, and assist people who had needs and problems, although his ministry would not be limited to one parish. From the outset Blake also made it clear that he did not become stated clerk in order to restrict his freedom to preach. "Every Presbyterian pastor has that freedom," Blake insisted. "I wasn't going to take this position and then have to request permission from the Moderator every time I wanted to speak."[15] Although some of his closest friends questioned the appropriateness of having the stated clerk speak "unofficially" for the entire denomination, Blake always reminded them that he could not remain silent when his conscience and common sense compelled him to speak.[16]

Blake saw two aspects of the stated clerk's position that had almost unlimited potential for his personal interests and abilities. By this point in his career Blake was firmly committed to the ecumenical movement and saw in his leadership of the Presbyterian church an opportunity to expand his denomination's historic commitment to ecumenical Christianity. So significant were Blake's contributions in this area that they have been discussed separately in chapters VI and VII. Blake also recognized the importance of church-state relationships and envisioned the unique position of stated clerk as an intermediary between his church and political power structures. In particular, his role in the struggle for civil rights and social justice, which brought him national attention, is described in chapter V.

Even before his inauguration as stated clerk, Blake was personally involved in a church-state controversy. On October 20, 1951, President Harry S Truman startled American Protestants by announcing his decision to send an ambassador to the Vatican and by transmitting to the Senate for confirmation the name of General Mark W. Clark. The following day Blake sent a telegram to Truman protesting the appointment and charging that it "deliberately flouted the expressed wishes and deeply held convictions of most Protestants." The protest, Blake concluded, was "both personal and on behalf of the Presbyterian Church in the United States of America."[17] Later Blake was appointed as a member of the National Council of Churches' committee of church leaders to help mobilize public opinion against the president's proposed ambassadorship. So effective was the opposition to Truman's action that General Clark requested that his name be withdrawn before the Senate had an opportunity to vote on the question.[18]

At a solemn ceremony held in Philadelphia's historic, high-vaulted First Presbyterian Church on October 23, 1951, Eugene Carson Blake was installed as stated clerk and Glenn W. Moore as secretary of the General Council. Blake's address focused on what he considered to be one of the most significant issues facing American society in the 1950s: "Freedom and Authority in Church and State." Blake's early words and subsequent actions aligned him with those who deplored the type of anti-Communism that engulfed the United States between 1948 and 1954 under the leadership of Senator Joseph R. McCarthy, Republican of Wisconsin. "McCarthyism" created such an atmosphere of suspicion that it seemed safer to conform than to disagree. So powerful was McCarthy's influence that many prominent people withheld criticism rather than risk being called "soft on Communism" or an "appeaser."[19]

In his address Blake described two basic principles from his Reformed tradition that he thought were relevant to the issue of freedom and authority in church and state. Central and foremost, Blake affirmed the principle of the sovereignty of God, a principle that has precedence in Reformed thought. All ideologies that denigrate freedom in favor of authority, Blake contended, would be most persuasive in modern society unless people remembered that Christian freedom is always freedom under God. "In the light of our heritage," Blake told his audience, "we have a grave responsibility always to be sure that the freedom and individualism we espouse is not that humanistic license that has done so much to the soul of modern man tired of what he thought was freedom to make and turn in his soul's sickness to tyranny old or new."[20]

As a corollary to this basic Calvinistic emphasis, Blake also stressed a second principle: "Authority in church and state, as a practical matter, must never be in the hands of any single person but must always be lodged in a group of freely elected representatives."[21] Referring to the position of stated clerk as a good example of this carefully preserved Presbyterian principle, Blake pointed out that the office was important only because it reflected the authority and prestige of the General Assembly whose servant the stated clerk is.[22]

Continuing his argument, Blake contended that within the church individual freedom must always be subject to the collective will and wisdom of the group. Christian faith and life, he stressed, is never a purely individual matter. It is a voluntary fellowship of people who must decide in some way the rules by which they can remain a fellowship. Blake opposed, therefore, the "rampant individualism" of either conservative or radical that disrupts the corporate fellowship of the church merely in the name of individual conscience. "Long ago," he said, "I chose to serve my Lord within the Church and not independent of it. And despite all discouragements and frustrations no experience within our Church has led me to believe that there is any better way."[23]

Blake's understanding of Presbyterianism was based on a faith or trust that God can and does work through institutional structures as well as through charismatic individuals.

> It is the faith that the Spirit of God delights to guide the affairs of men, not only through the mystic inspiration of lonely prophets but also and even more often through groups of men, who, with a common faith in Him, in the spirit of prayer and commitment to his will, in discussion and mutual forbearance, in the light of his word in the Scriptures, in listening to others and speaking out individual convictions, come at last to their decision which is more than their own decision and more likely to be the will of God than the individual insight of any single man. Yes, I boldly speak out faith: The Holy Spirit speaks through the actions and decisions of a Presbytery.[24]

Blake concluded his message by applying this theological principle to western democracy. Only where people believe that the group in serious consultation can arrive at better answers than an individual, Blake said, can representative democracy work effectively. Unless Americans really believe in representative democracy, Blake warned, "our world will become once more totalitarian, and I for one am as loath to accept the authority of Rome as that of Moscow. The hope of a free western world to bind men into a new unity of culture, faith, and all of life," he said in summation, "depends more than I like to think on the kind of faith in God and upon the kind of organization of government which we have inherited in our particular tradition."[25]

Although the Vatican ambassadorship controversy died down a few months after Blake's speech, another sensitive church-state issue arose to take its place. This time it involved the charge of Communism among American clergy, particularly in mainline Protestant churches. During the summer of 1953 J. B. Matthews, a hired congressional investigator, published an article in a religious periodical charging that "the largest single group supporting the Communist apparatus in the United States today is composed

63

of Protestant clergymen." Matthews also mentioned by name a distinguished Presbyterian minister, theologian, and educator, Dr. John A. Mackay, president of Princeton Theological Seminary and moderator of the General Assembly, and accused him of being a Communist collaborationist.[26]

At the September meeting of the General Council Blake and other officials expressed concern that no one had spoken out effectively in reply to Matthews' charges. They particularly resented what they considered to be completely unfounded allegations against Dr. Mackay. The council recommended that Mackay prepare a statement and present it to the council at its October meeting. After lengthy consideration of Mackay's statement, the council proposed that Blake and Mackay redraft the statement specifically as a general "Letter to Presbyterians" and submit it to a special meeting of the General Council for final approval. With some minor changes the letter was approved and November 2 set as the date for its public release.[27]

Besides his general support and encouragement of the council to speak out as a group in defense of Mackay, Blake also assumed responsibility for articulating the constitutional legality of such an action by the General Council. Blake personally wrote the first five paragraphs of the letter, which provided a context for the document, and set forth the ecclesiastical rationale for issuing the letter without first consulting the General Assembly itself. Blake cited a phrase in the Constitution of the Presbyterian church that instructed the General Council "to cultivate and promote the spiritual welfare of the whole church" and "to correspond with and advise the General Councils of Presbyteries. . . ." Moreover, Blake also quoted from a deliverance of the 165th General Assembly, which urged citizens to use their influence "to bring national life and all the institutions of society into conformity with the moral government of God, and into harmony with the spirit of Jesus Christ." Within the framework of these general guidelines, Blake concluded, the "Letter to Presbyterians" was consonant with Presbyterian precedent and government.[28]

In the body of the "Letter to Presbyterians" Mackay asserted that a "subtle but potent assault upon basic human rights was now in progress" in the form of congressional inquiries that tended to become inquisitions.

> These inquisitions, which find their historic pattern in medieval Spain and in the tribunals of modern totalitarian states, begin to constitute a threat to freedom of thought in this country. Treason and dissent are being confused. The shrine of conscience and private judgment, which God alone has a right to enter, is being invaded. Un-American attitudes toward ideas and books are becoming current. Attacks are being made upon citizens of integrity and social passion which are utterly alien to our democratic tradition. They are particularly alien to the Protestant religious tradition which has been a main source of the freedoms which the people of the United States enjoy.[29]

Mackay also identified another serious problem facing Americans in their attempt to deal with Communism. Pervading America, the "Letter" claimed, was a "fanatical negativism" against Communism that was "totally devoid of a constructive program of action" and was in danger of leading Americans into a "spiritual vacuum." In case of a national crisis there was a great danger that this emptiness could in the high-sounding name of "security" be easily manipulated by a fascist tyranny.[30]

The "Letter to Presbyterians" then set forth three basic principles to guide Presbyterians in dealing positively with this situation.

1. The Christian Church has a prophetic function to fulfill in every society and in every age. Its supreme allegiance is not to any nation or race or to any class or culture but to Jesus Christ. It has an obligation to speak out on the basis of this prophetic function.

2. The majesty of truth must be preserved at all times and at all costs. Fear of totalitarian Communism does not justify use of half-truth, rumour, and guilt-by-association in order to purge the country of suspected subversives.

3. God's sovereign rule is the controlling factor in history. Our greatest obligation is to make sure that what we mean by security and the methods we employ to achieve it, are in accordance with the will of God.[31]

In a concluding section the "Letter" suggested that Communism was by no means monolithic and that there were evidences that a "post-Communist mood" was actually beginning to emerge in many parts of Europe and Asia. It also asked Presbyterians to support efforts to meet around the conference table with Communist countries to attempt to work out solutions to basic political and economic problems.[32]

The "Letter to Presbyterians" had historical significance far beyond its denominational audience. It was the first public stand taken by any major Protestant group against the possible loss of individual freedom and constitutional rights in the name of patriotism and anti-Communism. It also provided support and guidance for church members in many different denominations who wanted to oppose the excesses of McCarthyism but had no theological foundation on which to build their arguments. The New York *Times* gave it front-page coverage and other major newspapers quickly followed suit. Although many editorials across the country hailed the "Letter" as an important contribution to national and world sanity and freedom, some newspapers like the Cincinnati *Enquirer* and the Los Angeles *Times* attacked it vigorously, claiming that the "Letter" aided and abetted the Communist cause and raised a false alarm about the danger of American fascism.[33]

On the denominational level, the "Letter to Presbyterians" evoked a flood of letters, postcards, and telephone calls to Blake, Mackay, and other members of the General Council. A majority of the communications were supportive but opposition was articulate, unified, and often highly emotional. When the General Assembly met in May 1954, however, it left no doubt where it stood in regard to the controversial letter. With a unanimous vote and thunderous applause, it supported Mackay and the General Council's action and urged local churches to study the document carefully. "It is our conviction," the assembly concluded, "that 'the letter' expresses the prophetic voice of God-guided men who have spoken to our age."[34]

Throughout the fifties Blake opposed encroachments on fundamental individual freedom even though some of his constituents worried about the possible politicization of the stated clerk's office. In 1955, for example, Blake testified before Senator Thomas C. Hennings, Jr.'s Senate Sub-Committee on Constitutional Rights. Speaking as a "churchman citizen," Blake outlined the theological ingredients of political freedom and castigated the Un-American Activities Committee for its failure to distinguish between allegations of disloyalty and proved disloyalty. Blake also listed a number of recent governmental actions which he thought were inconsistent with basic American traditions.[35]

In his testimony Blake touched on a subject that involved him in another sensitive area of church-state relationships—federal or state aid for parochial (church) educational systems. Affirming that Americans have always believed in freedom to establish private and parochial schools, Blake also stated that "most American Christians believe this right does not include governmental financial support for them."[36] Syndicated columnist David Lawrence tagged Blake as a "radical" for discrediting government security programs, attacking Roman Catholics, and discouraging the Senate from considering federal aid to parochial schools.[37] Blake defended himself against Lawrence's charges but remained firm on his position that the government should not become involved in the business of sectarian religious education. At the same time, however, he insisted that this did not mean that public, tax-supported schools must necessarily be irreligious, nonreligious, or antireligious. "The Constitution," said Blake, "ought to protect the public schools equally from sectarianism and secularism."[38]

Blake's disagreements with Roman Catholics on specific church-state issues never affected his ongoing concern for ecumenical cooperation and unity. Blake maintained his principles in an irenic manner and on a number of occasions publicly demonstrated that he was willing to discuss areas of agreement as well as points of opposition. At a meeting of the National Council of Churches in 1954, Blake interrupted one of the sessions to announce the serious illness of His Holiness, Pope Pius XII, and asked the delegates to stand for one minute in prayer to express "sympathy for their Roman Catholic friends." In 1964 Blake and the Reverend Edler Hawkins, moderator of the General Assembly of the United Presbyterian Church, paid a precedent-breaking call on Pope Paul VI. They were the first United States Protestant leaders to be received by Paul VI and were the first United Presbyterian officials ever to visit a pope.[39]

During the tense closing months of the Kennedy–Nixon presidential campaign, Blake opposed attempts to inject Kennedy's Catholicism into election issues. He and Bishop G. Bromley Oxnam were co-authors of a feature article in *Look* magazine in which they stated that their votes would be determined "by the quality of the candidate himself, by his campaign, his political record, his platform."[40] Blake and Oxnam also repudiated the prejudice that had characterized so much of the discussion of whether or not a Roman Catholic should be elected president of the United States. In addition, Blake signed an "open letter" sent out by thirteen prominent Protestant ministers condemning attacks on Kennedy for his religious preference and urging American clergymen to commend to their people "that charitable moderation and reasoned judgement which alone can safeguard the peaceful community of this nation."[41]

While Blake was stated clerk, America experienced the great cultural religious boom of the mid-nineteen-fifties when people attended and joined churches in unprecedented numbers. During the Eisenhower era, "under God" was added to the pledge of allegiance and cabinet meetings were opened with silent prayer. Billy Graham, Norman Vincent Peale, and Fulton J. Sheen captivated millions with their television appearances and syndicated columns, and top juke-box hits were: "I Believe," "The Man Upstairs," and "Count Your Blessings."[42]

Unlike many of his contemporaries, Blake viewed the general religious upsurge as a potential church-state problem. In 1954 he wrote an article for *Look* magazine in which he expounded "two basic facts that could very well keep religious leaders awake at night." One was that much of contemporary religion was nothing more than a superficial interpretation of the will of God "confusing or identifying American political interests with Christianity." The second was that some aspects of the "new religion" looked more like "old magic or superstition" rather than Christianity. People, said Blake, are trying to use God for their own purposes rather than trying to serve God and find His purposes. "The increase in religious interest," he concluded "becomes a possible danger. This increase may be tragic indeed if it becomes a prop and a justification to an essentially unreligious life instead of an aid to new moral and spiritual insights."[43]

Blake expressed his doubts about the quality of the religious revival of the 1950s even in the presence of some of its most distinguished success symbols. At the National Convention of Christian Men held in Cleveland, Ohio in September 1956, Blake appeared on the same program with Norman Vincent Peale, Billy Graham, Congressman Walter Judd, Elton Trueblood, and other national dignitaries. The convention's theme, "Ye Shall Be My Witnesses," generated real enthusiasm among some three thousand participants who sang lustily and listened attentively.

The conference, however, highlighted one of the basic problems of the new religious revival. Granted that Christians were to be witnesses, but witnesses to what? What content should be given to the gospel? Peale pushed for positive thinking: "Pray big. Believe big. Act big and you'll get big results." Graham stressed the essential simplicity of his gospel message: "God has set me at the gate of the kingdom to say two words: 'Enter in. Enter in. Enter in!' " H. Roe Bartle, mayor of Kansas City, said: "The great free enterprise system! There are some who say, 'Pay no attention to it,' but when my Lord walked the earth, he taught it."[44]

In contrast to the emotionalism and sloganism of other speakers, Eugene Carson Blake eschewed oratorical fireworks. His name had been inadvertently left off the program and his talk came early in the afternoon when many people were still straggling to their seats. "How do I find out what Jesus Christ wants me to do?" Blake asked. "I give you no new answers but repeat ancient and tried conclusions of the Christian Church."

> Every man must surrender himself to Jesus Christ as his own
> Lord and Savior. In short, he must be converted. He must
> seek Christ's will through reading and study of the Bible.

69

There is no other way. He must pray at the beginning and ending of each day, and in fellowship with his Christian brethren every week in the worship of the church. He must in the fellowship of the church receive the sacrament by which means Christ can be a very part of him. These are the traditional "means of grace" and there is no short cut, no gadget, no automatic technique by which they can be avoided.[45]

In addition to his role as spokesman for the Presbyterian church on issues of church and state, ecumenism, and social justice, as chief executive officer of a large denomination, Blake had an office to run, General Assemblies to organize, and numerous committees, boards, and agencies on which he was expected to function. Moreover, throughout the denomination, congregations and pastors looked to him for leadership, guidance, and advice on a whole gamut of ecclesiastical and personal problems. Presbyterians kept a steady flow of mail coming to his office with requests for appearances at dedications, groundbreakings, anniversaries, and other special services and events in the life of the church.

As stated clerk, Blake spent much of his time away from his desk. Shortly after his inauguration he left with David W. Profitt, president of the National Council of Presbyterian Men, on a trip undertaken to highlight special needs and worthy projects for the One Great Hour of Sharing sponsored by the Presbyterian church. The leaders visited Japan, Korea, India, Pakistan, Lebanon, Jordan, Switzerland, and Germany, with the heaviest concentration of time in Korea where they visited churches, military bases, and prisoner-of-war camps.[46]

Blake's domestic travel was no less extensive than his overseas itinerary. Since Blake spent much of his time living out of a suitcase, he quipped, "The trick is to keep the laundry going in all places at all times." A bulging briefcase and a stack of important notes tucked in his left-hand suit pocket became Blake's trademark as he criss-crossed the country representing his denomination and other ecumenical organizations. He told his colleagues that his theory of good administration was knowing how to keep the pieces of paper in his pocket in some semblance of order.[47]

At times Blake's travels were so extended that he was away from the office for nearly a month. During one such interim, his associate Otto Finkbeiner hired a new receptionist for the Philadelphia office. Blake came dashing into the office direct from the airport carrying his suitcase of dirty laundry and assorted papers. The receptionist, who had never met Blake, brought him up short when she barred his entrance with a polite but firm: "Excuse me, sir, with whom do you wish to speak?"[48]

Even with this heavy travel schedule, Blake ran an efficient and effective office in the Witherspoon Building in Philadelphia. With the help of his staff, Blake rewrote and reorganized the basic handbooks of church government so that they were up-to-date and easy to read and to interpret by church officers, who had found older constitutional handbooks to be outmoded and difficult to use. Assisted initially by Henry Barraclough and later by Otto Finkbeiner and Samuel W. Shane who became associate stated clerk after the United Presbyterian Church in North America union in 1958, Blake delegated most of the routine office business to his colleagues. Shane handled the legal correspondence and consulted Blake only on matters that he considered to be potentially difficult or problematical.[49]

Blake believed in delegating authority and encouraging the best efforts of those who worked with him. Shane recalled his first staff meeting with Blake in Philadelphia in 1958. Blake called in all the key personnel and in a one-hour meeting outlined what he wanted them to do. He told Shane, whom he would not see again for two months, "I have confidence in you that you are going to do your job well and effectively. If you do make any mistakes, remember that they are my mistakes. So don't make any mistakes!"[50] When the inevitable mistakes occurred, Blake accepted responsibility for them. Moreover, he never denigrated a colleague in public. Criticisms were made privately and then forgotten. As one of his co-workers summed it up: "Gene isn't the backslapping type, but he isn't standoffish. He's a warm human being. He's the kind of guy who makes you feel ashamed when you aren't putting out your best."[51]

Within the context of turning out a maximum amount of work in a minimum amount of time, Blake operated in an informal and personal style. The morning of his first day in the Philadelphia office, Henry Barraclough took a cup of coffee into Blake's private office. Blake looked up and said, "No, Barry, don't bring me the coffee—lead me to it." From that day on the coffee break became part of the office routine for the entire administrative and clerical staff. Blake also entertained his staff at least once a year and sometimes found time to take them to a baseball game when his childhood team, the St. Louis Cardinals, were in town.[52]

One of Blake's most important tasks as stated clerk was to supervise the complex arrangements for the annual meeting of the General Assembly, usually held in the month of May. Blake's correspondence shows the meticulous care and concern the clerk must give to every detail of the assembly: housing and travel, preparation of a docket, planning the recording, editing, and publication of the official reports and minutes, and organizing worship services and other special events. Blake drew up diagrams of seating arrangements for commissioners and dignitaries, provided detailed instructions for the assembly communion service, examined every script for plays, pageants, and presentations, and made corrections and changes to make every aspect of the program meet his high standards of excellence and good taste.[53]

During the two weeks of assembly activities Blake maintained an incredibly busy schedule, yet he rarely showed any signs of fatigue or physical exhaustion. Although active all day in plenary sessions, committee meetings, and private conversations, Blake would forgo his evening meal in order to visit a commissioner, visitor, or staff person who had been hospitalized by accident or illness during the assembly. Returning from the evening session Blake stayed up until two or three o'clock in the morning in the company of friends and acquaintances. With few exceptions the conversations centered on Blake's favorite subject—the church, what it should be doing, and how best to get it done. Blake had breakfast delivered promptly at seven A.M., no matter what time he had managed to get to bed. According to Dr. William Schram, who often assisted Blake with assembly responsibilities and shared a hotel suite with him, the breakfast never varied: two fried eggs, bacon, toast, orange juice, and coffee. "I know," said Schram, "because that's what he always ordered for me also!"[54]

When the full assembly was in session Blake took a back seat to the moderator, whose duty it was to preside at the business sessions. Nevertheless, it was usually Blake, not the moderator, whose presence dominated the proceedings. In complicated parliamentary questions, heated debates, or decisions affecting the basic structures of the church, most moderators turned to the stated clerk for help. Those who chose to "go it alone" often found themselves hopelessly entangled in motions and countermotions and had to ask Blake to bring some semblance of order out of a chaotic situation. Even Blake's most vocal opponents were willing to concede that he was a master of parliamentary procedure and was judiciously fair in giving minorities a right to be heard as long as the assembly was willing to listen.[55]

Blake saw it as his duty to enable every commissioner to consider the possible alternatives in framing a motion. "If you want to bring about this result," Blake would say, "then this is the motion you want. If, however, you want another result, then this motion would be appropriate." Blake consistently maintained one basic operating principle. "We must always be sure," he used to say, "that we do not permit the minority to deprive the majority of the right to act and to move ahead."[56]

Blake tried to be impartial in his role as parliamentarian on the assembly floor, but he did express his personal preferences in making recommendations for appointments to General Assembly committees. Although the stated clerk's responsibility is only to advise the moderator of the appointments which have to be made, nevertheless the moderator, who serves for only one year and who usually does not have extensive knowledge of the church at large, often relies on the stated clerk for suggestions. Thus Blake had a great deal of influence on committee appointments. Blake was scrupulous in making a distinction between two kinds of committees. When appointing an investigative committee, he urged the moderator to make it representative of all viewpoints. When appointing a committee to carry out a particular action, however, Blake encouraged the moderator to select only people who were known to favor that action. This distinction caused some misunderstandings of Blake's motivation in suggesting the composition of certain key committees.[57]

Although Presbyterian polity limited the stated clerk to an advisory role, Eugene Carson Blake made an impact on the Presbyterian church equal to any church leader whose power came from authority rather than personal influence. His commitment to making theological language intelligible to laypeople motivated his long service to the Committee on the Book of Common Worship. The new *Worshipbook*, published in 1970, was the final product of years of theological discussion and revision. Blake's interest in history was a decisive factor in encouraging the church to build spacious, modern facilities for the Presbyterian Historical Society, which today has one of the finest collections of religious manuscripts, official records, and other documents in the entire country. And Blake was also a moving force in the initial phase of creating regional synods so that church programs could be implemented more effectively than had previously been done at the national level.[58]

In the historic and precedent-breaking struggle to grant women full ordination rights, Blake gave progressive and supportive leadership. Although women had been serving as ruling elders in the Presbyterian church since 1930, efforts to expand constitutional provisions to include ordination to the gospel ministry did not crystallize until 1953 when an overture from the Presbytery of Rochester requested the General Assembly "to initiate such actions as may be necessary to permit the ordination of women to the ministry of Jesus Christ."[59] The assembly appointed a special committee to study the overture, with Blake serving as a special consultant. According to Dr. Margaret Shannon, Blake's guidance was an important factor in bringing the issue to a successful conclusion in 1956. At the time Blake himself said: "I am not a feminist, but I am committed to removing all legal barriers to women. When this is done, I believe the churches and the councils will gradually make fuller use of their leadership."[60]

Blake publicly supported the ordination of women by preaching the ordination sermon of Miss Wilmina Rowland on November 24, 1957. Blake selected a rather unusual text: "The women should keep silence in the churches; for they are not permitted to speak but should be subordinate, as even the law says" (I Corinthians 14:34). Blake used the occasion to explain how the Bible must be interpreted historically rather than literally and that the good news of God's grace and salvation should not be confused with particular social customs or mores.

> A central part of that gospel, is that in the Kingdom of which the church on earth is the foretaste and earnest, there is neither male nor female, bond nor free, Jew nor Greek. And this is why the Assembly of the Presbyterian Church, through the study of a committee of its elders and ministers, came to the prayerfully arrived at conclusion that the barrier against women being ministers ought to be broken down. . . .[61]

To many Presbyterians, however, no single change in the life of the church during Blake's leadership was more significant than the adoption of the Confession of 1967 along with other historic creeds as the new subordinate standards of the denomination. Since the seventeenth century Presbyterians had accepted the Westminster Confession of Faith as the *sine qua non* of Reformed creeds. Although over the years the Confession had been modified to make it more relevant to the American scene, it remained essentially the same document as produced by the Westminster divines in the seventeenth century. Blake and other leaders in the church had long been convinced that the Westminster Confession of Faith by itself was neither modern enough to be relevant to contemporary situations nor ancient enough to represent the rich heritage of a Christian past going back to the early centuries of church history.[62]

The union of the U.P.N.A. and the U.S.A. denominations in 1958 provided a natural opportunity to rethink the subject of standards subordinate to the Scriptures. At that time the General Assembly appointed a Special Committee on a Brief Contemporary Statement of Faith, which labored nearly seven years before presenting its final report in 1965. The report contained a proposal for a Book of Confessions and changes in the questions for ordination of ministers, elders, and other church officers. After much study and debate by judicatories throughout the country and revisions based on that study and debate, the 178th General Assembly gave final approval to alter the church's Constitution in May 1967.[63]

In place of the sole-subordinate standard of the Westminster Confession of Faith, the United Presbyterian Church approved a Book of Confessions containing the Apostles' and Nicene creeds, the Scots Confession of 1560, the Heidelberg Catechism, the Second Helvetic Confession, the Westminster Confession, the Shorter Catechism, the Barmen Declaration, and the new Confession of 1967. To Blake this action was the culmination of years of struggle within the Presbyterian church to align its standards with its understanding of the nature of the church in a broad, ecumenical context.

> No church in the twentieth century can cling to a seventeenth-century document, however great for its time or however often amended, without giving to its members and the world the impression that God died some time ago. . . . This does not mean that the Westminster Confession is to be repudiated. No, the Westminster Confession needs rather to be set in its proper place in the history of Christian thought. . . . Unless with courage, we are willing in our time and place to restate the faith in a language that can be understood, the witness of our church is obscured.[64]

In 1966 Eugene Carson Blake gave up his position as stated clerk of the United Presbyterian Church in the United States of America to become the general secretary of the World Council of Churches. One of his long-time associates, Dr. Paul Calvin Payne, former general secretary of the Board of Christian Education, who had worked with two previous stated clerks, described Blake's contribution as chief executive officer: "Eugene Carson Blake," he said, "gave the church back to the General Assembly."[65] All Presbyterians, however, did not share Payne's evaluation of Blake. One denominational official was heard to express relief when Blake resigned. "We couldn't have taken five more years of Blake's leadership," he said to a friend.[66] His negative opinion of Blake was not based on Blake's personality or his parliamentary procedures. Rather, it centered on Blake's strong stands on the controversial issues of civil rights and ecumenism. These two key aspects of Blake's career as stated clerk will be covered in the following three chapters.

· V ·

SPOKESMAN
FOR CIVIL RIGHTS

"Fellow jailbirds, the more I think about the wide publicity which I received as a result of my participation in the Baltimore demonstrations last year, the more troubled I become about the Church of Jesus Christ. It is tragic that the secular press finds so much news when a Christian does what he says."

Theologian Harvey G. Cox in his analysis of American religion in the 1960s characterized Eugene Carson Blake as "a hero of the 'New Breed' " of social activist clergy who became prominent in the civil rights movement.[1] Other commentators have said that without Blake's presence in the drive for civil rights for all citizens the involvement of mainline Protestant clergy and lay leaders would have been considerably reduced in size and significance.

Eugene Carson Blake grew up in a society that accepted racial segregation so routinely that he was scarcely aware that racism existed. "Theoretically," he said, "I knew about the wrongness of social prejudice. But as a small boy it never occurred to me that I was in a segregated school."[2] But as he matured Blake became increasingly sensitive to the plight of American minority groups who were denied basic constitutional rights and opportunities. At the same time Blake realized the impossibility of total or absolute justice. "I am Niebuhrian enough not to be romantic," he once

77

said. "Proximate justice is what we should seek."[3] Thus Blake proceeded to seek the goal of "proximate justice" as a pastor, administrator, and citizen.

Long before Blake became a national religious leader, he had demonstrated a concern for racial justice. Blake preached on the evils of racial prejudice and its inconsistency with the gospel of Christ. Sometimes he devoted entire sermons to the subject; frequently he interjected relevant illustrations into his commentary on biblical passages. For example, when dealing with John 6:66–67, which describes the falling away of Jesus' disciples when they found his teaching too difficult, Blake spoke of the problems of being a Christian in modern times when so much of what the world practiced was out of harmony with basic Christian doctrine.

> I have heard in the past few weeks professing Christians speak of the agitation for Negro rights in America in such terms that one could suppose they had forgotten all about Christianity if you did not hear them apply Christ's principles to our allies, the British in India. I don't foolishly think that the problems of race across the world are easy to solve, but I know that if in passion I decide that Negro, Hindu, Chinese or Jew is to be treated less than a child of God, I am no longer walking on the road with Jesus Christ.[4]

In a sermon based entirely on the Christian ramifications of racial prejudice, "Christianity and Racial Animosity," preached at Pasadena in 1946, Blake's text was I John 4:20, "For he that loveth not his brother whom he hath seen, cannot love God whom he hath not seen." Blake approached his subject historically. He described how the early church had not made a frontal attack on prevailing social evils but, rather, undermined them by its new spirit of brotherhood and companionship. After analyzing the theological aspects of his text, he concluded his sermon with these practical challenges:

> Let me take an illustration very close to home. In Pasadena, as some of you may know, there is a housing shortage. In two or three years it will be solved and you will have forgotten it.

78

But there are men and women in our community for whom it will not be solved and they won't be allowed to forget it. I refer to the Negroes and their housing. They are not in a position to speak where their voices can be heard. They are not in a position to exert their will against a complacent or hostile majority. Who is there to speak for them but a minister of Jesus Christ concerned with the plight of his dark-skinned brothers?

And I am asking this community, where are the Christian real estate men, the Christian voters, the Christian public opinion, the Christian capital that will associate together to solve this and other problems in such a way that our profession of Christian faith and brotherhood shall not be clear hypocrisy or in the stronger words of the apostle, a lie?[5]

Blake preached one of his best-known sermons on Christian attitudes toward race at Pasadena Presbyterian Church and it was published in *Presbyterian Life* in 1949. Blake recounted his "dream" about a young man who mysteriously appeared one Sunday evening at youth fellowship. Because of his biblical knowledge and his charismatic personality, he soon became an acknowledged group leader. Through his personal influence, young people of all racial, ethnic, and social backgrounds became interested in attending church. Many even began to contemplate some kind of Christian vocation. Before long, the congregation was literally overflowing with enthusiastic, responsive, and dedicated young people.[6]

Then trouble started. Some older members thought that the young leader was an agitator. Because he encouraged minorities to attend church and because he had unusual political ideas, some people branded him a Communist and an un-American radical. An FBI agent called on church members to investigate the young man's loyalty to his country. In his "dream" Blake interrogated the young man about his motives but found himself, instead, being questioned about the true purpose of an institutional church. Was it to maintain the status quo or to transform lives by the power of the gospel? The sermon ended with a skillful comparison of the young man's presence in the congregation with the career of Jesus, culminating in his arrest and crucifixion. Blake concluded:

Wide awake now, I wondered what would happen in my church if Jesus came to town. Would I and my congregation receive him? Or would we be the Pharisees, the Sadducees, the Pilate, Caiaphas and Judas of the tale, or, perhaps, just Nicodemus, who appreciated him as one who came from God, but wasn't able or willing to do anything about it all but visit him secretly by night? Would we help put him upon the Cross? Perhaps not, but might we not just stand by and watch?[7]

Blake carried out the principles he articulated when dealing with specific situations in the community. When the Blakes moved from Albany to Pasadena, they refused to sign a neighborhood covenant restricting the resale of their property to "undesirables," i.e., Blacks, Mexican-Americans, Orientals. As chairman of his presbytery's Social Education and Action Committee, Blake intervened when a minister in Los Angeles Presbytery participated in a civil suit to enforce a racially restrictive covenant in a neighborhood where he owned property. Noting that the presbytery already had a policy against purchasing racially restricted property, Blake moved that the presbytery direct all its ministers to refrain from any action that would involve, directly or indirectly, the sanction of racial discrimination through neighborhood property covenants.[8] At the next presbytery meeting the offending minister rescinded his participation in the covenant agreement and "if not humbly, yet with good spirit and full obedience" submitted to the wishes of his brethren.[9]

Blake utilized his chairmanship of Los Angeles Presbytery's Committee on Social Education and Action to stimulate racial brotherhood. During one of his frequent trips around the country to deliver a speech or sermon, Blake had seen a notice in a local newspaper stating that a certain church welcomed worshipers of all races. He thought that the use of such signs outside Presbyterian churches would symbolize their willingness to be genuinely integrated Christian congregations. Largely through his impetus Los Angeles Presbytery passed the following resolution in 1947 recommending that:

1. In publicity concerning the services of the local church the statement: "This church welcomes worshippers of all races" be included.

2. The statement be used in all media of publicity such as bulletin boards, calendars, newspaper advertisements.

3. Pastors and sessions be careful to carry out an adequate program of instruction to ushers and members of the congregation to assure a true welcome to worshippers of all cultural backgrounds into the fellowship of the church.[10]

Not all churches in the presbytery responded favorably to the recommendation. However, at Pasadena Presbyterian Church, Blake's session voted unanimously to proceed at once to its implementation. Beginning on Race Relations Sunday, February 8, 1949, Pasadena Presbyterian Church had a new sign on the front lawn: "This church welcomes worshipers of all races." Within a month the largest Methodist, Baptist, Congregational, and Christian churches, together with some other member churches of the local Council of Churches, officially decided to take a similar action.[11]

In reporting the results to Los Angeles Presbytery, Blake commented that the only evident disagreement was whether "worshipers" should be spelled with one or two *p*'s. Blake also noted candidly that the signs had no measurable effect on the racial complexion of any of the participating congregations. Yet Blake regarded the signs as a small step in the right direction. Since enforced racial segregation clearly had been recognized as an unacceptable pattern, the church was proclaiming to minorities, at least officially, "If you are segregated out of this particular church, you are doing it yourself. This is an open, definite, invitation."[12]

One of Blake's most prominent public stands on racial justice during his Pasadena pastorate was his leadership in the Interracial Commission of the Pasadena Council of Social Agencies, a pioneering community effort started in 1943 with a membership of three

Caucasians, three Blacks, three Mexican-Americans, and three Orientals. The commission had two basic objectives: "To secure for minorities the full rights and privileges of citizens of the community" and "To get members of minority groups to assume responsibility of citizenship within the community."[13] Community leaders chose Blake to head the commission because of his reputation for aggressive leadership and humanitarian concern. He soon discovered that he could not please everyone in such a delicate position. Some people accused the commission of being too progressive or even radical. Others said that it moved too conservatively and was not moving forcefully ahead to transform the situation in Pasadena.[14]

A major problem facing the newly formed commission stemmed from a successful law suit brought by the N.A.A.C.P. against the city of Pasadena charging that the municipality's swimming pool was illegally segregated. Pasadena had "white only" swimming Sunday through Thursday and on Friday had what residents euphemistically called "International Day" when minorities could swim. Officials then closed the pool on Saturday for cleaning. City leaders reacted to the court ruling by shutting down operations permanently on the pretext that malfunctioning equipment could not be replaced or repaired. So, for a number of years the city pool in the heart of town was out of service even when temperatures soared up into the 100s.[15] Blake's commission persuaded local officials that they should reopen the community pool under court guidelines no matter what their individual preferences were. It took some arm-twisting and patience but the Interracial Commission succeeded in giving Pasadena a truly municipal pool. This ended the anomalous situation where one family member could swim only one day a week because he or she had dark skin while another light-skinned member could swim all week![16]

Although the Interracial Commission had a continuing interest in promoting integrated recreational facilities, it did not confine its work to this one problem. Blake and other commission members quickly became convinced that the major issues in American segregation centered on housing, jobs, and education. Furthermore, these three issues were so interrelated that they thought it impossible to solve one without dealing with the other. Therefore, the commission encouraged large companies to employ minorities in positions other than custodial or menial tasks. It also met regularly with real estate boards to promote a distribution of minorities throughout the city to eliminate racial ghettos. In addition, the commission raised money to provide scholarships for minority students to attend Pasadena City College and constantly pressured the Pasadena Board of Education to provide quality education for all students under its jurisdiction regardless of race or ethnic origins.[17]

Despite its untiring efforts, the Interracial Commission could claim relatively few successes in breaking up deeply ingrained discriminatory practices in Pasadena. For Blake personally, however, it was a great learning experience. "During this period," he said, "I learned more about minorities and interracial problems than I had ever learned before."[18] He also discovered that some of the so-called solutions in turn raised other problems. For example, the Interracial Commission proposed a network of small parks throughout Pasadena in order to meet the desperate needs for recreational facilities in residential areas. At first minority leaders on the commission supported the idea as a step in the right direction. After encountering opposition from some of their constituents who viewed the scheme as a way of creating de facto neighborhood segregated parks, however, the commission changed its mind and withdrew support. This left Blake and other commission members in the difficult position of having to retract a program that had started out with unanimous support. Through it all, however, commission members remained friends and kept searching for other possible ways of cooperation and agreement.[19]

The Interracial Commission was certainly no radical organization, nor did its informal, indirect approach to solving racial discrimination issues produce many dramatic results. At that time, however, Blake thought that a gradual awareness of the evils of prejudice and the collective conscience of the Christian community would eventually bring satisfactory results. In 1948, for example, he articulated his approach to minority problems for a local magazine:

> It is not, I believe, a matter of legislation, because the feelings
> and sympathies of the people cannot be too far behind the law
> or there will be thus induced merely a disregard for the law,
> an attempt to get around it. The problems of minority con-
> sideration and privileges must be voluntary and self-
> instigated.[20]

When he was in Pasadena, Blake also opposed the harsh and unfair treatment of Japanese Americans during World War II. Because of wartime hysteria and strong pressure from Californians who feared that they would be attacked by Japanese bombers and submarines, moderate voices like Blake's were neither very loud nor effective. "I guess I was a little scared like most everybody else, including the general who gave the order," Blake later lamented. "I was not as quick on that as I wish I had been."[21] Nevertheless, through the Social Education and Action of Los Angeles Presbytery, Blake and his fellow Presbyterians passed a strong resolution protesting the forced movement of "large numbers of persons who are unquestionably loyal Americans" and expressed their "appreciation of and faith in the loyalty to the United States of the American citizens of Japanese ancestry."[22] Moreover, despite stiff opposition from many townspeople, Blake's church hired a retired missionary who had lived in Japan to assist Japanese-Americans [Nisei] in the Pasadena area to save their property and keep their families together.[23]

When Blake became stated clerk of the Presbyterian church in 1951, he continued to champion minority rights. Blake rejected any paternalistic approach to race relations. He felt that whites could not solve problems for Blacks or any other minorities but that leaders of various races should share in facing the issues and seeking solutions.

> The problem is not that Americans do not know what must
> be done under the law, but they are not quite ready to face all
> the implications of a small world in which the majority of
> people are of the darker races. The problem can be solved
> only by each community doing its very best to promote dis-
> cussion among the leaders of the various racial groups, com-

ing to common agreements as to what the next steps in improving race relations are in that community, and then trying to sell to the whole community their common decision. We cannot plan *for* minority groups; we must plan *with* their representatives.[24]

The United States Supreme Court desegregation ruling *(Brown v. Board of Education)* in 1954 had marked the beginning of a new era in civil rights history. Declaring that the segregation of Black children in public schools was unconstitutional, the ruling also rejected the doctrine of "separate but equal facilities" which had been propounded by the Supreme Court in 1896. In 1955 the Court issued a unanimous opinion that states should make a "prompt and reasonable" start toward implementing its ruling on segregated schools.[25]

As tempers flared and factions in communities polarized, Blake reacted and worked hard to be both an agent of change and a promulgator of reconciliation. In his capacity as stated clerk of the General Assembly and as president of the National Council of Churches (1954–57), he issued a number of statements supporting desegregation and pleading for common sense and compassion. In 1956 he and Moderator Paul S. Wright sent a letter to Presbyterian pastors and sessions asking leaders to "do all within their power to allay the panic and to cool passions, that understanding may grow and wisdom prevail in solving grievous social problems." The letter further requested that Presbyterians "not form hasty judgements, nor condemn others, nor assume partisan positions which will in no way work for peace, lest what we condemn in others we may discover within ourselves." The authors appended a prayer which pleaded for peace and reconciliation and asked for forgiveness and an end to fear, hate, anger, and revenge.[26]

Sharing Blake's concern, the General Assembly of the Presbyterian Church U.S.A. voiced its continuing support of a truly integrated society and condemned boycotts and other punitive reprisals directed at citizens who supported the Supreme Court's decision regarding segregated public schools. The 1956 assembly designated victims of such measures as "political refugees in our own country" and took action directing Blake as stated clerk to give persecuted church members "encouragement, counsel, and other assistance as he may judge appropriate."[27] Before the year was over, Blake implemented the general instructions of the General Assembly.

In August 1955 a group of eleven Black citizens, one of whom was Presbyterian pastor James Herbert Nelson, constituted an executive committee of the N.A.A.C.P. in Sumter, South Carolina, and attempted to effect a "nondiscriminatory" reorganization of two county school districts. As expected, reprisals and threats against the committee and its supporters quickly developed. To complicate matters, the attorney for the local school boards filed a libel suit against the N.A.A.C.P. executive committee for "actual and punitive damages" to his integrity as an attorney and his law practice. In a series of sessions before the Sumter County Court extending into 1956, the executive committee, fearing an exorbitant fine from an all-white jury that evidenced little sympathy for their cause, settled out of court on a consent verdict for $10,000. Since they did not have any funds, all eleven men faced a term in jail if they could not raise the money within thirty days.[28]

At this point Blake intervened. He consulted Paul Payne, general secretary of the Board of Christian Education, and secured from Payne a verbal promise of $5,000 from the board's funds. He borrowed another $5,000 from the General Council. Blake then sent Ben Sissel, a staff member of the Board of Christian Education, to a fund-raising rally at Shiloh Church in Sumter the night before the payment was due. Money in the form of small bills and coins had been trickling in from various individuals, but not one cent of the total money collected had come from a white person. Sissel described what happened when he gave the Reverend James Nelson the $10,000 check.

> The congregation rose as one person. They shouted. They clapped. They laughed aloud. Some wept. After the meeting was over, the Reverend M. A. Sanders said with unintentional exaggeration, "This is the greatest thing the Presbyterian Church has ever done down here. It means more than all the teachers, all the schools that our church has ever put in the

South. I have never been as proud of my church as I am tonight. I predict that before this episode is closed, it will not have cost the budget of the church a single penny."[29]

Sanders predicted correctly. Church people of both races voluntarily repaid the $10,000 with contributions. The General Assembly subsequently gave Blake a standing vote of confidence for his timely support of Nelson and his friends.[30]

Blake's willingness to risk $10,000 and to face criticism from segregationalists went unnoticed at the time but it had one side effect. Over the years a group of Black Presbyterians in the North and East had formed their own unofficial organization to promote Black causes because they felt that the General Assembly had not been taking consistent and positive action to implement its social pronouncements. Shortly after Blake sent the bail money to South Carolina, the Black caucus decided to end its separate existence and sent its treasury to Blake's office. This marked the beginning of a measure of confidence by the Blacks in the Presbyterian establishment that Blake nurtured and expanded throughout his tenure as stated clerk.[31]

In September 1957 Governor Orval E. Faubus called out the National Guard to prevent nine Black students from entering Central High School in Little Rock, Arkansas, and President Eisenhower dispatched federal troops to Little Rock so that public school integration could be carried out in an orderly manner. In a public address Blake called segregationalism "the revival of Protestant fascism" and rated it "the sharpest ideological challenge" facing the contemporary church. He also accused the segregationists of "utilizing the same scriptures by distortion to support almost an opposite ideology from our own."[32]

As controversy generated by the Little Rock episode continued to escalate, Blake and Theophilus M. Taylor, secretary of the General Council of the Presbyterian Church, released a statement to the press in October 1958, which spelled out their conception of Christian responsibility in the integration crisis. Blake and Taylor called for immediate solution to the problems of racial integration that would give the fullest measure of justice and cause the least amount of tribulation.

We are motivated by the fact that Negroes, not alone in the South but in all areas of our land, are discriminated against and oppressed, and denied rights that are morally and legally theirs. As Christians we cannot accept such a situation without protest, nor can we avoid the responsibility of trying to correct them. There is no segregation at the Cross, and the Church through its assemblies has repeatedly taken the stand that the segregation of people on the grounds of race has no place in a church or society that calls itself Christian.[33]

Blake and Taylor singled out Little Rock as an example of massive resistance to racial integration and predicted disastrous consequences for American society if such forces were not quickly suppressed. National wire services picked up the letter and featured one section of its contents, which brought a flurry of criticism.

At Little Rock, because of the policy of Governor Faubus, we are faced by a minority of political opportunists and racial extremists, we are faced in practical terms with a choice between two evils. But we believe that enforcing it with troops and tanks, if necessary, is a lesser evil—however undesirable—than the alternative of buying temporary peace at the price of: (1) continuing denial of rights to Negro American citizens; (2) increasing the pressure for integration; (3) setting a pattern of resistance that would be emulated elsewhere, again at the price of greater difficulty and pain; and (4) damaging the fabric of our democracy by permitting local extremists not only to contravene the law but to hold sway over the mass of law-abiding local citizens.[34]

The Chicago *Tribune* carried a headline: "Two Churchmen Back 'Tanks' at Schools" and *News and Views*, a popular right-wing publication, proclaimed: "Rev. Blake Advocates Force and Violence." Carl McIntire, fundamentalist, anti-Communist radio preacher, condemned Blake and Taylor for inciting violence and disrupting the American way of life. Other journalists, however, opined that the letter did nothing more than support constituted authorities and established laws, and that the basic issue was not bayonets and tanks but massive resistance in defiance of law.[35] Because of the

wide publicity generated by the letter, Blake became closely identified with Blacks in their efforts to implement the Supreme Court
ruling. In some circles this made him the target of derision and
bitter opposition. One anonymous writer sent the following sting-
ing rebuke to Blake:

> Your reckless statement proposing the use of troops to en-
> force racial integration in the schools of the South marks you
> a fanatic and troublemaker of the first order. Your warped
> racial views have no visible support in the ranks of the general
> membership of your (?) church. Most of the members would
> stand aghast at the sight of a Negro entering their church.
> The time has come for Presbyterians to take a good long look
> at some of the fanatics and lefties that have presumed to lay
> down the law on such non-related matters as racial mixing
> and religion. YOU should resign from the position of Stated
> Clerk of the United Presbyterian Church in the U.S.A. or be
> FIRED immediately.[36]

Although Blake continued to receive similar critical letters in the
1950s, he did not diminish his efforts to support the integration
and civil rights movement as they gained momentum. Before
criticizing others, however, he sought to put his own church house
in order. Early in 1954 he called Otto Finkbeiner, one of his
assistants, into his office and told him that the time had come for
the office staff to be integrated. It did not seem right, Blake said,
for the denomination to be speaking about an "inclusive church"
when the Office of the General Assembly had a "white only" labor
force. Finkbeiner replied that any effort to bring in a minority
person would probably cause serious problems among some staff
members who would find it difficult to work on an equal basis with
a member of another race. Blake decided to move ahead with the
hiring and instructed Finkbeiner to deal gently with people who
had misgivings about the innovation. Nevertheless, Blake concluded, "if the crunch comes, they will have to go. If they cannot
live out the principles in which we believe, they have no place in
this office." Finkbeiner hired a Black assistant secretary who over-
came some initial opposition and became a respected staff
member.[37]

In his capacity as stated clerk Blake also attempted to remove all vestiges of separatism and segregation from the *General Assembly Minutes* and other records. Robert Heinze, editor of *Presbyterian Life*, noted while looking up some statistics on western churches that after some congregations the abbreviation (col.) was employed. At first he thought that it meant that a certain church happened to be in Arizona but was actually under the jurisdiction of Colorado. A more careful reading showed that it stood for "colored" not Colorado.

Heinze went to one of Blake's aides and requested that such racist terminology be dropped from the *General Assembly Minutes*. The aide argued that a white person might apply for one of these vacant pulpits not knowing that it was a Black congregation. Heinze then wrote Blake a formal letter protesting the continuing use of the terminology and asked Blake to appoint a committee to study the matter. Heinze mailed his letter on a Tuesday. On Thursday he received a reply from Blake. Included in the envelope was a sheaf of carbon copies of letters sent to every church in the *General Assembly Minutes* designated "col." The letter expressed Blake's shock that this anachronistic labeling still existed in the Presbyterian church and conveyed his deepest apologies. Unless some civil charter required churches to be so labeled, and Blake indicated his willingness to go to court to contest such a requirement, as stated clerk he intended to drop all such designations unless local sessions specified otherwise. The terminology was dropped.[38] When the General Assembly met in Indianapolis in 1959, a local arrangements committee accepted responsibility for providing lodging for out-of-town commissioners. One hotel politely but unequivocally refused to register a Black United Presbyterian clergyman. When informed of the situation, Blake ordered: "Pull everybody out of that hotel and pull them out right away!" Accommodations were at a premium and only with extreme difficulty could commissioners find any kind of overnight facilities. Nevertheless, all who were involved thought that Blake had made a necessary and valid point in his action and did not resent the inconvenience of being unexpectedly uprooted from their rooms. Blake also saw to it that future housing arrangements for the General Assembly meetings were made through his office and that no hotel or motel could negotiate to supply rooms for blocks of commissioners unless they guaranteed that they would accept everyone regardless of racial origins.[39]

Blake's personal commitment to racial equality was as firm as the official commitment of his denomination. As early as 1946 the General Assembly had affirmed its support of a "non-segregated church and a non-segregated society."[40] Even a superficial glance at the General Assembly's social pronouncements from 1954, the year of the Supreme Court decision on segregated schools, to 1964 reveals that no area of economic, political, or social concern in the field of race relations escaped its notice. Presbyterians supported fair employment laws, open occupancy in housing, nonsegregated public facilities, aid to victims of reprisal for desegregation activities, nonracial evangelism, and the N.A.A.C.P. and various other social action groups. As Gayraud S. Wilmore, Jr., a prominent Black Presbyterian clergyman, expressed it in 1963, "No Protestant denomination has delivered more vigorous verbal blows against the citadel of segregation." All that remained, he concluded, was for the United Presbyterian Church to "put its body and its pocketbook where its mouth was."[41]

In 1963 Eugene Carson Blake and the United Presbyterian church had sufficient incentive to translate official pronouncements and personal proclamations into individual and corporate deeds. If any one year can be singled out as pivotal in the American civil rights struggle, certainly 1963, the Centennial Year of the Emancipation Proclamation, would be the choice of many. In February President John F. Kennedy forwarded proposals for new civil rights legislation to Congress and in May the Supreme Court ruled that the desegregation of public schools "with all deliberate speed" did not countenance indefinite delay in the elimination of racial barriers in schools or public facilities. And in August the March on Washington brought Blacks and whites together in a symbolic gesture of comradeship and commitment to the cause of racial equality.[42]

The same year also marked the opening of a major desegregation campaign led by Dr. Martin Luther King, Jr. in Birmingham, Alabama on April 2. Within three weeks more than four hundred persons had been arrested for parading without a permit, loitering, or trespassing. Among them was Dr. King, whose passionate "Letter from a Birmingham Jail" stirred millions of Americans, Black and white, to become personally involved in the struggle for justice, equality, and freedom in an open society. Sympathy demonstrations broke out in many northern and southern cities as the nation through the omnipresent television cameras kept its eyes fixed on Birmingham. Violence erupted during some of the demonstrations early in May. Police used trained dogs and firemen employed high-pressure water hoses to break up parades. An estimated 2,500 people were arrested by local authorities, whose rugged enforcement of segregation was symbolized in the figure of Birmingham's Public Safety Commissioner, Eugene ("Bull") Conner.[43]

Pictures of Blacks attempting to fend off canine assaults and to escape the spray of well-aimed fire hoses stabbed the consciences of white moderates who favored integration but had advocated restraint and patience. Eugene Carson Blake was one such leader for whom Birmingham, Alabama in 1963 symbolized the dividing line between moral support and direct action. "I decided that I just couldn't stand for such behavior any longer," recounted Blake. "I was angry and I went to the Des Moines General Assembly in that mood."[44] The collective "anger" of the United Presbyterian church encouraged the 175th General Assembly meeting in Des Moines, Iowa to establish the Commission on Religion and Race (CORAR) with three staff persons and an unprecedented $500,000 program budget.[45]

Blake's personal involvement in the struggle for racial justice also reached a climax in 1963. On Independence Day, with a distinguished group of Black and white leaders, he was arrested for attempting to integrate Gwynn Oak Amusement Park in Baltimore, Maryland. The park excluded Blacks and Maryland's law permitted the park to exclude whomever it wished. Maryland also had a trespassing law, which Blacks violated every time they appeared on park property seeking admission at the main gate. At the time it seemed a frivolous gesture to risk arrest for the sake of a roller coaster or a merry-go-round ride. But for the participants it went much deeper. The park owners had a long history of unabashed segregationalism. To local Blacks, pleas that integration of the park would result in economic loss was only a cover for deep racial prejudice. And to whites who participated in the march it did not matter if they were protesting a lunch counter, a department store, a school, or an amusement park. All blatant symbols of hard-core segregation were an affront to human dignity and stood equally in need of confrontation.[46]

Actually, the march to integrate Gwynn Oak Amusement Park was not planned by the United Presbyterian church or by the National Council of Churches but by the Congress of Racial Equality (CORE). Blake's participation in the July 4th confrontation came about in part because of aggressive questioning by a New York *Times* reporter rather than by some carefully calculated plan. As acting chairman of the National Council of Churches' newly organized Commission on Religion and Race, Blake had called a press conference to publicize what he considered a significant step forward in race relations. Just prior to the press conference, Jon Regier, a Presbyterian minister and temporary staff head of the new commission, informed Blake of a possible demonstration in Baltimore for which CORE was seeking support. "Check it out," Blake said as he hurried into the conference.[47]

In his remarks, Blake promised that the new commission would be a doing rather than a talking organization. "The time for talking is past," emphasized Blake. "Now is the time for action." George Dugan, veteran religion reporter for the New York *Times*, asked Blake a hard question: "Name one thing that you plan to do." His words caught Blake off guard. "I didn't want to have egg on my face," recalled Blake, "so all I could think of was the demonstration down in Baltimore. So I said we were considering going down there." When the reporters started scribbling notes, Blake could see that he had said something they thought newsworthy. As he left the press conference, Blake told his staff: "You'd better check that one out carefully because I think I have to go."[48]

Despite Blake's public commitment to participate in the Gwynn Oak demonstration, he privately reserved decision until he was assured by his staff that it was a legitimate, carefully planned venture. Once he was satisfied with the arrangements Blake took part in group strategy sessions. At the Metropolitan Methodist Church, where participants had gathered to discuss plans and to worship prior to the march, Blake was one of a number of leaders who spoke. Robert Heinze, who covered the event for *Presbyterian Life*, reported Blake's words:

> Human dignity is still abrogated in America. I think there is a new spirit abroad in the Churches. We have come to know that we can no longer let the burden of the day be borne alone by those who suffer the discrimination we contest. We who are white have been at best followers, certainly not the leaders. If I am asked why we are here today, I will gladly answer. I will be considerably embarrassed, however, if I am asked why we are so late.[49]

Both police and press were ready when the marchers made their move on the amusement park. The marchers divided into two groups, hoping that one or the other would penetrate the police line drawn up in anticipation of their arrival. Blake and nine other ministers, including such prominent leaders as Bishop Daniel Corrigan, Dr. William Sloane Coffin, Jr., Rabbi Morris Lieberman, and Monsignor Austin J. Healy, arrived first. Blake symbolically marched side by side with a Black Presbyterian elder, Mr. Furman Templeton, vice chairman of the denomination's CORAR and the executive of Baltimore's Urban League. As they approached the gate of the amusement park, Blake and Templeton nervously bantered about what they would do if they happened to get into the park. Blake did not like ferris wheels and Templeton did not like roller coasters. As it turned out, they did not need to worry. They never got past the main gate.[50]

One of the park proprietors read the Maryland trespass law to the demonstrators. When the reading was completed, Blake stated his desire to enter the park. The police chief said, "Go ahead." Blake added, "But I want to go with my friend, Mr. Templeton, here." The police denied Templeton entrance and Blake pressed them by saying that he and his Black comrade had decided that they wanted to ride the miniature Baltimore and Ohio Railroad. The police chief suggested that what they really wanted was a ride in the paddy wagon. Blake reiterated his intention to enter the park with Templeton at his side. They countered with the suggestion that they move instead to the waiting paddy wagon. "You'll have to take us," Blake replied. They were taken but in a very gentle and polite manner. In fact, the police offered to take Blake to the station in a private car. Blake refused. "No, I'm going with my friends." At the door of the van, police permitted NBC-TV to interview and photograph Blake at some length. The photograph of the tall, clean-shaven, dignified clergyman dressed in a dark suit, clerical collar, and dapper straw hat entering the police van was reproduced in newspapers around the world.[51]

In keeping with the dignity and prestige of many of the marchers, the entire demonstration proceeded in an orderly polite fashion. Even so, the possibility of bloodshed and conflict was never far away. Earlier in the day there had been rumors of violence. Only firm police action kept things under control. As the confrontation developed, a white crowd of some one thousand shouted: "Dump 'em in the bay," "Black nigger and white nigger," "Castrate 'em," and "Send 'em to the zoo!" There were some tense moments when some of the demonstrators refused to budge and had to be dragged into waiting buses for the trip to the nearby police station to be booked and fingerprinted. All things considered, however, neither police nor demonstrators could complain about unnecessary violence or disorderly conduct.[52]

After being fingerprinted, Blake and many other members of his group were released on bond. Later they pleaded "not guilty" to trespassing charges and were granted jury trials to be held at a later date. The charges were subsequently dropped. Before he left the police station, Blake spoke to some of the law enforcement officers present. He began by apologizing for being at least partly responsible for having so many of them on holiday duty and for causing them extra work and inconvenience. Then with a characteristic twinkle in his eye, Blake concluded: "But I want you to know that I had to give up my own golf date in order to come down here to Baltimore."[53]

Because of national and international publicity, Blake and his colleagues became a symbol of a new phase of racial involvement. Members of the ecclesiastical establishment had at last placed their bodies and reputations on the line for social justice. Blake and his entourage had status both in religious organizations and in society at large. They were well-respected, rational, responsible people who could not simply be dismissed as wild-eyed radicals. *Time* magazine captioned the photograph of Blake entering the paddy wagon, "The Timidity Is Gone," and the New York *Times* wrote under the same photograph, "Setting an Example."[54] Blake certainly was not the first minister to be arrested for opposition to segregation, but he was the first mainline Protestant executive to step out from the security of high office to put into practice what the church in theory had been proclaiming.[55]

Eugene Carson Blake paid a price for his symbolic involvement in the Baltimore Independence Day march. Although he had received criticism and verbal abuse before because of his outspoken defense of racial equality, the furor over his arrest caused him extreme personal anguish. Blake never relished the role of a "lonely prophet." He was primarily an organization man who prided himself on being a progressive leader rather than a frenetic radical. The latter tag bothered him tremendously as letters and telephone calls poured in from all over the country. Many, but not all, were from Presbyterians who were either shocked, dismayed, angered, or embittered about Blake's protest and arrest. Blake kept an orderly count on the responses by the following categories: complete approval, qualified approval, partly agree and partly disagree, complete disapproval, obscene and violent. Although the final tabulation showed a 2 to 1 approval of his action, Blake still received numerous negative letters and many certainly qualified as obscene or violent.[56]

A sampling of Blake's mail provides some indication of the excitement and turmoil of the times as social action in the sixties moved into high gear.

Dear Sir:
I see from the newspapers, specifically the New York *Times*, that you have succeeded in your ambition of getting your mug in the three column cut on the front page. I am delighted to learn that you are in jail. If we could keep you there it would be a boon to Christianity. You are a disgrace (that's right) a disgrace to the Presbyterian Church and it makes me

ashamed to identify myself as a Presbyterian when we have
such scallywag as you acting as the Chief Executive Officer.
The longer you stay in jail the better I'll like it.

Dear Sir:
In your program, having driven our Christ out of the
Church, and our Bible out of our schools, the capstone is to
be putting the Negro on the roller coaster with our
daughters—challenging the rights of private property, and
also of individual decisions and tastes as to social contacts.
Frankly, dear Apostate, your inordinate thirst for the lime-
light in the "post-Christian era" gives us a sharp nausea.[57]

On the other side, clergy and laypeople communicated their
approval of Blake's witness. One minister wrote: "Seldom has
anything done the church at large so much good in so short a
time."[58] Another commented, "Your recent action is probably the
most obvious sign we have had for some time that the church is
able to act as well as speak."[59] Professor Elwyn Smith, who was
overseas at the time, wrote:

Dear Gene:
Time tells me of the very significant step which you have
taken in conference with other churchmen at Baltimore. I
think it was a most important action and will do immense
good, both within our church and in regard to its bearing on
the hearing our church will have among some informed
people. It seems to me that our church is resuming the role
that it enjoyed in colonial and revolutionary times; at close
grapple with the great public issues, not afraid to move, able
to discern the movement of history, and willing to act. You
carry the church with you in such moments.[60]

Many of the letters came from young clergy who had been
sympathetic to the civil rights movement but could not find the
courage to participate directly in demonstrations and protests.
Blake provided them with an example of respectable, judicious,
and positive involvement. One such letter expressed appreciation
for Blake's decisive and exemplary action.

I am deeply grateful for your recent forthright and courageous words and acts in behalf of racial justice. Your frontline
involvement has helped to shatter the myth that the church's
preservation demands expediency, and has helped to chart a
new course for a church that does not deserve to survive if it
fails to follow such an example. . . . Our experience here
. . . is proving to be an exciting challenge. Civil rights in-
volvements occupy most of the extra hours we can find and
make our life very full indeed.[61]

On a personal level Blake had to cope with the ambivalent
feelings of many of his close friends. They still admired him as a
man of integrity but they wondered if he had not just "gone off the
deep end" on the racial question. A few of his golfing friends
suddenly became unavailable for matches, and several speaking
engagements were withdrawn because of unforeseen "scheduling
conflicts." At a church auction, Blake's straw hat worn during the
Baltimore arrest went for a paltry one dollar! There were some
compensating moments, however. Shortly after his Baltimore arrest, Blake had arranged a meeting with his good friend and denominational attorney, George McKeag, at the Union League in
Philadelphia. McKeag noted that Blake had a bemused look on his
face as he entered the dining room. "George," he said, "something
happened today that has never happened before. The Black atten-
dant who checks our hats and coats just shook my hand and said,
'Thank you for what you are doing for us.' "[62]

Although Blake had learned over the years to accept both
criticism and praise, he could not evade a basic issue raised by his
involvement in the Baltimore demonstration. Does a private citizen have the right to disobey a law simply because he or she does
not consider it to be right or just, especially when local, state, and
national governments offered constitutional machinery by which
laws could be modified and suspended? Newspapers had played
up one of Blake's comments made when he was wiping fingerprint
ink from his hands in the Baltimore police station: "I would not
know whether the law is constitutional. All I know is that it is not
right."[63] This was a particularly difficult question for Blake to face
because over the years he had appealed to Americans to obey the

law of the land, i.e., the Supreme Court decision of 1954, even though they personally disagreed with it or found it difficult to implement. Now he found it necessary to compose an apology for Christian civil disobedience.

On a popular level Blake defended himself in *Monday Morning*, a Presbyterian magazine designed primarily for Presbyterian clergy, and in a sermon preached at the Riverside Church in New York City shortly after the Independence Day arrest. In both places he based his civil disobedience on the Bible and in the gospel. In Acts 5:29 Peter and the apostles answered: "We must obey God rather than men."

> So let us be entirely clear that law is not God. It has always from the first been a basic Christian conviction that there are times when a Christian ought to break a law, any law. . . . As Christians Peter and the Apostles believed that they must not obey any order, however legal, which would stop them from making their witness to the Lord Jesus Christ.[64]

Blake also appealed to tradition and ecclesiastical precedent for his action.

> It is quite clear that all of the highest authorities in the Church of Jesus Christ do so believe. The General Assembly of my own Church has repeatedly made it clear that the white man's treatment of the Negro in our free nation is morally and spiritually wrong and that our normal treatment of the Negro even in the church itself is morally wrong. The World Council of Churches said this summer it is "a betrayal of Christ." The Pope has made it clear that this is also the Roman Catholic understanding. The Presiding Bishop of the Protestant Episcopal Church, based on the Scriptures and the actions of their convention, spoke most eloquently and officially this Spring in the same vein. So all the major Churches in the whole world.[65]

Blake concluded that justice was always more important than law. As a Christian and a citizen, however, he had to be prepared to pay the penalty for his disobedience and to face openly and fairly the possibility that he indeed might be wrong in his assessment of the situation. But Blake's conviction remained firm. "It is not easy always to know how to obey God," he said, "but no one who is failing to try to find the way to change the racially segregated pattern of American life, can claim these days to be trying very hard to obey God."[66]

On a more scholarly level, Blake explained his ethical stance as one that accepted both an absolute and a relative dimension to moral decisions. Writing in *The Annals of the American Academy of Political and Social Science*, Blake defended an objective ethical code as one that had validity no matter whether anyone accepted it or not. It would also be unaffected by changing circumstances and individual whims or desires. On the other hand, Blake also argued that because of human pride all human laws and rules are subject to selfishness and sin; therefore they cannot be taken as ultimate and final. Moreover, he contended that ethics in public life must be recognized as relative because compromise is the only practical way to achieve good in public life.

> Note that compromise is not the same as appeasement. A public figure who has no code of ethics should not be thought of as a compromiser. Such a man has no principles to compromise. Only a man of moral principles can compromise.[67]

From Blake's perspective, the most serious charge leveled against his civil disobedience was that as a follower of the Prince of Peace he was paradoxically cast in the role of agitator and fomentor of violence and revolution. Blake transferred the onus of agitator to the supposedly "law-abiding" element in American society that used the law as an obstacle to genuine justice. "My conviction," he told a friend, "is that those who are responsible for extremist action are those who refuse to create new patterns of racial relations in this country."[68] These obstructionists, not the protestors, Blake concluded, were the real source of violence and discord in contemporary American society.

Into the early months of 1964 Blake continued to receive a barrage of letters, telegrams, telephone calls, and personal confrontations relating to his arrest and civil disobedience. Although evidence suggested that most Presbyterian leaders applauded Blake's action, Blake faced a haunting question about the "silent majority" who had not clearly expressed themselves. Blake wondered if he had misread or misinterpreted the mood and mind of his church. "I am no radical," he said later. "I don't like to go up against the majority—especially in the church."[69] He expected to find out just where he stood when the 176th General Assembly of the United Presbyterian Church convened in Oklahoma City in May 1964.

Prior to their arrival, commissioners to the General Assembly had been carefully studying a number of important overtures on which they would have to vote. Overture 22 from the Presbytery of West Tennessee had particular significance for Eugene Carson Blake. The overture condemned the activities of Dr. Martin Luther King, Jr. and chastised Blake for his "unwise" actions and his "apparent disregard for the dignity of the United Presbyterian Church as a whole." In particular the presbytery recommended:

> That this General Assembly remind the Rev. Eugene Carson Blake, that, by virtue of his office his actions reflect on the United Presbyterian Church as a whole and request and require him to cease and desist from all violations of duly enacted laws of this land, and from any action that would bring disrepute or lower the dignity of the United Presbyterian Church in the United States of America during such time as he is known as "the chief executive officer of the General Assembly."[70]

Some commissioners speculated that Blake would be a victim of what the press was then calling "white backlash" because of his prominence in civil rights agitation. The backlash was not in evidence at an opening-day breakfast sponsored by the Presbyterian Interracial Council where some eight hundred people saw awards presented to civil rights activist and professional comedian Dick Gregory (in absentia) and to Eugene Carson Blake. Many in attendance that morning were Presbyterian ministers who had been jailed for civil rights activities. In his brief remarks, Blake acknowledged their witness and offered this observation about his arrest in Baltimore:

101

Fellow jailbirds, the more I think about the wide publicity which I receive as a result of my participation in the Baltimore demonstrations last year, the more troubled I become about the Church of Jesus Christ. It is tragic that the secular press finds so much news when a Christian does what he says.[71]

When the commissioners met, Overture 22 was still on the agenda as a test case not only for Blake personally but for the Presbyterian church at large. In its first act, the assembly proceeded to dispel any doubts that it had abandoned its quest for a "non-segregated church and a non-segregated society" by electing Dr. Edler Hawkins, a Black Presbyterian clergyman, as moderator. Then, instead of supporting Overture 22 or even debating it, commissioners accepted almost unanimously a substitute proposal commending Blake for his "courageous action and witness in the area of race relations" and affirming his "duty to speak and act in consonance with the pronouncements and actions of the General Assembly."[72] In making the substitute proposal, commissioner Omar R. Buckwalter complimented Blake for "putting his body where the General Assembly's mouth was." When Blake returned to the platform, he received prolonged and thunderous applause. By these actions, Blake realized he had not misread the temperament of his church.[73]

In the years following his arrest, Blake continued to be very active in the civil rights movement. He helped to plan and participated in the historic March on Washington for Jobs and Freedom held on August 28, 1963. On that occasion some 60,000 whites and 150,000 Blacks united in a peaceful demonstration in the nation's capital culminating in a mass rally on the steps of the Lincoln Memorial. For Blake, the march signified that victory in the civil rights crusade was finally at hand. "I detected a new mood in the churches in the Washington march," he said. "It was the changing from a minority of blacks asking for equality to a majority of blacks *and* whites asking for justice."[74]

Historians remember the march as the setting for Martin Luther King, Jr.'s classic and unforgettable "I have a dream" speech. As one of the recognized and respected white leaders, Blake also spoke briefly and eloquently. He spoke for himself but also for his church. He spoke of frustration but also of faith. He spoke of repentance for past failures but also of hope for future accomplishments.

> We come and late we come, but we come to present ourselves this day, our souls and bodies, to be a living sacrifice holy and acceptable to God which is our reasonable service in a kind of tangible, visible sacrament which alone in times like these can manifest to a troubled world the grace that is available at communion table or high altar. We come in prayer that we in our time may be more worthy to bear the name our tongues so fluently profess. We come in faith that the God who made us and gave His Son for us and for our salvation will overrule the fears and hatred that so far have prevented the establishment of full racial justice in our beloved country. We come in hope that those who have marched today are but a token of a new and massive, high determination of all men of religion and patriotism to win in this nation under God liberty and justice for all. And we come—late we come—we come in that love revealed in Jesus Christ which reconciles into true community all men of every color, race and nation who respond in faith and obedience to Him.[75]

Blake was also an energetic interfaith lobbyist for President Kennedy's proposed civil rights legislation, which eventually became law in 1964 under the Johnson administration. Appearing before a House Judiciary Sub-Committee on July 24, 1963 along with Father John F. Cronin, S.S. and Rabbi Irwin M. Blank, Blake gave an "unprecedented and historic" testimony in that he represented the social and racial action departments of the National Council of Churches, the National Catholic Welfare Conference, and the Synagogue Council of America. Blake warned legislators that unless they took immediate action the present social revolution could easily degenerate into civil chaos. He also warned against underestimating "the demand for justice regardless of color, race, or national origin. The time is past," he reiterated, "for tokenism or demands for endless patience." Blake also endorsed the establishment of a federally operated Community Relations Ser-

103

vice and a Commission of Equal Employment Opportunity and supported other measures to prevent discrimination in federally assisted programs.[76]

When President Lyndon B. Johnson signed the new Civil Rights Bill on July 2, 1964, legislative leaders acknowledged how significant support from the interfaith coalition had been in the long legislative process. Senator Hubert Humphrey, floor manager of the bill, said after its enactment: "We never would have broken the filibuster without the support we got from the clergy." And Senator Richard Russell, opposition leader, admitted, "The preachers did us in."[77] In a letter thanking Blake for his untiring efforts on behalf of civil rights legislation, Senator Jacob Javits of New York handwrote this personal postscript: "You have been an outstanding 'hero' in this struggle."[78]

Recognition of Blake's decisive role in the civil rights struggle came from other sources. In 1964 he received the America's Democratic Legacy Award from the Anti-Defamation League of B'nai B'rith. The University of Dubuque, a Presbyterian-related institution, made Blake an honorary rector. President Gaylord Couchman described Blake as a man "whose witness to Christ and the Church possesses the ring of the contemporary grounded in the authority of the church while retaining a deep and compassionate concern for humanity."[79] The Catholic Interracial Council of Chicago gave its coveted John F. Kennedy Award to Blake in 1964. It marked the first time that the stated clerk of the United Presbyterian Church had been honored by any Catholic group. In making the award, Monsignor Daniel M. Cantwell complimented Blake for proving that he was prepared to say with deeds what he and other church leaders had been saying with words concerning the application of Christian principles of equality and fair play.[80] And Dr. Martin Luther King, Jr. thanked Blake for his generous contributions to the Southern Christian Leadership Conference in a personal letter to the stated clerk.

> Nineteen sixty-three was a significant year for the civil rights movement. We were able to make greater strides in that year than ever before. It goes without saying that your creative witness and magnificent support went a long, long way to-

ward making 1963 the momentous year that it proved to be in civil rights. Let us hope that 1964 will be an even greater year and that our long trek toward the realization of the American dream will be brought nearer to fulfillment.[81]

Despite these words of praise for Blake's contribution to the civil rights movement, he realized that minority people wanted and deserved much more. Black power and liberation theology both signaled the beginning of a new era of racial relations with new leaders and new goals. Speaking in 1972, Blake observed, "The race situation is both more complicated and more important [than it was in 1960]. We don't know how to say 'power' and 'identity' and 'community' all at once."[82]

Blake's admission that the civil rights movement of the 1950s and the 1960s did not achieve all its goals does not diminish the significance of his leadership during the era of social unrest. One who participated with Blake said, "There was both a heroism about Gene Blake, without which Protestantism would have been even more cowardly than it was in those hectic days, and an arrogance about him so necessary to do what needed to be done."[83]

· VI ·

ECUMENIST OF
GROWING INFLUENCE

"I suggest to you that something no less drastic than a new reformation, a new ecumenical reformation must be envisaged and established."

The life of Eugene Carson Blake and the history of the modern ecumenical movement have striking parallels. In a sense, Blake and modern ecumenism grew up and matured during the same time period. In 1906, the year of Blake's birth, American church leaders approved theological bases for the Federal Council of Churches, which organized in 1908. In 1910 the Edinburgh Missionary Conference proved to be the first step in bringing Christians together on a worldwide basis. During the period when Blake was receiving an education and entering the pastorate, a number of landmark ecumenical events occurred. The Life and Work Movement conference in Stockholm (1925) and the Faith and Order Movement meeting in Lausanne (1927) laid the groundwork for the Edinburgh and Oxford conferences in 1937 and for the eventual formation of the World Council of Churches at Amsterdam in 1948.[1]

By the time Blake became stated clerk of the Presbyterian church in 1951, the National Council of Churches had been organized, giving American ecumenism a unified voice for the first time in its history. Also, significant assemblies of the World Council of Churches met in Evanston, Illinois (1954) and New Delhi,

India (1961) where delegates engaged in theological dialogue and organized social projects of international scope. Blake himself made ecumenical history in 1960 with his famous church union proposal in San Francisco and, as general secretary of the World Council of Churches, presided over the pivotal Uppsala Assembly in 1968.[2]

Chronological parallels, however, cannot of themselves explain Eugene Carson Blake's ecumenical interests. Other clergy grew up during the same time period and did not become ardent ecumenists. Probably one important factor in shaping Blake's ecumenical outlook was the influence in his young life of the Presbyterian church. There he learned that Presbyterianism did not constitute "the church" but was only one small part of a much greater spiritual reality. Another factor was his educational experiences at Lawrenceville, Princeton, Lahore, and Edinburgh where he encountered different customs and thought patterns from those of his midwestern upbringing and an appreciation of the complexity and diversity of Christianity.

Beyond these educational experiences, Blake's personality made him receptive to ecumenism. He detested parochialism in any form—intellectual, social, esthetic, or religious. He enjoyed meeting people of different backgrounds and interests even though he himself did not share their convictions or emulate their lifestyles. Moreover, Blake always thought in terms of how to broaden the base of involvement in any worthwhile cause or organization. This meant an ever-widening circle of contacts and cooperation with people of different racial, ethnic, social, and religious backgrounds.[3]

Early in his pastoral ministry Blake displayed an interest in ecumenical projects. He began reading J. H. Oldham's *Christian Newsletter* and *Christendom* (predecessor of the *Ecumenical Review*) and became conversant with international ecumenical activities. At the local level, Blake broke with tradition and promoted ecumenical youth rallies with nearby churches, although not all his colleagues shared his enthusiasm for cooperative youth work. When Blake asked the senior pastor of one of the prestigious collegiate churches for his support, he was rebuffed: "Young man, our young people meet in this church at 6 P.M. every Sunday

107

evening and that is that. Good day." Blake nevertheless mustered enough support to hold a successful rally.[4]

In Albany (1935–40) Blake helped to organize a local council of churches and participated in an ecumenical association of Protestant clergy. He also pioneered an interdenominational community Thanksgiving service, which continues to this day as a meaningful religious tradition in Albany. Virtually all of his ecumenical activity at this stage, however, was limited to Protestant clergy and laypeople. During his five-year Albany pastorate he never met the resident Roman Catholic bishop and had only limited contact with parish priests through his work with the local Community Chest. "At that stage of my ecumenicity," Blake recalled, "I explained the priests' presence as being due to their desire to use Protestant and Jewish money for separatist Catholic welfare programs."[5]

A survey of Blake's early sermons indicates that he was still in the formative stages of developing an ecumenical theology and seeing its relevance to the problems of parish life. None of his sermons was devoted entirely to ecumenism. When the subject did come up, it was usually tangential to his main argument. For example, in a sermon preached in 1937 with Ephesians 2:20 as a text ("Jesus Christ himself being the chief cornerstone"), Blake listed various ecclesiastical substitutes for the centrality of Jesus Christ.

> Historically look at the crazy variety of things which we Protestants have substituted for Him. Baptists a tank of water. Episcopalians a prayer book. Lutherans the Bible. Methodists a method. Presbyterians, O yes, we are just as vulnerable as the rest—Presbyterians the *Institutes* of John Calvin.[6]

On occasion Blake gave evidence of a growing awareness of the international ecumenical movement. In a preparatory lecture based on John 15:1–17 (Jesus as the true vine and His people as the branches) Blake related the concept of unity and dependence suggested in the text to the ecumenical movement. "Do you realize, I wonder, how truly thrilling is this growing consciousness of unity of all the branches of Christendom as part of the central vine which is Jesus Christ?" He concluded his remarks by reading at length an affirmation of church unity from the Second World Conference on Faith and Order held in Edinburgh, Scotland in 1937.[7]

At Pasadena, California (1940–50) ecumenism became an increasingly important part of Blake's ministry. The more he became involved in community activities and social problems, the more he became convinced that a divided Protestantism was an ineffective instrument of social amelioration. Even though Protestants constituted a majority of the American people, they had very little voice in important political decisions. Blake once called a friend in the mayor's office in Los Angeles to discuss an issue raised by the Interracial Commission of which he was chairman. His friend candidly responded: "Gene, to be honest we really don't pay much attention to you and your group. There are only two people we listen to in Los Angeles: One is the Archbishop and the other is Aimee Semple McPherson. They produce votes. You don't produce any votes." At that point, Blake said to himself, "Okay, we'll produce some votes!" Blake became convinced that ecumenical Protestants could more readily "produce votes."[8]

For the first time in his career Blake also became involved in the programs of the Federal Council of Churches, one of the forerunners of the National Council of Churches. Encouraged by ecumenically minded Presbyterians such as Roswell P. Barnes and Samuel McCrea Cavert, Blake attended his first biennial meeting of the Federal Council of Churches as an official delegate at its 1946 meeting in Seattle, Washington. Because of Blake's preaching ability, Barnes asked the Pasadena preacher to give an address on evangelism. Blake spoke on "The Evangelization of America" and linked proclamation of the gospel with cooperation and ecumenism.

> We will not evangelize America until under God such Christian leadership is raised up in all our churches that will lead us on to a church cooperation in America such as just now none of us is really contemplating. The churches we represent are watching us, my friends. They are saying to us: "In the face of the pagan challenge of America, what do you have to offer in the way of leadership?" If we reply with mimeographed

109

sheets in white and pink and green full of high sounding phrases on which we say what big things we are going to do together when all the time we intend to compete with each other, beware. The index of the progress of the evangelization of America is easily watched by the share of our national benevolence budgets we can organize ourselves wisely to spend together.[9]

Many delegates were impressed with the dynamic young preacher who spoke with conviction, theological acumen, and insight about the role of evangelism in American life. One Presbyterian pastor who heard Blake's message on evangelism was so aroused that he returned to his congregation and instituted a program of visitation evangelism. In a few years his congregation grew from forty to 450 members and became one of the strongest churches in that particular presbytery. The pastor commented on Blake's influence on his ministry.

> I have often wondered where I would have been and where the congregation would have been had I not heard Gene Blake that day in behalf of evangelism. I think the point of all this is that Blake has been accused of being so much in the forefront of social action that he has forgotten the importance of evangelism. Nonsense! Blake never lost sight of evangelism. He simply included in that profoundly wealthy term both personal relationship to Jesus Christ and social responsibility under the Gospel.[10]

A pivotal event in Blake's commitment to international ecumenism came in 1948 when the World Council of Churches was formed in Amsterdam at an assembly attended by 351 delegates representing 145 churches from 44 countries. On August 23, 1948 at a plenary session chaired by the Archbishop of Canterbury, Dr. Geoffrey Fisher, delegates unanimously affirmed the constitution of the new world organization, which defined itself as "a fellowship of churches which accept our Lord Jesus Christ as God and Savior." The memorable moment marked the beginning of the modern era of ecumenical history.[11]

Eugene Carson Blake's association with the World Council of

Churches began inauspiciously. He went to Amsterdam as an "accredited visitor" along with his good friend Tom Holden, and they both were officially entitled to one-half of a seat. Fortunately for Blake, Holden unexpectedly found another permanent seat so that the Pasadena pastor was able to attend the meetings. "I came to Amsterdam," Blake said, "because I had read enough to believe that the First Assembly of the World Council of Churches would be a great moment in Christian history. I wanted to be part of it."[12]

The opening liturgy and communion service held in the New Church of Amsterdam made a great impression on Blake. He was awed by the solemn procession of ecclesiastical dignitaries as they made their way into the ancient cathedral: Orthodox priests with full beards, uncut hair and flowing robes, and great gold crosses hanging on chains about their necks; nonconformists in business suits; Lutherans and Calvinists in white bands and Geneva gowns; and Anglicans in surplices and colored stoles. Within the garb were people of every race and ideological position known to the religious world: radicals, liberals, conservatives, revolutionaries, activists, and fundamentalists—all representing an understanding of the Christian faith influenced in part at least by different cultural contexts.[13]

Inside the cathedral Blake heard Dr. D. T. Niles of Ceylon preach the sermon, although he could not see him. Blake's seat was at the end of the transept with a great Gothic column separating him from a clear view of the magnificent high pulpit. Niles' address set the tone for the entire assembly. Focusing on Acts 1:8, Niles reiterated the searching question: "Who are we here gathered that we should be Christ's witnesses?" Then as never before, said Blake, "I knew that Jesus Christ was far greater than any interpretation of Him, and that our common Lord was calling us all to a broader and deeper ecumenical understanding of our faith."[14]

At Amsterdam, Blake also learned that the road to Christian unity was filled with ideological conflict that transcended theological traditions. He heard John Foster Dulles, United States foreign policy adviser, and Dr. Josef L. Hromadka, dean of the Jan Hus Theological School in Prague, Czechoslovakia, clash over differences between eastern Communism and western democracy. Dulles attacked Communism and warned that unless the Christian church discharged its "inescapable" responsibility in the present-day world, "political leadership can scarcely hope to succeed." Hromadka countered that fear of Soviet advances was depriving the West "of an adequate understanding of what is actually going on" and charged that westerners were "restless, confused, scared, nervous" and have "not much to offer along lines of moral, philosophical or spiritual leadership."[15] Although Blake appreciated their honest struggle to put political insights under the larger truth of Jesus Christ, he left Amsterdam realizing that ecumenical involvement would likely precipitate controversy as well as cooperation.[16]

Prior to the Amsterdam meeting, Blake also represented the Presbyterian Church in the U.S.A. at the World Presbyterian Alliance (now the World Alliance of Reformed Churches—Presbyterian and Congregational) meeting in Geneva. William Barrow Pugh, stated clerk of the Presbyterian denomination, appointed Blake as a delegate to the meeting when he learned that Blake was paying his own overseas travel expenses. Pugh asked Blake to attend the World Presbyterian Alliance meeting, lead a Bible study group, and become acquainted with Reformed theologians from the continent and elsewhere. This was Blake's first real contact with leaders in his own theological tradition who were not English-speaking. He made some good friends and began a long association with the World Alliance that extended through his own term as stated clerk of the Presbyterian church and as general secretary of the World Council of Churches.[17]

Blake returned from Amsterdam with a new enthusiasm for ecumenical Christianity. He reported on his experience in a sermon delivered at the First Presbyterian Church in New York City just a few weeks after the initial assembly of the World Council of Churches.

> All thoughtful Christian leaders agree that we must newly realize and re-assert the sovereignty of the Lord Jesus Christ. That was a common thread in every great address I heard at Amsterdam. Not merely Jesus as a teacher and prophet. Not merely Jesus as sacrificial priest. But rather the *Lord* Jesus

Lulu Carson Blake, c. 1894
(*Presbyterian Historical
Society photo*)

Orville P. Blake, c. 1910
(*Presbyterian Historical
Society photo*)

Howard, Eugene,
and Rhea Blake, c. 1911
(*Eugene Carson Blake photo*)

Eugene Carson Blake, 1917
(*Presbyterian Historical
Society photo*)

Blake, Princeton University, 1926 (*World Council of Churches photo*)

Valina Gillespie Blake
and Eugene Carson Blake, c. 1940
(*Presbyterian Historical Society photo*)

Blake during special outing of
Pasadena Presbyterian Church, 1948
(*Presbyterian Historical Society photo*)

Blake on visit to Jordan in 1952 *(World Council of Churches photo)*

Blake as Stated Clerk with Paul Wright, Moderator of the General Assembly, 195
(*Presbyterian Historical Society photo*

Blake with President Dwight D. Eisenhower at Interchurch Center, New York,
October 12, 1956 (*World Council of Churches photo*)

Bishop James Pike and Blake outside of Grace Episcopal Cathedral following
Blake's historic sermon calling for church union, December 4, 196⟨
(Presbyterian Historical Society photo⟨

Vice President Hubert H. Humphrey, Blake, and Sargent Shriver,
Director of the Office of Economic Opportunity, 1965
(*Presbyterian Historical Society photo*)

Blake with Dr. Martin Luther King, Jr.
(*World Council of Churches photo*)

Blake welcoming His Holiness Athenagoras I, Ecumenical Patriarch (Constantinople
to the World Council of Churches Headquarters in Geneva, 196
(*World Council of Churches photo*

Blake in his World Council of Churches office, 1970
(*World Council of Churches photo*)

Blake with youth leaders at the Uppsala Assembly, 196
(World Council of Churches photo

The three General Secretaries of the World Council of Churches since inception. Left to right: W. A. Visser 't Hooft, 1948-1966; Blake, 1966-197 Philip Potter, 1972- *(Religious News Service photo*

National Council leaders discussing civil rights legislation with President Lyndon Baines Johnson in 1963. Left to right seated: J. Irwin Miller and Senior Bishop Reuben H. Mueller; left to right standing: Bishop B. Julian Smith, Dr. Robert W. Spike, and Blake *(Religious News Service photo)*

Blake at March on Washington for Jobs and Freedom, 1963. Among others on the platform are, left to right: Whitney M. Young, Jr., Dr. Martin Luther King, Jr., and Walter P. Reuther *(Religious News Service photo)*

The first four presidents of the National Council of Churches. Left to right
the Rt. Rev. Henry Knox Sherrill (1950-52); Bishop William C. Martin (1952-54)
Blake (1954-57); and Dr. Edwin T. Dahlberg (1957-61) *(Religious News Service photo*

Blake at Geneva Life and Work Conference, 1966, with, left to right
Bishop Vladamir, M. le Pasteur Richard Andriamonjato, Margaret Mead
and M. M. Thomas *(World Council of Churches photo*

Blake with Pope Paul VI
on his arrival at the
Ecumenical Centre, June 10, 1969
(*World Council of Churches photo*)

Blake with participants at the
opening service of worship,
Fourth Assembly of the World
Council of Churches, Uppsala,
Sweden, July 4, 1968.
Left to right: Rev. Dr. Martin Niemoeller,
one of the WCC presidents;
Rev. Dr. Ernest A. Payne,
Vice Chairperson of the
WCC Central Committee;
Blake, General Secretary of the WCC;
Metropolitan Nicodim of the
Russian Orthodox Church;
and Bishop Hans Lilje of the
Evangelical Church in Germany
(*World Council of Churches photo*)

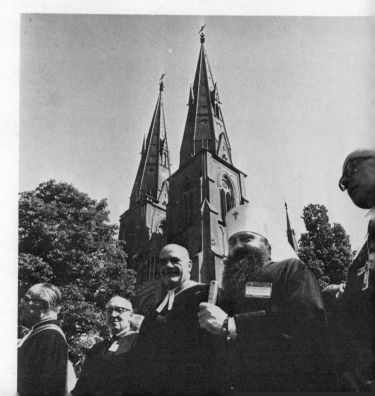

Blake at his retirement from the World Council of Churches, 1972. Left to right: Pauline Webb, Vice Chairperson of Central Committee; M. M. Thomas, Moderator of Central Committee; and Bishop Hans Lilje, one of the six presidents of the World Council of Churches *(World Council of Churches photo)*

Jean Ware Hoyt Blake (left) and Eugene Carson Blake at their wedding, June 14, 1974. Standing with them, Rhea Harvey Blake and Howard Blake *(Diddo Clark photo)*

Christ who is prophet and priest. If the Christian minority all over the world will affirm a new loyalty to him as they bow their heads and say their prayers, there will come a new power and direction to all Christian life.[18]

Back in Pasadena, Blake became an active participant in American ecumenical activities. When George Emerson Barnes, a Presbyterian alternate delegate to the United States Conference for the World Council of Churches, died shortly after the Amsterdam assembly, the stated clerk asked Blake to fill the vacant slot. This put Blake into the inner circles of the American ecumenical movement as plans were made to organize the National Council of Churches in 1950. In the meantime, Blake helped to organize and became the first president of the Pasadena Council of Churches in January 1949. In accepting the position Blake told reporters: "One echo from Amsterdam keeps ringing in my ears, that the only way to make the new promise of unity envisioned at Amsterdam become real is that all of us, wherever we are, whatever our church, realize that unity in our cooperative relationships."[19]

When the merger of the Federal Council of Churches, the International Council of Religious Education, the Home Missions Council, and other national interchurch agencies met in Cleveland, Ohio in December 1950 to form the National Council of Churches, Eugene Carson Blake was already being recognized by senior ecumenists as a rising star in the unity movement. He was one of the west coast leaders invited to attend the historic Cleveland organizational meeting. On the closing night of the assembly, Blake shared the platform with Episcopal Bishop Henry Knox Sherrill, the newly elected president of the National Council of Churches. Prior to Sherrill's presidential address, Blake preached a sermon calling for the end of the religious competition that was so much a part of the American denominational scene. All the high-sounding words of the convention, Blake proclaimed, "would be insincere unless they mean that no longer are we going to continue in the old paths of denominational rivalries." He concluded, "Free churches in America are stronger and will remain stronger than any religious rivals, not by attacking others, but by increased devotion to their own tasks and to Him who leads them."[20]

From its inception, Blake took part in the decision-making procedures of the National Council of Churches. As stated clerk, Blake served as one of the chief Presbyterian representatives to the council's General Assembly and its ad interim policy-making General Board. In addition, he was chairman of the Washington Office Committee and a member of several other important committees including Policy and Strategy, Study and Adjustment, and the Maintenance of American Freedom. Blake also represented his denomination on the National Council's Division of Christian Life and Work.[21]

Blake's participation in the National Council of Churches made him a leading candidate for the prestigious office of president when Methodist Bishop William C. Martin's term expired in 1953. Council leaders agreed informally that the honor of a three-year term as president should go to a Presbyterian, since the first two presidents had been Episcopalian and Methodist bishops respectively. Because the Presbyterian church had no hierarchy, however, there was no one group of persons among whom a selection could easily be made. A number of prominent Presbyterians had long been active in ecumenical circles: Paul Payne, Herman Morse, Charles Leber, George Buttrick, and Henry Sloane Coffin, to name only a few, but Payne and other Presbyterians involved in the selection process were reluctant to bypass the office of stated clerk, since it was the denomination's chief executive position. With their support Blake was unanimously elected to serve as the third president of the National Council of Churches for a term of three years (1954–57).[22]

As president of the National Council of Churches and stated clerk of the Presbyterian Church in the U.S.A., Blake gained national and international recognition. Blake's rise to prominence paralleled the nationwide interest in religion of the 1950s featuring the "piety on the Potomac" of the Eisenhower administration, the "positive thinking" of Norman Vincent Peale, and the "decision-making" rallies of Billy Graham. Magazines, newspapers, and television stations were anxious to give religious leaders a free forum for their particular ideas. Eugene Carson Blake, very much conscious of the potential impact of the various media on American public opinion, utilized his natural talent for communication so effectively that by 1955 he was widely known and respected by both professional and lay church members.[23]

When the National Broadcasting Company (NBC) began broadcasting its "Frontiers of Faith" program on national television in 1951, the Broadcasting and Film Commission of the National Council of Churches, the National Council of Catholic Men, and the Jewish Theological Seminary of America all accepted responsibility for planning an allotted number of programs during the year. Blake led one of the Protestant segments in 1952 and did so well that NBC officials asked him to host the Protestant series in 1953 under a new and more experimental format. Television executives wanted to move away from the traditional preaching service to a "new look," featuring discussions of important religious and secular issues and innovative use of music, art, and literature in communicating religious themes. Albert Crews of the Broadcasting and Film Commission asked Blake to accept the position of host on the new program. "We have wanted it to be a scholarly person," he wrote, "a very composed and articulate person and yet one with a sense of the dramatic and a vigor of approach which will give the program stature. We all feel here that you are the one person who best fits that role."[24]

Blake accepted and for nearly five years planned and participated in the Protestant portion of "Frontiers of Faith," about twenty-eight programs a year. "Frontiers of Faith" was carried over some sixty-five stations in the NBC chain reaching across the American continent and into Alaska and Hawaii. Blake moderated panel discussions on such subjects as: "Why Church Union?" "Ethics in a Business Society," "The Church and Juvenile Delinquency," "The Church and Labor," "National Security and Individual Liberty," and "The Negro in Higher Education." In addition programs featuring nontraditional worship experiences such as "The Dance of Religion," "Religion and Art," and "Religion in the Theatre," featuring Helen Hayes, provided both innovation and variety. For its high standards of production and presentation, "Frontiers of Faith" annually won awards from such groups as the National Conference of Christians and Jews, the Institute of Education at Ohio State University, and the Freedoms Foundation. By the middle 1950s, wherever Blake spoke, church members immediately recognized him from seeing him on television.[25]

Blake also gained prestige as an ecumenical leader through his frequent contact with the White House in the 1950s and 1960s both as stated clerk of the Presbyterian Church in the U.S.A. and as president of the National Council of Churches. Because of his ecclesiastical position, Blake was acquainted with all the United States presidents from Truman to Nixon. Blake, along with other religious leaders, was often pictured in major newspapers shaking hands with the president, conferring over some important national or international issue, or attending some ceremonial function of state.

Blake enjoyed a close relationship with Dwight Eisenhower, who was baptized into the Presbyterian faith shortly after he became president. During the eight years (1954–60) of Eisenhower's leadership, Blake was a frequent visitor to the White House. In particular he appreciated the president's unpretentious religious faith. Eisenhower explained that his mother utilized card-playing as a means of religious education. She used to tell young Dwight, "God deals the cards, but you have to play them."[26]

Shortly after John F. Kennedy became president, Kennedy invited Blake and other Protestant leaders to the White House for an informal conference. Kennedy sat in his famous rocking chair and fired questions. "Gentlemen," he said, "tell me the difference between the Protestants in New England and the Protestants in Oklahoma. I think I understand Protestantism in New England but I've been down in Oklahoma recently and I'm not sure that I understand that phenomenon at all." With his long experience in the fundamentalist ethos of the midwestern Bible Belt, Blake was able to assist the young president to grasp some of the distinctions of American Protestantism. Blake was impressed with Kennedy's penetrating questions and attentiveness to the answers.[27]

Blake was frequently in contact with President Lyndon B. Johnson, especially after the chief executive launched the "War on Poverty" in the mid-sixties. Although Blake had always been concerned for the poor, his identification with Johnson's poverty crusade was more intense and public than his previous efforts. In sermons and addresses, such as "Poverty Is Embarrassing" and "The Moral Aspects of Poverty," Blake challenged his "affluent Christian friends" to prove that "we are really the brothers in Christ of the poor."[28] He served on a top-level White House commission to advise the government on antipoverty programs and held leadership positions in the Citizens Crusade Against Poverty and the Inter-Religious Committee Against Poverty.[29]

Blake's endorsement of domestic policies was in sharp contrast to his disappointment with President Johnson's handling of the escalating American involvement in the war in Vietnam. By the summer of 1965 Blake had such strong misgivings about the direction of American foreign policy that he wrote an urgent letter to Secretary of State Dean Rusk, a Presbyterian layman, requesting a private meeting to receive a "frank interpretation" of the Vietnam situation. As chief executive officer of the United Presbyterian Church and as a member of the Executive and Central committees of the World Council of Churches, Blake wrote Rusk before his summer trip to the annual meetings:

> Our dilemma is that since we dare not be silent about a matter of so great human concern, we find ourselves faced either with being publicly critical of the policy in which you three Christian men [Rusk, Robert McNamara, and Adlai Stevenson] are so intimately involved, or of later finding ourselves in the impossible position of having uncritically supported the policy as it develops, even though, with the information available to us now, we have grave questions about it.[30]

In August 1965 Blake met with Dean Rusk, Robert McNamara, and George Ball (Stevenson had died in the interim). From these officials Blake received assurances that the administration intended to limit the use of force in Indochina and that they had good reason to believe that the conflict would be resolved quickly. Nevertheless, a month later he sent a confidential and personal letter to President Johnson raising questions about the moral and practical implications of the continuing American involvement. In his letter Blake assured President Johnson, "I shall continue to refrain from joining the public, church, and university criticism which on the whole has seemed to me to be irresponsible."[31]

During the following year the United States became more deeply committed to supporting the widening conflict in Vietnam. Blake could no longer remain publicly silent. In December 1966, at a press conference following the announcement of his election as general secretary of the World Council of Churches, he declared that "whatever victory" the United States might have in Vietnam "will have a racial stigma." He predicted that "basically the more successful the U.S. policy seeking victory in Vietnam, the greater will be the disaster in the long run." Blake concluded by asking for rapid de-escalation of military involvement and for concerted efforts to arrange peace negotiations.[32]

After his open break with government foreign policy, Blake's accessibility to the White House diminished. In the last years of the Johnson administration and during the latter part of Richard M. Nixon's presidency, Blake found it virtually impossible to make personal contact with the chief executive or his staff members. He later discovered that his name was included on a list of several hundred politicians, journalists, labor officials, entertainers, scholars, and business persons whom the Nixon White House staff considered to be domestic enemies.[33]

In addition to his television appearances and Washington contacts, Blake kept the National Council before the public by means of a number of well-publicized overseas trips. Just three days after his election as president of the National Council of Churches, Blake made an extended tour of Korea and Japan where he visited American service men and women stationed abroad. In subsequent years he traveled to Europe and Alaska. Serving as a representative of American Protestants much as Cardinal Spellman did for American Catholics, Blake mixed informally with the soldiers, inspected religious facilities, and counseled with chaplains about their particular problems and needs. Upon returning, Blake conveyed his impressions to appropriate government and church officials so that they could take steps to improve the conditions of Americans serving overseas.[34]

No single trip that Blake ever took evoked as much coverage and controversy as his visit to Soviet Russia in 1956, undertaken in an era of "McCarthyism" and "Cold War" and "Iron Curtain" rigidity. Although he did not originate the idea for the Russian visitation, Blake did figure prominently in its planning and implementation. For a number of years Dr. Walter W. Van Kirk, executive director of the National Council of Churches Department of International Affairs, had been working to promote world peace through the spiritual influence of Christian churches. Van Kirk recognized that an important step in this direction would be reestablishing contact between so-called Iron Curtain churches and American congregations. Largely through his efforts the National Council's governing General Board voted in June 1955 to take the initiative in proposing a visit to the U.S.S.R. by a widely representative group of American church leaders "as a manifestation of the spiritual fellowship binding all Christians."[35] As president of the National Council of Churches, Blake proposed the visit in a letter to Patriarch Alexei of the Russian Orthodox Church. He received a favorable reply, with an additional proposal: "We would also like to visit you and get acquainted with church life in America."[36]

An American delegation of nine persons including Blake left New York for Moscow on March 9, 1956. After a brief stop in Prague where they were guests of Czech Protestant and Eastern Orthodox church leaders, the delegation flew to Moscow where they were greeted with much fanfare by Metropolitan Nicolai. A busy week of conversations, interspersed with receptions, sightseeing, and sidetrips in the Moscow area followed. The talks, held mainly in the hundred-year-old residence of the patriarch, brought Americans in contact with Russian and Armenian Orthodox churchmen, Russian Baptists, and Lutherans from the Baltic states. Ten days after their arrival, the American delegation left Moscow for the trip back to New York.[37]

In their wide-ranging conversations the Americans and Russians discussed how their respective churches could promote the causes of world peace, religious freedom, the relationship between Christian faith and modern science, and relations between churches in the United States and the U.S.S.R. Although Blake candidly admitted at the time that the conversations skirted many controversial issues and often were nothing more than each side stating its own view of theological and political issues, he thought it was an important step in establishing contact between Russian and American people.[38]

Because the Americans went to Russia simply as Christians and private citizens and not in any official governmental capacity, they were able to lay the groundwork for the eventual participation of the Russian Orthodox Church in the World Council of Churches. Dr. Franklin Fry, one of the nine delegates, held private conversations with Russian ecclesiastics about possible World Council relationships. These initial contacts later led to the Russians and other Eastern Orthodox churches officially joining the World Council of Churches in 1961.[39]

Based on his Russian experience Blake wrote a feature article for *U.S. News and World Report* entitled, "A Churchman's Plan for Dealing with Russia." Blake advocated a "competitive coexistence" between East and West and contended that anyone who refused to accept coexistence with Iron Curtain countries was "asking for a mutual . . . destruction so widespread that civilization itself will be wiped out with untold human suffering and loss of life." Blake also argued that unless Americans sharply modified their hardline, monolithic approach to Communism the end result would be tragedy for both East and West.[40]

Blake set forth a three-point program designed to ease East-West tensions. First, he said, Americans should stop trying to sell freedom as a way of life merely on the grounds of prosperity and productivity. "It is a strange paradox," he said, "that the Marxist materialists talk much about justice and freedom and peace, while again and again we 'Christians' fall into the trap of talking about order and wealth and material advantages." Second, Americans should give financial and technical assistance to other nations without demanding that they become our satellites or follow our political or economic policies. "To exert power politics and dollar diplomacy and call it Christian generosity, and then to expect the poor to love you for it is about as foolish as people can be." Third, Blake called for an increased commitment to the values of a free society instead of opposing Communism. He saw little hope that America could maintain its strength simply by being negative about Communism.[41]

Blake's outspoken support of efforts to open relationships with Communist countries made him a target of political and religious groups who labeled him many things, including Communist sympathizer, socialist rabble rouser, and theological heretic. Blake and the other delegates risked this kind of criticism in making the Russian trip and when they returned they were met with a barrage of unfavorable publicity generated primarily from right-wing sources.

Most vocal and persistent of Blake's critics was the Reverend Carl McIntire, ex-Presbyterian U.S.A. clergyman who was expelled from the church in 1936 charged with "defiance" of church discipline and disturbing the "peace of the church." McIntire later became a leader in the ultra-fundamentalist Bible Presbyterian Church and the American and International Councils of Christian Churches, which he organized to counteract comparable ecumenical organizations. Through his "Twentieth Century Reformation" broadcasts and editorials in the *Christian Beacon*, McIntire, operating out of Collingswood, New Jersey, attacked Blake for his integration efforts, his ecumenical theology, and his fraternization with church leaders in Iron Curtain countries. He also published an "Ecumenical Coloring Book" with drawings by Vic Lockman, *Christian Beacon* cartoonist, which featured unflattering sketches of Blake advocating cooperation with Red China, flapping his arms in flight to Russia, and embracing Archbishop Nikodim over the dead bodies of Siberian peasants who had drowned in "the gulf of godlessness."[42]

McIntire also frequently protested outside meetings of the General Assembly of the Presbyterian church and usually scheduled meetings of the American Council of Christian Churches and International Council of Christian Churches to compete with gatherings of the National Council of Churches and the World Council of Churches attended by Blake. In 1962 McIntire publicly challenged Blake to debate the question of Communist control of the Russian Orthodox church and whether or not it had any right to be in the World Council of Churches. In response to the request Blake wrote:

> If the International Council of Christian Churches had, during the past years, evidenced a positive, evangelistic worldwide program by its actions and statements, I would have been inclined to accept your invitation. However, it has been clear that the program of the International Council of

121

Christian Churches has been almost entirely negative, planning its activities to weaken the World Council of Churches without any positive substitute. It is for this reason that I refuse your invitation.[43]

Although Blake often smarted under McIntire's attacks, he resisted the temptation to engage him in debate. On numerous occasions, however, Blake did make a public defense of the National and World Councils of Churches when the two organizations were challenged by extremist groups. When charged in a press conference that some Russian Orthodox bishops were Communists in disguise, Blake quipped: "Fine. We'll convert them!" And when an anonymous group distributed literature to the parishioners of the Presbyterian Church of Santa Barbara, California, questioning the loyalty of the National Council of Churches to democratic institutions, Blake came to Santa Barbara and answered questions raised by the unsigned communication. Preaching on Exodus 20:16 ("Thou shalt not bear false witness against thy neighbor"), Blake responded point by point to the accusations, correcting errors of fact and indicating unwarranted assumptions. In his conclusion he said: "If there appears in this congregation real differences of conviction about any matter touched on in this sermon, I suggest your session proceed to handle it under the law and constitution of this church." No one responded to Blake's challenge.[44]

Concurrent with support and defense of the National Council of Churches, Blake assumed leadership roles in the activities of the World Council of Churches. He attended the Third World Conference on Faith and Order at Lund, Sweden, in 1952 as a delegate from the Presbyterian Church U.S.A. and wrote an incisive summary of the meeting for the religious press.[45] In 1954 at the Second Assembly of the World Council in Evanston, Illinois, Blake was elected to the powerful Central and Executive committees and at the same time became chairman of the Committee on Finance of the World Council. In the latter position he quickly became knowledgeable about the inner workings of the World Council and acquired a reputation as one who could raise money and balance budgets. One delegate to the 1954 assembly described how Blake managed to raise the budget almost by one-third and did it so tactfully that everyone felt good about it. Convinced that the World Council was too dependent on the North American churches for financial support, Blake challenged the European and Third World churches to increase their contributions by 50 percent as a demonstration of their commitment to the World Council of Churches. They readily accepted the challenge. Blake then spoke to the North American churches. "Seeing what these churches have done, despite their poor financial condition," he said, "shouldn't we raise our contributions at least 25 percent as a recognition of their sacrificial giving? I am only asking you to do half as well as they are doing." No one pressed Blake on his logic or his technique as the assembly enthusiastically affirmed its intention to follow through on the proposed budget.[46]

At the Third Assembly in New Delhi (1961) Blake was appointed chairman of the World Council's Division of Inter-Church Aid, Refugee and World Service, which had been given a new mandate by the assembly "to express the solidarity of the churches . . . especially in their service to the world around them." Under Blake's leadership the division provided funds for assistance in a number of Muslim and Christian countries including the Mississippi Delta Ministry in the United States. In 1964 the division launched the Ecumenical Program for Emergency Action in Africa (E.P.E.A.A.), which designated $10 million over five years to finance a program of urgent nation-building projects and the relief and rehabilitation of refugees throughout the continent. Blake also participated in preliminary discussions which led to a joint effort of the World Council and the Roman Catholic church to provide emergency and relief aid for famine-stricken India. Up to that time it was the largest cooperative aid project ever undertaken between the World Council of Churches and the Roman Catholic church.[47]

The period between the Second and Third Assemblies (1954 and 1961) was especially significant in the development of Eugene Carson Blake's ecumenical theology. At his first Central Committee meeting Blake listened impatiently while some of his fellow Presbyterians held forth on the Reformed understanding of ecumenical issues. The next morning at breakfast he noted W. A. Visser 't Hooft, general secretary of the World Council of Churches, sitting alone at the breakfast table. Blake joined the affable Dutchman and said, "You had a hard time with the Presbyterians yesterday, didn't you?" Visser 't Hooft looked up with his characteristic grin and replied, "Yes, I did. It would help some if they didn't confuse themselves with God all the time!"[48]

Blake particularly claims to have listened to and learned from Orthodox Christians in the World Council of Churches. This was his first in-depth exposure to "catholic" Christianity other than the familiar western "Roman" version. At first Blake found it difficult to penetrate the cultural and intellectual barriers between eastern and western theological systems. At many sessions of the World Council of Churches the Orthodox leaders would sit quietly until an agreement had been reached on a particular issue. Then they would say, "We don't oppose the consensus you have reached. It is a good answer to the questions you have raised. The only problem is that we would not have raised those questions."[49]

Blake soon realized that despite some obvious cultural differences between East and West there were some very common theological bases for ecumenical understanding and theological discussion. He credited this prolonged contact with Orthodox leaders with giving him a new appreciation of the potentials of "catholic" Christianity. "It was not until I had listened to Orthodox theologians for some years," he recalled, "that it finally came home to me how much my own Church needed the continuity with all the past, the joy in the Eucharist, and the transcendence of the culture that are common in Orthodoxy."[50] Moreover, Blake's new appreciation of Roman Catholicism came through his understanding of Orthodoxy rather than through direct contact with Roman Catholics. His association with Orthodoxy also laid the foundation for his formulation of a future proposal for church union at San Francisco in 1960.[51]

In addition Blake benefited from the Faith and Order studies of the World Council of Churches conducted during the 1950s, which clarified for him some of the basic problems of the relationship between the authority of Scripture and the authority of tradition. Blake believed in the principle of *sola scriptura*, the Bible as the sole basis of religious truth, but his studies convinced him that, despite claims to the contrary, every Christian group had its own particular *traditio* by which it consciously or unconsciously interpreted Scripture.

> I began to realize that everyone was in the same boat on the relationship between scripture and tradition. No one in the World Council wanted to say that his position was unscriptural. You didn't find that some people were always misusing scripture and that others were always using it correctly—not at all—They were always trying to fit it into their own structure or tradition.[52]

His association with the World Council of Churches also taught Blake that social and cultural factors, sometimes miscalled "nontheological factors," did more to keep Christians divided than all the creeds, confessions, and orders and practices of worship put together. He thought that as long as these differences were permitted to limit or prevent open discussion of theological issues there would be little progress made in Christian unity. Reflecting once on an unsuccessful colloquy of distinguished theologians from all parts of the world, Blake offered this suggestion to help break down cultural differences. "I wonder," he said, "if it would not be a good idea to try an ecumenical conference at which theological discussion would be strictly forbidden, and the whole time was spent in teaching one another the languages we do not know and playing and praying together."[53]

These insights helped Blake to formulate what he later called an "ecumenical consensus theology," not based on the lowest common denominator of Christian agreement but, rather, on the conviction that Christian truth has been reduced and distorted by the divisions of the church.

> "You cannot rightly hear the word of God without the insights of your brother Christian" is the true motto of ecumenism rather than "Let us unite the Church forgetting the dogmatic differences of the past." The enrichment of every Church's apprehension of the Truth in Christ is the aim of truly ecumenical unity, not, I repeat, the reduction of truth or its relativisation.[54]

Blake summarized his ecumenical consensus theology in four major convictions:

1. There is a transcendent God, who has revealed Himself in Jesus Christ.

2. Knowledge of this God is found in reading the Bible and understanding what it says in historical context.

3. The heart of the Christian faith remains what it always has been. God, who created the universe, is Redeemer through Jesus Christ and He is fulfilling His purpose in history.

4. "Time makes ancient good uncouth," which fact requires us radically to revise our understanding of what should be expected of followers of Jesus Christ today as contrasted to what was required fifty years ago.[55]

Based on this traditional statement of faith and armed with the conviction that the only future for the church of Jesus Christ was an ecumenical future, Eugene Carson Blake gave ecumenism top priority in his ecclesiastical career. Speaking at the inauguration of the Program of Advanced Religious Studies at Union Theological Seminary (New York) in 1955, Blake called for the beginning of a new era in modern ecumenism that would capitalize on the great strides made during the first half of the twentieth century.

> I suggest to you that something no less drastic than a new reformation, a new ecumenical reformation must be envisaged and established. An attitude of ecclesiastical business as usual will either put off the day of the coming unity of the Church of Christ or will leave us in the position of the leaders of the counter-reformation while others became the heroes, martyrs and builders of the new day.[56]

Blake gave substance to his call for a "new ecumenical reformation" by leading his own Presbyterian U.S.A. denomination into a successful organic union with the United Presbyterian Church of North America (U.P.N.A.), a church whose origins went back to an 1858 union of Associate and Associate-Reformed Presbyterian bodies. There had been intermittent talk about such a union since the end of the Civil War but discussions had never produced any concrete actions. After negotiations in the early 1950s on a three-way union (Presbyterian Church U.S., U.S.A., and U.P.N.A.) ended in failure, many observers thought that Presbyterian re-union would be unlikely. Along with other leaders, however, Blake was not willing to accept an impasse in union negotiations. Moving ahead without the southern church, the U.S.A. and U.P.N.A. General Assemblies in 1955 authorized the drafting of a plan. In May, 1958 both General Assemblies met in Pittsburgh, Pennsylvania to constitute the United Presbyterian Church in the United States of America with a membership of more than three million. Blake was unanimously elected stated clerk and Dr. Samuel W. Shane, stated clerk of the U.P.N.A. church, assumed the position of associate stated clerk.[57]

The 1958 union had important ecumenical significance. It marked the creation of the Commission on Ecumenical Mission and Relations (COEMAR), which for the first time in Protestant his-tory saw a major denomination eliminate its Board of Foreign Missions in favor of an agency that would handle the church's diplomatic and mission relations together. As part of the union proposal, COEMAR replaced the boards of Foreign Missions and three agencies dealing with various aspects of interchurch work. The new commission represented a new concept of mission work that stressed the joint participation of churches in this country and overseas in programs of evangelism, education, literacy, and medi-cal work. As one writer expressed it, COEMAR "brought ecu-menical missions and relations where they belong—together."[58]

As the 1950s drew to a close, Blake's call for a "new ecumenical reformation" went largely unheeded by other major Protestant churches in the United States. Ecumenical progress came very slowly. Even though *The Christian Century* had approvingly com-mented that there was a "wonderful restlessness" in Blake's brand of ecumenism, Blake had yet to see very tangible evidence that his influence was going to effect the basic structures of American Prot-estantism.[59] It would take more than "restlessness" to break the pattern of a divided Protestantism.

·VII·
ARCHITECT OF
CHURCH UNION

---

*"We must believe that if church union is
according to the will of Christ, now is the
time to get on with it. We dare not excuse
ourselves, or abdicate our responsibility by
leaving its accomplishment to the next generation or after so many years, a dozen, or
twenty-five, or fifty, as some have
suggested."*

$\mathbf{F}$ew religious leaders are ever considered sufficiently newsworthy to be featured on the cover of *Time* magazine. Eugene
Carson Blake became a member of an exclusive group on May 26,
1961 when his portrait appeared on the cover of that widely read
periodical. In the same year Blake was recognized by the Religious
Newswriters Association as "religious newsmaker of the year."
The reason for these honors was not because of Blake's civil rights
activities, nor for his leadership of the United Presbyterian Church
or the National Council of Churches. Instead, both honors
stemmed from a single sermon preached on December 4, 1960 in
Grace Episcopal Cathedral in San Francisco where Blake proposed
the merger of four mainline Protestant churches—Episcopal,
Presbyterian, Methodist, and United Church of Christ—as the
initial step toward the reuniting of America's fragmented Christian churches and eventually that of the entire world.[1]

Behind Blake's sermon lay a series of events that began on September 14, 1960. On that date Bishop James Pike invited Blake, his good friend and respected ecumenical statesman, to be the guest preacher at the 11 A.M. service in Grace Cathedral on December 4, preceding the opening of the fifth triennial General Assembly of the National Council of Churches in San Francisco. "I feel that your appearance here in connection with the National Council Assembly," Pike wrote, "would go a far way in dramatizing for the community the oneness that we hold in Christ."[2] Blake had to adjust some of his prior commitments but on October 3 notified Pike that he would be able to accept the invitation.[3]

Blake welcomed the opportunity to speak on such an auspicious occasion, but as stated clerk of the United Presbyterian Church he had little leisure time in which to prepare an appropriate sermon. He knew that he could not wait until the last minute because his crowded schedule of committee meetings and speaking engagements would not permit it. "I had the sense enough to know that an old sermon wouldn't do," Blake recalled, "but I hadn't fixed in my mind exactly what I wanted to say."[4] Given the setting, the time, and the speaker, however, there was little question that the sermon would focus on Blake's favorite topic—the ecumenical movement and the reunion of Christ's church.

As Blake began preparations for his sermon, the Kennedy–Nixon presidential campaign was drawing to a close. Although both candidates attempted to avoid the issue of Kennedy's Catholicism, there was much discussion in the country of the role of religion in American life. Most of it, from Blake's perspective, generated more heat than light. Blake felt that the election campaign raised a basic point. "Never before," he said, "have so many Americans agreed that the Christian churches, divided as they are, cannot be trusted to bring to the American people an objective and authentic word of God on a political issue. Americans more than ever see the Churches of Jesus Christ as competing social groups pulling and hauling, propagandizing and pressuring for their own organizational advantages."[5] This context was important in shaping Blake's sermon.

Nevertheless, a specific incident rather than a general context crystallized Blake's thoughts. While mulling over possible sermon topics, he attended a gathering of Republicans at the Union League in Philadelphia, where he had been asked to give the invocation at dinner. Before ceremonies began, a man walked up to Blake and said, "Good evening, Father, what is your name?" "Don't let the clerical collar confuse you," Blake replied, "I'm not a Catholic priest. I'm a Presbyterian minister." "That's interesting," the man responded. "My wife is a Presbyterian and I am an Episcopalian. My wife and I go to each other's churches and get along fine. Why don't you fellows get off the dime? Why do you keep on perpetuating this separateness?"[6] Because of this conversation, Blake decided to propose a church union that would bring together Presbyterians, Episcopalians, and other Christians who shared a common faith and could see little sense in maintaining divisions that dated back to the sixteenth century.

On October 14 Blake wrote Bishop Pike a two-page letter, sketching out the broad lines of his proposed sermon.

> Ever since I was able to arrange to accept your good invitation to preach at Grace Cathedral on December 4th, I have been turning it over in my mind what I ought to say. A rather exciting possibility has come to me which I want to share with you. Would you think that the occasion might warrant my attempting in the sermon to open up the question of a possible union between our churches, with a definite attempt to see if we could get both Churches to move from the impasse in which we have found ourselves since the breaking up of negotiations in 1946?[7]

Blake then outlined a proposal of church union involving Presbyterians, Episcopalians, Methodists, and the United Church of Christ based specifically on the following points: "1. The Church would be catholic, which is to say, it would have a visible unity with the whole Church in all ages. 2. The Church would be as explicitly reformed as it is catholic." Blake admitted that he had "not yet thought through thoroughly" his entire proposal but he wanted Pike's response before moving ahead. He concluded:

> I have been feeling over these past months an increasing sense of responsibility to try to see if there is not a new and creative ground for a church union in this country which transcends

the Reformation of 400 years ago. You are one who I know shares a desire to move out of the situation in which we find ourselves. My real question to you is whether the occasion that the invitation has graciously offered me to preach in Grace Cathedral should be used in some such manner as I have suggested.[8]

Blake's letter sat on Pike's desk unanswered for several weeks because the bishop was away on an extended speaking tour. On his return, Pike responded with an enthusiastic telegram urging Blake to follow through with the sermon and promising unqualified cooperation and support. By early November Blake had a rough draft ready which he sent to Pike and Dr. James I. McCord, president of Princeton Theological Seminary, for corrections and suggestions. To Pike, Blake said:

I am particularly concerned as to the principles I have outlined as important to the Catholic tradition. Have I left any important word out? Can you suggest improvements in my formulae? The sermon is already pretty long and I am afraid somewhat dull. It is very difficult to cover as much ground, except abstractly, and sermons need to be as concrete as possible.[9]

After Pike had studied the sermon draft, he and Blake had a lengthy telephone conversation during which they went over the sermon point by point. Pike offered a number of minor suggestions most of which were designed to make the proposal more acceptable to evangelicals. Only at one point did he ask Blake to make any substantive change. Blake had included some critical words in the original draft about great cathedrals, rich vestments, and complicated liturgy. "Can't you ease that just a little," Pike queried. "This cathedral isn't paid for yet!" Blake softened his terminology and Pike was satisfied.[10]

Despite Blake's consultation with Pike before writing a final draft, the term "Blake–Pike Proposal" employed by the religious press and popular historians is a misnomer. From beginning to end it was Blake's project. He proposed the idea and had the sermon in nearly finished form before Pike had any input. As indicated,

Pike's suggestions resulted in only minimal modifications to the text. However, because Pike made a formal response to the sermon and because it was given in Grace Cathedral, the New York *Times* and *Time* magazine linked both names with the reunion message and other newspapers and magazines followed their example. The hyphenated title persisted despite disclaimers from Pike. Blake never made a public issue of the terminology and to this day reputable journals continue to link Pike with Blake's sermon.[11]

Although Blake consulted with Pike and McCord beforehand, he did not share the contents of his sermon with the moderator of the General Assembly or members of the General Council of the United Presbyterian Church. (Blake telephoned the moderator, the Reverend Herman L. Turner, and informed him he was going to say something important in San Francisco.) He followed this procedure because he did not want the sermon to be an "official" pronouncement. Rather, he wanted to speak to the San Francisco congregation as a minister who believed that "God requires us to break through the barriers of nearly five hundred years of history, to attempt under God to transcend the separate traditions of our Churches, and to find a way together to unite them so that, manifesting the unity given us by our Lord Jesus Christ, His Church may be renewed for its mission to our nation and to the world 'that the world may believe.' "[12]

When Blake entered the high pulpit of Grace Cathedral on December 4, 1960 there were no empty seats. Although Blake had managed to keep the text of his sermon a secret, he did let it be known that he intended to say something of significance. People came with a sense of expectancy, wanting to be witnesses to an important event. Parishioners, delegates to the National Council of Churches Assembly, visitors, and a press corp of more than one hundred men and women were on hand to hear him preach.

Immediately after the sermon, Bishop Pike responded to Blake's proposal, calling it a "prophetic proclamation [that] is the most sound and inspiring proposal for unity of the church in this country which has ever been made in its history."[13] As the congregation made its way out of the cathedral at the conclusion of the service, Harold Fey, editor of *The Christian Century*, remarked to a friend:

"You could go to church for a decade—maybe for this century—and not see a service as unique and as important as this one."[14] Both supporters and opponents of Blake's proposal admitted that Fey and Pike were correct—Eugene Carson Blake had set the ecumenical agenda in American Protestantism for the next decade and beyond.

Blake prefaced his proposal with a caution that he was speaking as an individual Presbyterian minister and not as stated clerk of the Presbyterian Church in the U.S.A. However, he claimed historical precedent for support from his own Reformed tradition, citing a statement issued by the World Alliance of Reformed Churches in 1959 that challenged constituent churches to "put their traditions and systems under the judgement of Christ" and to be alert for "new forms with which an eternally re-creating God can startle us while he secures his Church." He did not mention, however, that the chairman of the committee that drew up this statement was a minister named Eugene Carson Blake![15]

Before explicating the basic principles of his proposal, Blake defined his understanding of the key word "catholic." He did not, he explained, mean catholic in the common usage of "Roman Catholic" referring to a particular Christian church. Nor did he mean catholic in the sense of the Apostles' Creed: "I believe in the Holy Catholic Church," i.e., the confession that "Jesus Christ has established one universal Church in all ages and in all places and that we are at least part of it." Instead, Blake offered a third definition.

> I refer to those practices and to those understandings of faith and order, of church and sacraments, which are catholic in contrast to the protestant or evangelical practices and understandings. . . . When I say then that the proposal I make is to establish a Church both catholic and reformed, I mean one which unites catholic and reformed understandings and practices in an even broader and deeper way than that already present in your communion.[16]

Blake next described the principles of reunion that he considered to be important to Christians of the "catholic" tradition.

1. The reunited Church must have visible and historical
   continuity with the Church of all ages before and after
   the Reformation. This will include a ministry which by
   its orders and ordination is recognized as widely as possible by all other Christian bodies.[17]

Blake began with this principle because he saw it as the only
possible basis on which the broad reunion he was proposing could
take place and because he knew that it would be a thorny theological issue for noncatholics. Blake proposed to cut the Gordian knot
of years of theological controversy by establishing a united church
with a historical ministry recognized by all participants without
question or mental reservation. Blake's understanding of episcopacy (the office of bishop) derived from his experience with Eastern
Orthodoxy, and the Orthodox understanding of bishop as pastor of
the congregation seemed to Blake to hold possibilities for organic
union that none of the western, hierarchical forms could express so
well.[18]

2. The reunited Church must clearly confess the historic
   trinitarian faith received from the Apostles and set forth
   in the Apostles' and Nicene Creeds.[19]

Although trinitarian Christianity was not a controversial issue
with the groups involved in Blake's proposal, Blake wanted to
provide a creedal basis for the new church that would satisfy
"catholic" Christians while at the same time would not deter those
who feared the imposition of some restrictive, required confession. Blake thought that the Nicene and Apostles' creeds
provided both a base of theological agreement and a way of defin-
ing historic Christianity over against contemporary secular,
humanistic, and atheistic ideologies.

3. The reunited Church must administer the two sacraments, instituted by Christ, the Lord's Supper (or Holy
   Communion, or Eucharist) and Baptism. These must be
   understood as truly Means of Grace by which God's
   grace and presence are made available to His people.[20]

134

In this principle Blake eschewed a precise description of sacramental theology. He acknowledged, however, the catholic concern for the reality of the sacraments so that they are recognized as true means of grace rather than as symbolic memorials. Further definitions of the nature and function of sacraments, Blake admitted, would have to come later. In the meantime, Catholic Christians could rest assured that the reunited church would enable them "to worship and witness joyfully and in good conscience."[21]

Blake then described principles of reunion important to Christians of the Reformation tradition.

1. The reunited Church must accept the principle of continuing reformation under the Word of God by the guidance of the Holy Spirit.[22]

Speaking to religious communities where the watchword was *sola scriptura*, Blake recognized the fundamental authority of Scripture in the life and doctrine of the church. Although the Bible is "God's instrument to speak His saving Word to Christians and to the Church," Blake cautioned that it is not and cannot be interpreted in a vacuum. There will always be an interaction of Scripture, sacrament, and tradition. Blake envisaged a new church where the principle of the reforming power of Scripture is acknowledged but is constantly understood and appreciated in the context of sacrament and tradition.[23]

2. The reunited Church must be truly democratic in its government, recognizing that the whole people of God are Christ's Church, that all Christians are Christ's ministers even though some in the church are separated and ordained to the ministry of word and sacrament.[24]

In discussing this principle, Blake articulated the fears of nonepiscopal churches whose deep-rooted suspicions of aristocratic and authoritarian hierarchies reached back to the reformation of the sixteenth century. While emphasizing that episcopacy in this country was committed to democratic principles, Blake stressed that it was essential to the new church that decisions generally be made by groups of people under the guidance of the Holy Spirit rather than by one individual who has authority to impose on others his/her decision or judgment. Above all, Blake emphasized the importance of protecting the responsible freedom of congregations to elect pastors and of ministers to respond to calls from God. Defense of these freedoms historically had been the source of denominational schism and strife. This Blake was determined to avoid in the new church organization.[25]

> 3. The re-united Church must seek in a new way to recapture the brotherhood and sense of fellowship of all its members and ministers.[26]

Blake deals here with what can be termed "ecclesiastical linguistics." Although it is inevitable that there would be various levels of authority in the new church, Blake saw no need in perpetuating anachronistic terminology and protocol. "My brother or my sister" would be a better form of Christian address than "your grace or my Lord." Blake's plea for simplicity in nomenclature appears on the surface to be far less significant than other basic principles. To church members, however, such practical matters are of paramount importance, and Blake let them know that he shared their concern. For the clergy Blake also proposed that the reunited church would attempt to avoid unreasonable inequities in ministers' salaries and perquisites "lest the poor be alienated or the world concluded that luxury has sapped the soul of the Church."[27]

> 4. Finally the reunited Church must find the way to include within its catholicity (and because of it) a wide diversity of theological formulation of the faith and a variety of worship and liturgy including worship that is nonliturgical.[28]

Blake anticipated the charge that church union automatically meant church uniformity. Neither creedal rigidity nor liturgical formality were part of Blake's vision for the new church. "True church union," he said, "can become a reality only when churches appreciate better than they have the liberating and creative inspiration of the Holy Spirit" in ordering their doctrine and worship. Rather than a sterile uniformity the proposed church would provide a framework for a more diverse Christianity than any single denominational tradition could possibly offer.[29]

Before his closing remarks, Blake clarified one other important assumption in his proposal. The reunited church, he emphasized, must remain in the mainstream of the ecumenical movement and recognize that its reunion is but a "stage and a step toward that unity which Christ requires His Church to manifest." The proposal was not intended as an end in itself but, rather, as a meaningful move "*toward* the reunion of Christ's Church." This latter reunion Blake saw as a continuing process involving interrelation with national and international conciliar movements as well as other major Christian traditions not included in his specific proposal.[30]

Probably no single sermon in modern times prompted such a widespread reaction and exchange of opinion as did Blake's San Francisco address. Both the religious and the secular press gave it front-page coverage. *Time* called it "a landmark in Protestant history," *Newsweek* devoted its religion section to a detailed analysis of Blake's proposal, and *Life* gave one of its rare religious editorials on Blake's "fresh idea" for ecumenical progress. A few weeks after the sermon Blake and Pike were interviewed on "Face the Nation" (CBS), an invitation extended because of the excitement stirred up over the possibility of church merger. Even Roman Catholic journals and newspapers joined in a response to Blake's proposal as it related to possible developments in the impending Vatican II ecumenical council.[31]

Not all the immediate response was favorable. The Reverend John Huess, rector of Trinity Episcopal Church in New York, said that the proposal was "so unrealistic and unbiblical that it borders on fuzzy-headed thinking." He also called it "a reunion based on a theological vacuum" and charged Blake with "dealing with a serious subject in a trivial way."[32] Bishop Gerald Kennedy, president of the Methodist Council of Bishops, commented: "I don't think Blake has proposed anything. There is nothing new here. . . . We are exactly where we have always been."[33] Dr. Norman Vincent Peale, pastor of Marble Collegiate Church in New York City, asked: "What good will it do to merge weakness and decadence? It only makes for bigger weakness and decadence."[34] Dr. L. Nelson Bell, founder of *Christianity Today*, saw in Blake's proposal the possibility of a step toward "the eventual creation of a super-Church" that would "appeal to the unregenerate of the world." What was needed, Bell insisted, was not unity at the organizational level but a "spiritual unity of believers which transcends denominational, racial, and national borders."[35]

Why did such an ordinary sermon evoke so immediate and sustained a theological response? Most of what Blake said was not new or original. Numerous pronouncements, proposals, and ecumenical study documents could be cited as sources for Blake's address. One noted Roman Catholic scholar reached back as far as 1898 to a book written by William Reed Huntington entitled *A National Church* for a concept of church union similar to the one proposed by Blake. What was new, however, was the setting in which the proposal was made and the climate of receptivity present in 1960 that was not there in 1898.[36]

There were several reasons for its impact. For one thing, the timing and setting of Blake's sermon virtually guaranteed that it would get maximum possible exposure. The conjunction of a meeting of the General Assembly of the National Council of Churches and a sermon by Dr. Billy Graham in the Grace Cathedral pulpit at 3 P.M. following Blake's address attracted a swarm of eager secular and religious reporters.[37] In addition, Blake carried sufficient stature in religious and ecumenical circles to command attention and had the backing of American church leaders who themselves had gained the respect of millions of Christians—Lichtenberger, Hoskins, Wagner, Lord, and Pike to name only a few."[38]

Second, the reunion proposal itself was very practical and thus appealing. Blake did not offer some mystical oration on the general values of "spiritual ecumenism." His proposal was that one significant step "toward the reunion of Christ's church" be undertaken. In effect Blake threw down the gauntlet to four major Protestant denominations whose leaders and laity had been committed to ecumenical Christianity. By precedent and principle they could hardly sidestep Blake's concrete proposal without losing face in the religious world. Furthermore, Blake had selected four denominations whose history was deeply intertwined. Methodism had sprung from Anglicanism in the eighteenth century and the United Church of Christ had a Puritan and Reformed background that came from the same Calvinistic sources as Presbyterianism. Finally, the size of the proposed reunited church—approximately twenty million members—was large enough to excite the imagination but manageable enough to remain within the realm of actual implementation.[39]

A third factor underlying the impact of Blake's reunion proposal was Pope John XXIII's convocation of Vatican Council II. In 1959, only ninety days after he became pope, he startled the Christian world with the announcement that he planned to convoke the Church's twenty-first ecumenical council, the first since Vatican I in 1869–70. Pope John also proposed that Protestant observers be invited to attend the sessions as the Roman Catholic church "opened up its windows to the world" and focused its attention on *aggiornamento*, updating Catholicism for the twentieth century. Although the council did not open until 1962, there was already in 1960 an air of excitement and expectancy of changing Catholic–Protestant relationships and the possibility of rapprochement between the Church of Rome and its separated brethren. Blake himself frequently acknowledged the impetus that Pope John gave to honest consideration of the San Francisco sermon: "Pope John got me off the hook," Blake said, "by calling Vatican II and making Catholic a good word again."[40]

Without one other essential ingredient, however, Blake's proposal would have disappeared in the oblivion of most ecclesiastical pronouncements. It is impossible to account for the lasting national response to Blake's message solely on the basis of publicity and charismatic leadership. If the vast majority of American Protestants had not been receptive to the possibilities of church union, or at least confused, dismayed, and uncertain about existing denominational divisions, no amount of bureaucratic manipulation could have evoked such an overwhelming response of interest. Blake himself evaluated the situation in these terms: "I was flabbergasted. I knew my sermon wasn't all that good. It simply released a great impatience with disunity which was latent among the church members of America. As usual, the people were way out ahead of their leaders in their readiness to move forward."[41]

In the aftermath of the dramatic reunion sermon, the one immediate reaction that most concerned Eugene Carson Blake was not the opinions of learned theologians but the feelings of the leaders, pastors, and churchmembers of his own denomination. Unlike other pronouncements on race and church and state, Blake had not sought approval from the General Council or the moderator of the General Assembly. He had simply exercised his perogative as a Presbyterian minister in a free pulpit to speak his mind on an important subject.

He knew the test would come at the meeting of the General Assembly of the United Presbyterian Church in the U.S.A. scheduled for Buffalo, New York in May 1961. Commissioners to that assembly would in effect decide the fate of Blake's proposal, for if his own denomination did not overwhelmingly move to expedite reunion negotiations, there was little likelihood that the other churches involved would give the proposal serious consideration.

Events proved that Eugene Carson Blake had read the mind of his constituents correctly. Before the General Assembly convened, about sixty out of two hundred presbyteries forwarded overtures designed to set in motion union negotiations along the lines suggested by Blake in San Francisco. The only serious obstacle to Blake's proposal was an overture by the Presbytery of Chicago which sought to require in advance an agreement by the Protestant Episcopal Church that it would recognize other denominations as "true churches possessing a valid ministry" before commencing reunion explorations. Commissioners rejected the overture, however, on the grounds that the question of episcopacy should itself be a subject of negotiation and that the Presbyterian union committee would be severely weakened if the General Assembly loaded it down with reservations prior to discussions.[42]

A Committee on Church Union of the General Assembly then recommended that an overture on church union by the Presbytery of Albany be adopted with several clarifying and broadening amendments so that the United Presbyterian Church could "ex-

plore the possibility of organic union" with the other named denominations. An important clarification was the addition of
"evangelical" to the distinguished characteristics of the proposed
united church. The church would be "truly catholic, truly reformed, and truly evangelical." Blake concurred with the addition
of "evangelical" because informal conferences with Methodist,
Episcopal, and United Church of Christ leaders had convinced
him that this would make the proposal more acceptable and would
eliminate any misinterpretation of his ecumenical theology. Blake
cautioned, however, that the word *evangelical* "refers to the gospel
of Jesus Christ and must not be abandoned to those who choose to
interpret it narrowly."[43]

After some sharp debate, most of which centered around the
role of bishops and the mutual recognition of the validity of ministry, commissioners agreed to create a nine-person committee,
chaired by Dr. James I. McCord, to explore reunion possibilities
and report back to the next General Assembly. With only a few
dissenting votes, the General Assembly passed the following
resolution:

> The United Presbyterian Church in the United States of
> America, meeting in Buffalo, New York, May 17–24, 1961
> . . . invites the Protestant Episcopal Church, meeting in
> General Convention in Detroit, Michigan, in this same year to
> join with us in an invitation to the Methodist Church and the
> United Church of Christ to explore the establishment of a
> united Church, truly Catholic, truly Reformed, and truly
> Evangelical.[44]

In response to the Presbyterian initiative, the other three denominations in Blake's proposal indicated their willingness to
cooperate in conversations about church union. Representatives
held their first full meeting in Washington, D.C. in April 1962,
and constituted themselves the "Consultation on Church Union,"
which became known as COCU. Plenary sessions met annually to
discuss substantive issues and to make decisions regarding the progress of church union. During Blake's active involvement in
COCU, additional meetings were held at Oberlin (1963), Prince-

ton (1964), Lexington, Kentucky (1965), and Dallas (1966). As discussions progressed, other denominations accepted membership in the consultation: Evangelical United Brethren Church and Disciples of Christ (1962), African Methodist Episcopal Church and Presbyterian Church in the U.S. (1965). African Methodist Episcopal Zion Church (1966), and Christian Methodist Episcopal Church (1967).[45]

Once the Consultation on Church Union became a reality, Blake did not dominate the committee, nor did his San Francisco sermon determine the agenda. Blake had not intended it as a blueprint for a facile merger of four major denominations and it was not so employed. It was, however, the starting point for a series of ongoing and developing theological discussions about church union. Blake did not serve as chairman of the consultation but as a member of the executive committee, and as an active participant he exerted considerable influence and direction. Dr. Truman Douglass of the United Church of Christ pinpointed Blake's role in consultation discussions: "On many occasions when we might have bogged down or given up, Gene Blake got to the root of the problems, smoothed over the ruffled feelings, and started us moving again."[46]

Agreement on basic theological issues came more quickly than critics of the plan had predicted. One of the first breakthroughs in COCU came in the Oberlin session where the participants reached agreement on the dual authority of Scripture and tradition in the life of the church. Later plenary sessions dealt with the sacraments and the nature of the ministry, the latter being one of the most difficult subjects to reconcile with different denominational interpretations. A threefold ministry of bishop, presbyter, and deacon was accepted, but in each case the offices were defined so that they did not represent only one church's historic definition or common practice.[47]

Despite progress in the COCU discussions, opponents of the merger plan maintained a steady stream of opposition in the religious press. A major criticism was that the sheer mechanics of church union might sap the energy of the churches at a crucial point in American history when a united effort was needed to deal with pressing social problems such as race and poverty. Also, the size of the proposed church (twenty million) frightened many people who saw specters of an inefficient, cumbersome, and ineffective "super-church" instead of a tight-knit community of believers witnessing for Jesus Christ. Moreover, opponents insisted that bigger churches meant authority structures, hierarchies, organizational flow charts, and mountains of red tape. Inevitably, they said, a large organization spends considerable time, money, and talent just keeping the organization itself functioning. As for bishops, there were many who responded with: "Over my dead body" or some other more colorful expletive.[48]

In the years immediately following his proposal, Blake dealt publicly with these objections as he traveled about the country. He drew larger audiences then than he had ever previously or since. The people seemed enthusiastic about his proposal and were anxious to hear his rebuttal of the major arguments set forth by his opponents.

To the charge of unnecessary "bustle" Blake responded personally by his deep commitment to the struggle for racial justice. His arrest in 1963 for attempting to integrate a public amusement park was proof that ecumenical fervor and social involvement could go hand-in-hand. Blake told one audience:

> If I had not been for church union before becoming fully involved in the churches' effort to be rightly involved in the civil rights movement, my experience in trying to mobilize the troops of Jesus Christ for this engagement would have converted me to church union. Nothing, in my considered opinion, stands so much in the way of the churches' proper involvement and witness in the world than the present denominational division of the Church.[49]

As an administrator Blake felt qualified to comment from experience on the charges of "bigness and bureaucracy" in the reunited church. Admitting that in organization of any institution it is difficult to keep means and ends in proper perspective, Blake still contended that the proposed church could cope with potential structural problems. Blake thought unity of commitment, program and purpose, and administration in small-enough geo-

143

graphical areas to promote intimacy and democracy could be achieved with wise leadership. Even so, Blake always insisted that people should not think of the church as a conglomerate or a food-chain store. The new church, Blake said, "won't be cheaper. It won't be more efficient. But it will have integrity. And that is what we are after. That is what is basic."[50]

The question of bishops in the reunited church was not so easily dismissed, especially by lay persons in the Reformed tradition whose ancestors had fought tenaciously with episcopacy to secure religious freedom and diversity in worship practices. Blake stressed the role of bishop as "pastor" (as in the Eastern Orthodox tradition) and assured his audiences that he was committed to a ministry that would enable people to "worship and witness joyfully and in good conscience." Blake delineated common theological grounds in Catholic, Reformed and Evangelical traditions that supported a threefold ministry of bishop, presbyter, and deacon with no repudiation of any previous ordination. Agreements reached at COCU plenary sessions confirmed his thinking on this point.[51]

After three years of productive discussion, COCU members agreed that sufficient progress had been made in theological agreement that the time had come to draft "an outline of a possible plan of union." For some time Blake had been urging such definite action. Speaking at Grace Episcopal Cathedral in January 1965, Blake gave some "second thoughts on church union" and concluded with a plea for immediate implementation of a definite reunion plan.

> We must believe that if church union is according to the will of Christ, now is the time to get on with it. We dare not excuse ourselves, or abdicate our responsibility by leaving its accomplishment to the next generation or after so many years, a dozen, or twenty-five, or fifty, as some have suggested. I believe we ought to proceed with all seriousness now to solve the theological and organizational problems that prevent union. If we are serious in our obedience, I have faith that Jesus Christ will illumine our way. There is no reason to believe that any later time will be a better time.[52]

At Lexington, Kentucky in 1965 COCU appointed Blake chairman of a six-member special commission to finalize a workable plan of union. Blake's commission had its report ready for the fifth plenary session of COCU which met in Dallas, Texas, in May 1966. In a new format, the "Outline for a Possible Plan of Union" presented most of the theological agreements reached in previous years. Chapters on the church's faith, worship, sacraments and ministry required little discussion. A fifth section on the structure of the church, however, was returned for further study, "since this topic was not discussed in earlier meetings and had no consensus statement to draw upon."[53] Moreover, another chapter, "Steps and Stages Toward a United Church," outlining a definite timetable of church union in the near future was approved for discussion purposes but was removed from the main body of the report and placed in an appendix. Significantly, the title of the report was changed from "Outline for a Possible Plan of Union" to the less specific title "Principles of Church Union."[54]

Despite his best efforts to bring together differing viewpoints and to resolve them into a workable consensus, Blake could not secure the votes necessary to implement a reunion timetable. When the final vote came and some of the basic elements of his report were eliminated or modified, Blake accepted the decision with dignity and reserve. If he experienced any bitterness or disappointment, he did not visibly show it. After leading the session in a closing prayer for continued guidance and perseverance, Blake waited outside of the conference room for an elevator to take him up to his room. As he waited, he turned to one of his associates and said, "Well, what do you think of that?" "Without vision," came the reply, "the people perish!" Blake simply nodded in agreement. The elevator door opened and Blake stepped inside. Since this was his last meeting before leaving to become general secretary of the World Council of Churches, COCU's future would be in other hands than those of Eugene Carson Blake.[55]

Neither COCU nor Blake's interest in it stopped in 1966. As the consultation moved ahead to implement some of the steps leading toward organic union, Blake kept in touch and offered encouragement. Following his retirement in 1972, Blake was asked by COCU (now Churches of Christ Uniting) to serve on its theological commission. This he has done with his usual vigor and enthusiasm although he has continued to express questions about the prolongation of discussion and the ever-widening circle of activities embraced by COCU. Blake still remains firm about his priority for union. Speaking in 1976 he said:

> I've always said that when you get a good plan of union or as good as you can make it, I think you should send it out to a vote and have it voted up or down. That's the first step. If you haven't got anything and they all vote it down, then you start again. But you don't just go on talking.[56]

A final evaluation of the impact and effectiveness of COCU obviously cannot be made now. For that matter, neither can Blake's San Francisco sermon be fully appreciated. However, Blake's sermon did much more than create COCU. It provided a catalyst for unprecedented grassroots ecumenical discussion among Protestants. Through the initial impetus of Blake's proposal, Christians of various denominations and traditions began to "get together" to discuss the possibility of church union and to learn more about each other. Moreover, through their conversations they also found new ways to cooperate on educational, social, and community projects. With the added thrust of Vatican II, ecumenism at the local level in the early 1960s reached a level that has not been equaled.[57]

Although questions about the future of COCU remain, there are few ecumenists who would not agree with the observation of the late Samuel McCrea Cavert, distinguished churchman and participant in more than a half-century of ecumenical activity:

> Whatever may be the final outcome, the Consultation on Church Union has served the American churches well by probing the issues of union in a more penetrating way than ever before. It has not been content merely to draft a plan for merging existing structures but is also exploring the fundamental questions of what the Church of Christ ought to be in the world today. It is seeking to conserve all the values inherited from the past and at the same time to make a flexible and imaginative approach to the future.[58]

· VIII ·
GENERAL SECRETARY
OF THE WORLD
COUNCIL OF CHURCHES

> *"We are not allowed the luxury of ecclesiastical structure in the ecumenical movement any more. We cannot spend our time trying to put together the broken pieces of ecclesiastical structure. We can only do that if we are ready to work together in the common service of the world."*

At the age of fifty-nine, when most church administrators are anticipating retirement, Eugene Carson Blake was taking an intensive course in French at the University of Grenoble to prepare himself for the position of general secretary of the World Council of Churches. When questioned about how it felt to be embarking on such a new and demanding career, Blake answered: "At my age it is nice to be asked to do something different."[1]

Blake's election as general secretary of the World Council of Churches on February 11, 1966 came after several years of indecision and controversy in the World Council. The incumbent general secretary, W. A. Visser 't Hooft, had announced at the New Delhi Assembly in 1961 that he wanted to retire when he reached the age of sixty-five in 1965. In 1963 the Central Committee of the World Council considered appointing a representative nominating committee but abandoned the plan primarily for reasons of economy.

147

Instead, it delegated the search for a new general secretary to its fourteen-member Executive Committee under the leadership of the American Lutheran ecumenist, Dr. Franklin Clark Fry.[2]

The Executive Committee first asked Dr. Lukas Vischer, who had joined the World Council in 1961 as research secretary of the Department of Faith and Order, to become general secretary. (Blake had previously eliminated himself from consideration.) Vischer declined, stating that he preferred work of a scholarly nature rather than an administrative position. The Executive Committee then selected the Reverend Patrick C. Rodger, a priest of the Scottish Episcopal Church and co-director of the World Council's Faith and Order Department, as its sole nominee for general secretary. Before the Executive Committee reported its decision to the Central Committee in January 1965, however, word of Rodger's nomination appeared in the religious press. Many members of the Central Committee who might otherwise have voted for Rodger balked because the premature press release made Rodger's nomination appear tantamount to election. Others, although they respected Rodger's abilities, indicated they did not consider him of sufficient international stature and experience to replace the distinguished W. A. Visser 't Hooft. Despite these pressures, Fry and his committee (including Blake) were not willing to withdraw Rodger's nomination to be chief executive of the World Council.[3]

When the Central Committee met in early 1965, opposition to the Executive Committee's well-publicized recommendation had solidified. In closed sessions the Central Committee could not resolve the conflict either by approving Rodger or by reaching agreement on some other candidate. In order to break the deadlock, Dr. John Coventry Smith of the United Presbyterian Church proposed three motions: first, to take no action on Patrick Rodger; second, to have Visser 't Hooft continue for at least one more year as general secretary; third, to set up a nominating committee of eighteen members to begin anew the process of selecting a general secretary. All three motions passed, and a committee with Bishop John Sadiq of India serving as chairman renewed the search for an acceptable candidate.[4]

When the nominating committee met in the summer of 1965, it had no one person to recommend. After several hours of discussion, however, a consensus seemed to emerge: the candidate should be an older, respected, and experienced veteran of ecumenical service. With this criterion established, the committee drew up a list of candidates. By secret ballot vote, the members reduced the list first to sixteen, then to five, and finally to three names. On the concluding unsigned ballot, each member wrote one name. Eugene Carson Blake was a near unanimous choice.[5]

Blake deliberated some time before giving an affirmative answer to the nominating committee. His wife's ill health precluded any possibility of her coming to Geneva with him, and Blake was reluctant to accept an overseas appointment that would mean prolonged separation. However, Valina Blake encouraged her husband to accept the position if he considered it to be a call from God. In what he termed "one of the most difficult decisions of my entire life," Blake finally accepted on the condition that he could, at his own expense, plan to visit the United States about once a month in order to be with his wife. On August 28, 1965 Blake formalized his decision in a letter to Bishop Sadiq:

> My wife and I have decided that, if I am elected General Secretary of the World Council of Churches with near unanimity by the Central Committee at its meeting in February, I will accept such an election as a call from God. We have come to this decision despite the fact that such acceptance will involve a great deal more separation from each other than either of us desires to contemplate.[6]

At a press conference following the public announcement of his election Blake told a reporter: "The reason I became General Secretary was that they couldn't agree on anyone else." Although there was some truth to this statement, Blake could not have emerged as the candidate without a broad base of support in the ecumenical world. Among the members of the World Council, the American representatives respected Blake as a courageous advocate of civil rights and as an articulate ecumenist. British and European leaders on the Central Committee admired his outstanding work as chairman of the Finance and the Interchurch Aid committees. The Greek, Russian, and other eastern leaders appreciated his willingness to listen and to learn from Orthodox representatives and his efforts to integrate them into the structures of the World Council. Asian and African members saw him as an international symbol of racial justice and equality, and as a person whom they could respect and trust.[7]

Reactions from the religious press regarding his election were favorable. *The Christian Century* endorsed Blake as one whose "proved administrative decisiveness, firmness, inventiveness and durability" would guarantee a well-run and forward-moving Council.[8] *Christianity Today* described Blake as "the best known ecumenical engineer in the Western Hemisphere" and as a man who "readily commands respect."[9] Among the many congratulatory letters and telegrams he received was one from Martin Luther King, Jr.: "Men of all colors and from various positions of servitude and affluence throughout the world take a firmer grip on hope for overcoming the evils of racism and poverty as you assume the role of General Secretary. We regard you as our gift to the world, and with you we shall overcome." Blake's long-time critic, Dr. Carl McIntire, cabled enigmatically: "You're just the man for the job."[10]

When Blake assumed leadership of the World Council, the world was caught up in revolutions, riots, and racial unrest. In Asia, hostilities and fighting raged in Vietnam, India, Pakistan, Indonesia, Laos, and Cambodia. In Africa, the issue of apartheid in South Africa and Rhodesia meant volatile situations. Belgium faced deteriorating relations with the Congo. Violence in the Middle East intensified in June 1967, when the conflict there burst into open fighting and raised the specter of World War III.

Like other institutions during this time, the World Council of Churches was in a period of transition and self-examination. The so-called Third World representatives were calling old assumptions, attitudes, and procedures into question. These representatives saw institutional paternalism to be contrary to the goals of freedom, equality, and justice. Reflecting similarly divided attitudes in the secular world, some World Council leaders wanted to de-emphasize traditional ecumenical theological interests in order to promote social action, while others wanted to limit social involvement so that existing ecclesiastical structures would not be adversely affected. The challenge was to keep these two positions from polarizing and causing schism within the World Council itself.

Blake had other problems to face. For one thing, he was succeeding the prestigious W. A. Visser 't Hooft, an accomplished linguist and scholar who had helped to create and then led the World Council since its founding in 1948. Despite Blake's administrative experience and personal popularity, he could not emulate his predecessor's theological acumen and knowledge of complex ecumenical protocol. Realizing this, Blake made no such attempt, but rather sought Visser 't Hooft's advice and counsel on matters affecting the future of the World Council. Blake offered Visser 't Hooft an office in the Geneva headquarters, provided him with a secretary, and met with him regularly throughout his tenure as general secretary.[11]

Blake began in Geneva with the handicap of being labeled a typical American "activist and financial wizard" by many of his European colleagues, who therefore tended to discount Blake's abilities as a serious theologian. They soon discovered, however, that Blake was more complex and theologically proficient than American press releases had led them to believe. While Blake never functioned as a traditional, academic, systematic theologian, he had the ability to reflect on problems and to respond to them theologically. Moreover, he consulted with people of varying theological orientations before passing final judgment on a policy or program. Significantly, Blake's first official speech to the Central Committee as general secretary in 1967 was a theological analysis of transcendence as a basis both for revolutionary new obedience to Christ and for the conservation of the ancient Christian gospel.[12]

Blake's age caused many ecumenical observers to see him as a compromise, interim appointment. Indeed, with the precedent already set for retirement at sixty-five, Blake had only a little more than five years to serve, a short time to create staff loyalty and cohesiveness. Like Pope John XXIII, however, Eugene Carson Blake believed that much could be done in a brief period of time. His outgoing, affirming personality gained him admiration and support from colleagues and staff, and his physical stamina and drive belied his fifty-nine years. He neither looked nor acted old, and many younger staff members could not keep pace with Blake's seemingly inexhaustible energy.

The most immediate, pressing problem facing Blake was to make final preparations for the Fourth Assembly of the World Council of Churches to be held at Uppsala, Sweden, July 4 to 20, 1968. Because of the delay in electing the new general secretary, Blake had only about eighteen months in which to supervise the structure and content of what many theologians were calling the most pivotal assembly in the history of the World Council of Churches. Although the Central Committee had determined the basic agenda of the Uppsala meeting, Blake had the responsibility of making last-minute changes in the program and the tremendous job of coordinating the largest gathering in the history of the World Council: some 700 delegates, a staff of 330, a press gallery of about 750, and 900 other participants such as advisers, youth partici-pants, fraternal delegates, and guests.[13]

Beyond guiding the mechanics of the assembly, Blake knew that what the World Council decided at Uppsala and how it arrived at its conclusions would be closely watched, and that since this would be his only assembly as general secretary, his name would be linked, positively or negatively, with its results. Blake was concerned for the international reputation of the World Council and knew the ramifications of an indecisive assembly. Two months before Uppsala, Blake voiced his concern at the dedication of the Institute of Ecumenical and Cultural Research in Collegeville, Minnesota: "We are not allowed the luxury of ecclesiasticism in the ecumenical movement any more. We cannot spend our time trying to put together the broken pieces of ecclesiastical structure. We can only do that if we are ready to work together in the common service of the world."[14]

The agenda for the Uppsala Assembly reflected the interplay between the concerns of Faith and Order and Life and Work, two divisions of the World Council. The former focused on such issues as ministry, sacraments, and tradition as theological bases on which church union could be consummated. The latter stressed specific issues affecting church and society—education, peace, church and state relationships, and the ethical dimensions of economic systems. World assemblies in 1948, 1952, and 1961 gave both emphases considerable attention.[15] However, even though the World Council formalized Life and Work activities in a Department on Church and Society and sponsored many consultations on important social themes, a Life and Work conference had not attained the prominence of Faith and Order meetings such as Lund (1952) and Montreal (1963) until a conference held in Geneva in July 1966.

This Geneva Conference had as its theme: "Christians in the Technical and Social Revolutions of Our Time." The makeup of the conference was unique in that laypeople outnumbered professional theologians and nearly half of the representatives were from "developing" or Third World countries. In addition, there were eight officially designated Roman Catholic observers and three guests. It also marked the first time that serious attention was given to the possibility of Christian participation in violent revolution. As one participant observed, the 1966 Geneva Conference "loaded the ecumenical conversation with the vocabulary of revolution," and set the standards by which the Uppsala Assembly was constantly being measured.[16]

The real dichotomy that emerged at the Geneva Conference was between what Catholic laywoman Barbara Ward, one of the key speakers, termed "the rich nations and the poor nations." Editor of *The Christian Century*, Harold Fey, who attended the Geneva Conference, said that the meeting "profoundly shocked most Americans who were not prepared to hear what we call 'foreign aid' characterized as altogether self-serving, often more of a handicap than a help, and something which the recipients were planning to do without anyway."[17] Another American observer said that the conference clarified what Third World countries had been saying to the rest of the world for some time: "If you really have a spiritual concern for me, get off my back."[18] Most Americans and Europeans were surprised, sobered, and sensitized by the Geneva discussions. For the first time in their lives they knew what it felt like to be a member of a minority group.[19]

Blake attended the Geneva Conference as general-secretary-elect but had no role in planning the event, nor did he make any addresses. Unlike some of his American and European contemporaries, he previously had been exposed to the language of revolution theology and had been involved in situations where minority opposition to white leadership had been expressed passionately. Yet Blake acknowledged that he learned a great deal from the Geneva Conference. He acquired a feeling for the source of the "Christian" voice in the world. The conference startled westerners, Blake recalled, "because the words were spoken by the people who were the subjects of colonialism and not by advanced, liberal westerners." The importance of the event, Blake said, was not so much that it created a new social emphasis, but that "at last we heard." By listening carefully to the voices from all over the world, Blake was able to make more appropriate and informed preparations for Uppsala than he might otherwise have done.[20]

The months preceding Uppsala were exceptionally chaotic. Martin Luther King, Jr., scheduled to be preacher at the opening service at Uppsala, was killed in the spring, and Robert F. Kennedy was assassinated in June. Both deaths triggered rounds of marches, sit-ins, and occupations of office buildings by minority groups. Ecumenical observers tried to predict how the assembly would respond to these unsettling conditions. Some thought that Uppsala would repudiate or at least blunt the radical language of the Geneva Conference. Others suggested that Uppsala would usher in an entirely new era of ecumenical activity in which Third World leaders would set the pace and determine the priorities. Aware of these conditions, Eugene Carson Blake simply said: "I assure you that prophet and priest, revolutionary and reactionary, will confront each other at Uppsala."[21]

In many respects, Uppsala reflected the ambivalent attitudes of its participants as Blake had described them. On the one hand, notwithstanding its overall theme, "Behold, I make all things new" (Revelation 21:5), much about the convocation was predictble, traditional, and essentially conservative. In an age when many prominent theologians were announcing the "death of God" and heralding an age of "religionless Christianity," the Uppsala Assembly affirmed the worship of a transcendent God and a continued dependence on Scripture as the source of wisdom for coping with contemporary problems. The first of six study sections covered by the assembly dealt with "The Holy Spirit and the

Catholicity of the Church," and concluded that "we must continue to seek the union of all Christians in a common profession of faith in the observance of Baptism and the Eucharist, and in recognition of a ministry for the whole church."[22] Although the report acknowledged that the church must develop a "new openness to the world in its aspirations, its achievements, its restlessness and its despair," it held firm to the presupposition that the basic questions facing Christians in the twentieth century were theological and not secular: What does Jesus Christ mean for humanity and what is the Holy Spirit saying to the churches?[23]

Previous world assemblies had been marked by the blossoming of new theological jargon. By contrast, Uppsala's verbiage tended to be predictable and even tiresome to some participants who had hoped that some exciting new "Uppsalalia," a term contrived by Professor J. Robert Nelson, might emerge from the assembly.[24] One observer at Uppsala noted that the biggest problem at the assembly, especially in its early and middle days, was boredom. One item on the graffiti board in the lobby of Fyris Hall, the sports palace in which the assembly's plenary sessions were held, attested to this feeling of ennui:

GOD IS NOT DEAD!
HE JUST FELL ASLEEP
IN THE MIDDLE
OF DOCUMENT 329

Beset by this "documentitis," many participants felt that they spent entirely too much time reading lengthy transcripts and trying to rewrite them, instead of engaging in lively dialogue.[25]

Despite efforts to make Uppsala a representative world assembly, statistics indicate that "old guard" leadership was still firmly in control of the ecclesiastical machinery. One writer noted that Uppsala was top-heavy with clerical potentates, many of them senior citizens. Of those accredited to the entire assembly, only 10 percent were youth delegates and they had no vote. Only 4 percent of the delegates were under thirty-five and 22 percent were over sixty. The average age of voting delegates was 51.7 years. Most were ordained and male. In another sensitive area statistics show that North America and Europe accounted for 69 percent of the delegates. Considering the priorities that Uppsala gave to Third World problems, it seemed unusual to many observers that only three out of ten delegates represented that community. Although Blake claimed that "these hoary, aged ecclesiastics" had actually ratified at Uppsala the vital worldly concerns raised at Geneva in 1966, it appeared obvious that future assemblies would have to pay more attention to youth in a world where half the population was under twenty.[26]

On the other hand, the Uppsala Assembly recognized and responded to signs of newness. "Hoary, aged ecclesiastics" notwithstanding, there was an outburst of political action from the under-represented: women, laypeople, youth, Black Americans, and Third World representatives. The youth were the most visible and vocal, and from the outset they made their presence felt. The colorful opening procession of some seven hundred delegates had just gone inside the Uppsala Cathedral when Theodore Buss, a Swiss theology student and former president of the Swiss National Student Association, mounted a ladder and proclaimed, "Religion is in trouble!" He invited curious bystanders to discuss "what they're doing inside." Before Buss had an opportunity to gather much of an audience, however, a few Swedish policemen pulled him down and took Buss and a companion into custody.[27]

Youth also made their mark on the assembly in more organized ways. About 150 youth participants had been invited to the assembly by the Executive Committee of the Central Committee according to a plan based on national and regional representation. The assembly budget provided considerable subsidy for their travel and entertainment. Their applause from the "youth area" of the balcony, their participation in section meetings, and their publication of a mimeographed news sheet, "Hot News," provided the "over thirty" participants with clear examples of their feelings. In uninhibited language they criticized the assembly for not granting youth voting privileges and for becoming enmeshed in theological rhetoric rather than developing creative programs. One issue of "Hot News" contained this admonition: "Get beyond the words, get down to deeds, put your bodies where your words are, in God's name *do* something."[28] In the evenings at "Club 68," an informal youth headquarters, young people bombarded World Council leaders night after night with radical challenges and proposals.[29]

As general secretary, Eugene Carson Blake tried to bridge the so-called generation gap with the student contingent. At a pre-assembly meeting, Blake welcomed the young people and promised to cooperate with them to the best of his abilities. He identified with their criticism of "the establishment" but stated his own personal conviction that there were signs of greatness and relevance within the contemporary institutional church. He concluded by asking the young people to work with him and not against him. Younger World Council staff members who heard Blake's informal remarks thought that the general secretary had done an excellent job in conveying an attitude of openness, receptivity, and understanding in a very difficult situation.[30]

By his own admission, however, Blake had moments when he almost lost his temper attempting to deal with demands from student leaders. He shared his ambivalent feelings in his address at a plenary session.

> I am glad that students all over the world are scaring the establishments with their demands. This does not mean that I am happy with the programmes proposed by extreme black power advocates any more than I approve the apparent anarchism and irrationality of many student demands. But I suggest that an Assembly such as this, representative of an ecclesiastical establishment that is world-wide, had better look hard to try to discern what God is now requiring of us as we are disturbed by the "rods of His anger."[31]

Blake had a tense moment at the end of the assembly when youth delegates made a last-minute demand to participate in the closing worship service in the Uppsala Cathedral which was to be led by Blake and the Reverend Professor John Meyendorff of the Russian Orthodox Greek Catholic Church. Youth leaders wanted to have a procession of placard-bearing young people form part of the liturgy. Anxious that the worship service not turn into an ecclesiastical circus, Blake was reluctant to alter arrangements to accommodate them. When the youth leaders refused to yield and threatened to go ahead without official sanction, Blake conceded: "I'd rather have them picket with my support than picket without my support," he confided to a friend. Blake also invited a youth leader to give the only address made at the worship service.[32]

Many observers considered the concluding service to be one of the most impressive moments of community worship in the entire assembly. After hearing Scripture read in five different languages, the young people came in silent procession bearing placards that reminded worshipers of some of the challenges to practical obedience that the assembly had previously expressed: "Racism is a blatant denial of the Christian Faith"; "The longing for a just society is causing revolutions all over the world"; "It is the duty of churches to challenge governments"; "Applause of Kaunda is no substitute for 20 years of inaction"; and "Christ works alone in the world while the church worships." The students stood silently in the nave facing the congregation throughout the remainder of the service.[33]

Another new ecumenical trend that Blake fostered, the presence of Protestant churches that were not yet in the World Council fold, was evident at Uppsala. Attending were thirty-six delegated observers from twenty-four Protestant churches such as the Lutheran Church, Missouri Synod, and the Reformed churches in the Netherlands. In addition, there were a number of other non-member churches present with observers not so officially or formally designated. Blending in the ecumenical milieu were representatives from churches such as Adventist (Finnish and Seventh-day American and Polish), Assembly of God, Lithuanian Evangelical Reformed, and Pentecostal (Brasil para Cristo).[34]

The impact of these new Protestant groups was miniscule compared to the significant Roman Catholic presence at Uppsala. In contrast to previous world assemblies where Roman Catholics attended incognito or under the threat of Vatican discipline, some two hundred Catholic observers and guests moved about freely and participated vigorously in assembly activities. Among the official observers and guests were: Bishop Jan Willebrands, head of the Secretariat for Promoting Christian Unity; Monsignor Charles Moeller, a leader in the Congregation of Sacred Doctrine; Fathers

Jerome Hamer, O.P., Pierre Duprey, and Thomas Stransky, C.S.P., of the Secretariat for Christian Unity; Monsignor Joseph Gremillion, head of the Pontifical Commission on Justice and Peace; Father George Dunne, S.J., chairman of the Exploratory Committee on Society, Development and Peace; and Father Robert Tucci, S.J., editor of *Civilta Cattolica*.[35]

Father Tucci's speech to the assembly illustrated how far the Roman Catholic church had come on its journey from a Counter-Reformation to an *aggiornamento* ecumenical outlook. Tucci was the first Roman Catholic to give a platform address at a world assembly of the World Council of Churches and the first to raise openly the issue of Roman Catholic membership in the World Council fellowship. Tucci affirmed that Roman Catholics "no longer regard themselves as outside spectators who are indifferent or merely curious . . . but as partners engaged in the same joint fraternal quest for the unity that is Christ's will for His Church." He also pointed out that this ecumenical perspective was not confined to a small minority in the church but was widely held by Catholics throughout the world. Citing documents from Vatican II (especially the *Decree on Ecumenism*), Tucci offered his personal opinion that Roman Catholic membership in the World Council of Churches was possible in the near future. In the light of Rome's new expression of ecumenism as "restoring unity" rather than "returning to Rome," Tucci concluded that Christian unity "cannot be the victory of one Church over another, but the victory of Christ over our divisions."[36]

The Uppsala Assembly displayed a willingness to channel the new Protestant–Catholic ecumenical spirit into concrete action. It adopted a recommendation that an earlier Exploratory Committee on Society, Development and Peace become the Joint Roman Catholic–World Council of Churches Committee on Society, Development and Peace (SODEPAX). The assembly approved the appointment of Father George Dunne, S.J. to head the new commission and provided funds for an expanded staff. The founders of SODEPAX envisioned an ambitious educational campaign to mobilize Christians to help overcome the growing gap between rich and poor nations as the only adequate basis for the long-range establishment of world peace.[37]

Although overshadowed by the developments taking place in Roman Catholicism, Orthodox ecumenicity also displayed unusual vigor in the Uppsala proceedings. As Blake pointed out in his closing press conference, Orthodox Christians had participated fully in the work of the sections and the committees and in the preparation of reports. Unlike previous occasions, they did not want to make declarations as a separate group. Moreover, Orthodox leaders impressed the audience with insightful theological presentations on contemporary ecumenical themes. Metropolitan Ignatios Hazim of Latakia, for example, delivered the main-theme address. He called for churches to be "the prophets of the new, the visionaries of the resurrected Christ," and challenged all religious institutions, rich or poor, to be "the living, prophetic conscience of the drama of the present time."[38]

Another mark of newness about Uppsala was its decided emphasis on "secular ecumenism." The Life and Work themes of the earlier Geneva Conference permeated virtually every aspect of Uppsala's deliberations. As Blake said in his analysis of Uppsala, "every report received, document approved, and program envisaged was affected by the state of the world even more than by the state of the Church." Whether consciously or not, Blake continued, "each member of the Assembly knew in his depths that radical change, creative and destructive, was the mark of the times forcing all to re-examine the foundations, to dream new dreams, to build new structures in order to be relevant to the ultimate fears and hopes of man."[39]

Study Section III, "World Economic and Social Development," is probably the clearest expression of "secular ecumenism" made at the Uppsala Assembly. The report described the basis of Christian concern for development, the dynamics of development, the political conditions of world development, and the task of Christians, churches, and the World Council of Churches to work for a worldwide responsible society. It stressed that developed nations "must shed all tendencies to exploit economically or to dominate the poorer, and therefore weaker, economics of other nations." It called upon developed nations to deal with regional and world economic planning involving the stabilization of the world market and an international taxation system to provide funds for development. The document also summoned Christians to be "in the forefront of the battle to overcome a provincial, narrow sense of solidarity and to create a sense of participation in a worldwide responsible society with justice for all."[40]

Even Uppsala's severest critics considered Section III to be the best section document produced at the fourth world assembly. The youth participants, for example, who had been negative about many assembly pronouncements, seemed to be basically satisfied with Section III. One of the student leaders, Robert Maurer, commented: "Only this section document will be remembered years hence."[41] Blake himself agreed that Uppsala would likely be remembered longest for its emphasis on development and concluded that the Section III report would stand for many years as "the charter of the newest task of all the Churches and the ecumenical movement itself."[42]

Another prominent feature of "secular ecumenism" at Uppsala was a concern to deal with the problem of racism. Some Europeans accused Blake of introducing American ideas into the world racial scene. "I didn't have to introduce them," Blake countered. "They were already there and were more radical than anything I had ever been involved in."[43] No speaker at the assembly sparked more interest and evoked more controversy than did James Baldwin, the Black author, who lectured on "White Racism or World Community." At a luncheon prior to the address, Blake had talked candidly with Baldwin and urged him to pull no punches: "Be as persuasive as you can," Blake urged. "We need what you can say to us."[44]

Apparently Baldwin needed little encouragement to speak his mind freely and forcefully. Although he repudiated institutional Christianity, Baldwin spoke out of a Christian understanding of the theological dimensions of racism. He addressed himself to his audience as "one of God's creatures whom the Christian Church has most betrayed." Recapitulating a long tale of racial injustice, Baldwin charged that "long ago, for a complex of reasons, but among them power, the Christian personality split itself into two—into dark and light, and is now bewildered and at war with itself. . . . I wonder," said Baldwin, "if there is left in the Christian civilizations the moral energy, the spiritual daring, to atone, to repent, to be born again?" Baldwin also accused the church of telling lies "to itself, about itself" and concluded that "the destruction of the Christian Church as it is presently constituted may not only be desirable, but may be necessary."[45]

In a structured approach, the Committee on Church and Society urged the Uppsala Assembly to implement the findings of the World Conference on Church and Society held at Geneva in 1966. The committee singled out "white racism," defined as "the conscious or unconscious belief in the inherent superiority of persons of European ancestry . . . which entitles all white peoples to a position of dominance and privilege, coupled with the belief in the innate inferiority of all darker peoples . . . which justifies their subordination and exploitation."[46] The committee also challenged the World Council to undertake a crash program to guide the council and member churches in the urgent problems of racism. Included in the program were comprehensive reports on racial situations throughout the world, regional and international consultations on race, and the production of educational materials on racism. The committee also projected the establishment with the General Secretariat of the World Council of a "coordinated secretariat on the elimination of racism, and the appointment of an ecumenical commission to supervise this programme."[47]

The assembly was less successful in its efforts to produce a single document that would spell out the World Council's opposition to racism. A hastily prepared manuscript that had been drafted by Policy Reference Committee II in consultation with two members of a subcommittee of the Department on Church and Society failed to gain assembly approval. The statement spoke in such general terms that many delegates could see no point in adopting recommendations that showed little promise of action. Others felt that the emphasis on "white racism" failed to take into account the complexity of international racial problems. Although Blake had hoped that the assembly would take a strong stand on racism, he recognized that the assembly's indecision left no choice but to defer action. The assembly finally moved that "the question of a statement on Racism be referred to the Central Committee for consideration and action."[48]

In addition to concerns of development and race, the Uppsala Assembly also committed the World Council to several new ecumenical ventures. It approved a new constitution for the Commission of the Churches on International Affairs (CCIA) which provided for a larger and more representative staff and closer relationships with world confessional families and national and regional councils. It also voted to establish an Office of Education to cope with the "education explosion" that was taking place throughout the world. This new venture was advanced largely through Dr. Theodore A. Gill's labors in a two-year stint as executive secretary of the Joint Study Commission on Education. The assembly also authorized a special three-year study on the *humanum* in a changing world. A new pattern of inquiry to be coordinated through all divisions of the World Council planned to confront these questions:

> Is there a distinctive Christian view of man? In what way is Jesus Christ the true revelation of authentic humanity? What are the characteristics of the "new man in Christ" and the new humanity, the church? What anthropologies are implied in modern sciences, secular ideologies, and non-Christian religions? How does the church enter into dialogue with them?[49]

As the Uppsala Assembly worked out its new programs and attempted to deal realistically with the pressing demands of "secular ecumenism," Eugene Carson Blake labored behind the scenes to keep the complex activities moving according to schedule despite bewildering logistical problems, unexpected protests, and breakdowns in communication. Blake also made his own formal theological contribution to the assembly in a major address on the second day of the convocation. Although he dealt with a variety of topics, Blake clearly had in mind a response to the criticism of the World Council that its social, economic, and political involvement was leading churches away from their central task of proclaiming the gospel, worshiping God, and offering eternal salvation to a dying and sinful humanity. As he had done throughout his entire career, Blake refused to accept the premise that social action and evangelistic outreach were antithetical rather than complementary.

> I want to be sure that this assembly understands that this kind of activity has always been the proper business of the church. . . . I want to be sure that we understand that this emphasis on humanity is not a turning away from God but a turning towards the God who most fully revealed himself in Jesus Christ, our Lord and Savior. . . . I hope that no member of this assembly will be able to go home still supposing that the concern here with white racism, for example, is somehow a diversion from the proper and central concern of the church.[50]

Blake also made two basic points about his understanding of the quest for newness stated in Uppsala's theme and demonstrated in its proposals.

1. The new emphasis on the social, economic and political that the Uppsala Assembly presses upon the churches is not new in the sense of being novel (and therefore rightly suspect), but rather in the sense of renewal in the life of the churches of the most ancient truths of the Christian faith.

2. The new in the sense of novel of modern up-to-date arises from the radically changed world of the late twentieth century in which the churches of Jesus Christ must do their proper work and make their proper witness.[51]

It is difficult to form any "objective" estimate of what the 1968 Uppsala world assembly did or did not accomplish. A study of the documents produced, for example, does not necessarily convey the spirit of those who drew them up. Moreover, the informal contacts and personal experiences which are important in determining individual attitudes are beyond the reach of detached historical analysis. Perhaps one of the most objective statements about the Uppsala Assembly was made by Blake himself: "A strong case for the success of the Uppsala Assembly can be made on a purely negative basis. What the prophets of gloom predicted did not happen."[52] In more colorful language, Alan Geyer of *The Christian Century* captured the ambivalence of Uppsala:

Uppsala! An Assembly burdened with the old but bursting with the new. God must have been terribly bored at times and mightily outraged, too; but he seems to have been there, after all, leaving his tracks all over the place.[53]

As a postscript, some of the most important decisions came after the assembly had adjourned. The newly elected Central Committee chose as chairman Mr. M. M. Thomas, an Indian lay theologian and social scientist and a critic of churches that were not responsive to the revolutionary challenges of Third World countries. At Blake's insistent urging, the new Executive Committee was more representative of Asia and Africa. One vice chairman was Orthodox: Metropolitan Meliton, ecumenical patriarch of Constantinople, and the other was a woman: Pauline Webb, an English Methodist.[54]

The diversity of the new Executive Committee was symbolic of the new direction suggested by Uppsala. Nevertheless, Uppsala had to go beyond symbolism if it was to be taken seriously by the secular world. As James Baldwin had expressed it: "At this moment in the world's history, it becomes necessary for me, for my own survival, not to listen to what you say, but to watch carefully what you do."[55] Much of what the World Council would do in the critical years following Uppsala would depend on the leadership exerted by Eugene Carson Blake.

· IX ·

LEADER OF
CONTINUITY AND CHANGE

---

*"As a former 'hierarch' in a member church,
I have tried to use the fruits of that experience to persuade the official church leaders of
the World Council to support through the
Council those movements of which they were
afraid, . . ."*

A lthough the Uppsala Assembly was pivotal in the history of
the World Council of Churches and in the life of the general
secretary who directed it, the major evaluation of Eugene Carson
Blake's leadership must focus on his activities following the world
convocation. As events at the assembly showed, the church would
have to make its witness in "doing," not in "talking." The slogan of
youth at Uppsala, "For God's sake *do* something!" provided a
mandate for the World Council of Churches and its constituent
ecclesiastical bodies to transform theological reflection into functioning programs. More than ever before, both ecclesiastical and
secular communities were testing ecumenical Christianity's credibility. Although the watchword of many church bureaucrats at
the time was "Caution!" Eugene Carson Blake challenged Christian leaders "to run the risks that true renewal of the churches and
of the Council requires."[1]

A crucial question was what the World Council would do with
the Uppsala recommendation that a crash program on racism
should be undertaken immediately. If the World Council vacil-

lated, skeptics could reopen the charge that ecclesiastical machinery was too cumbersome and anachronistic to be an effective agent of social reform. Blake was chairman of the Staff Coordinating Committee on Racism, and thus he could give priority to the racial issue. One of the committee's first acts was to make preparations for an "International Consultation on Racism" which was held at Notting Hill, London, the scene of many racial conflicts. At a planning session for the Notting Hill consultation, a few World Council staffers expressed fears that efforts to initiate an aggressive race program might cause some important member churches to dissociate themselves from the World Council just at a time when the ecumenical organization was in a precarious financial situation. Blake reportedly listened briefly to these fears but ended the discussion by stating: "That may be true, but I'm not prepared to help to keep the World Council going if it is to be at the expense of what the World Council should be standing for."[2]

Representatives from all the world came to Notting Hill in May 1969 to struggle with the problem of racism. Senator George McGovern, Democrat of South Dakota who had been a Methodist delegate at Uppsala, served as chairman of the consultation and Blake was secretary. Although the conference made significant progress in preparing recommendations to the upcoming Canterbury meeting of the Central Committee, it made headlines not for the documents it produced but because of an interruption of its proceedings by Black Power leaders. At a plenary session, a group of American and Nigerian Blacks took the microphone from the scheduled speaker and read a "Declaration of Revolution," which included a demand for reparations of sixty million pounds sterling in the form of a legal document committing the World Council to make payment. As general secretary of the World Council, Blake was given until eleven the next morning to comply.[3]

After a long night of discussion, conference leaders, including Blake, prepared a report, which Blake then delivered the following morning to the militants. He acknowledged the long history of racial oppression and injustice but saw unrealistic demands for reparations as contributing nothing positive to ultimate solutions. "If we believed all that your statement says about the church," Blake added, "we would hardly be here as church members in this

167

consultation." He pointed out that the consultation was arriving at collective decisions on such things as reparations and radical change but that the Notting Hill conference had no authority whatsoever to commit the World Council or its member churches to any promises about anything. Blake assured the militants, however, that he would bring their statement before the Central Committee at its August meeting in Canterbury. Despite such unscheduled interruptions, the Notting Hill consultation did manage to draw up "A Plan for an Ecumenical Programme to Combat Racism" (PCR).[4]

A few months later at the Canterbury meeting Blake personally presented the PCR proposal to the Central Committee. In his remarks, Blake admitted that the whole issue of racism was complicated by psychological and sociological difficulties, as events at Notting Hill had clearly illustrated. "Nevertheless," he said, "the nature and urgency of the problem demands a new initiative." He urged the Central Committee to give the new program its approval so that staff members could begin immediately to implement the proposals.[5]

Even with Blake's endorsement, some World Council staffers were still worried that the race program was too radical to secure unqualified support from the Central Committee. Some of the staff felt that the whole question of "white racism" and the theology of liberation, in which language much of the document was expressed, was a potential stumbling block to acceptance. It did appear at times that the PCR might fail because of questions on language and details. Blake was confident that the majority of the Central Committee would endorse the new program. His concern was to get as large a majority as possible. An Asian member of the Executive Committee, Indonesian General Simatupong, gave vital behind-the-scenes and floor leadership, which helped the proposal pass by a wide margin. There were no negative votes and only six abstentions.[6]

In adopting the new race program, the Central Committee called upon participating churches to "move beyond charity, grants and traditional programming to relevant and sacrificial action leading to new relationships of dignity and justice among all men, and to become agents for the radical reconstruction of society." It outlined a five-year program and agreed to provide finances for a staff and in addition a special fund made up of $200,000 from the World Council's own limited reserves. To this was added an appeal for at least $300,000 more from member churches. The Central Committee further resolved that "this special fund be distributed to the organizations of oppressed racial groups or organizations supporting victims of racial injustice whose purposes are not inconsonant with the general purposes of the World Council."[7]

In 1970, a little more than a year later, the Executive Committee of the Central Committee made the first distribution from the special fund in a meeting at Arnoldshain, Germany. Beneficiaries included liberation movements in Angola, Guinea-Bissau, Mozambique, Rhodesia, and South Africa, some of which were politically banned and committed to the overthrow of white ruling minorities. The public release of the list of aid recipients touched off a furor that did not die down for several years. Groups in South Africa, Germany, the Netherlands, and Great Britain launched widespread propaganda attacks against the World Council of Churches and the PCR because of their support of revolutionary organizations. Later, strong opposition also came from various groups in the United States.[8]

As general secretary under whose direct guidance the PCR was being implemented, Blake absorbed much of the political and personal indignation at the use of church money to support revolutionary causes. He spent a large amount of his time defending the PCR as well as granting interviews and making speeches.[9] One encounter came when Bishop Hermann Dietzfelbinger, chairman of the Council of the Evangelical Church in Germany, raised public objections to the World Council's race program. Blake responded in a detailed statement in which he noted that "in the course of history, Christians often used force to free themselves from oppression." He also assured the bishop that gifts were not used to purchase machineguns, as some sources had alleged, but rather, for such humanitarian projects as education, health, and aid to political prisoners' dependents—strictly what the groups requested. Blake later appeared on German national television to defend the PCR, but his appeals for a calm, rational approach to the facts of the case failed to quiet the opposition.[10]

Despite unfavorable reaction to the PCR, Blake continued to serve as a spokesman for the goals and methods of the World Council in its efforts to foster racial justice. While acknowledging the validity of many specific criticisms of the race program, Blake insisted that these criticisms should not be used as an excuse to avoid the main issue—that racism was prevalent in the life and structures of the churches, in the World Council of Churches, and in the world as a whole. Blake welcomed the controversy as a means of generating interest in the problem of racism, especially the moral, ecclesiological and theological aspects of the question of violence and nonviolence. More important, Blake contended that the PCR had given the World Council of Churches a measure of credibility among constituents in various minority groups struggling for recognition. By 1975 the PCR had distributed more than one million dollars to oppressed groups throughout the world and had become a permanent part of the work of the World Council.[11]

Other than the administration of special funds to revolutionary groups, the PCR provided opportunities for consultation and dialogue with leaders of the oppressed and developed an annual Program Project List, administered separately from the special fund, to support local, national, and regional churches and other groups with projects for the racially oppressed. In areas where minority groups could not present their own cases through conventional avenues, the PCR supplied them with the necessary literature. The PCR also attempted to bring economic pressure on corporations investing in apartheid countries and compiled a list of banks in various countries that provided loans to the South African government and its agencies. Projects undertaken in the years since Blake's departure from the World Council demonstrate a continuing concern for racial equality and justice.[12]

Indirectly, the Program to Combat Racism helped to produce the negotiation of a peace agreement in 1972 that ended a seventeen-year war between northern (Muslim) and southern (Christian) groups in the Sudan. It began when Blake received an unsolicited invitation from President Boumedienne of Algeria to bring a World Council delegation to visit his country. Even though more than 90 percent of Algerian residents were Muslim,

170

Boumedienne had been so impressed with the World Council's efforts to promote racial equality that he wanted its advice on how to mobilize popular faith in God to support the Algerian government's aims of equality and justice for all people. During conversations with Boumedienne and his staff, Blake and World Council representatives asked Boumedienne if he would use his influence to assist the council in its efforts to distribute food in southern Sudan. Boumedienne made contacts and arranged for a World Council delegation to visit Khartoum to work out details. To their surprise, Sudanese Muslim leaders not only promised to help with the transfer of food but also indicated their willingness to work out a peace agreement with the Christians in the south.[13]

By following up this peace gesture, a three-man World Council team consisting of Burgess Carr, Kodwo Ankrah, and Leopoldo Niilus assisted in the mediation between Sudanese Muslims and the rebel Christian leaders. Meeting in Addis Ababa, Ethiopia in the spring of 1972, representatives from both sides composed an agreement that ultimately resulted in a stable, peaceful situation. Blake secured a draft of the treaty just as he was leaving for the United States. When he arrived in New York, Blake met with Kurt Waldheim, secretary-general of the United Nations, and gave him a copy of the negotiations before Waldheim had secured one through regular United Nations channels. Impressed with the efficiency and effectiveness of World Council mediation efforts, Waldheim asked Blake with a smile: "Now, how about going to the Middle East for us?"[14]

At the same time that he was supporting the program on race, Blake was also helping the World Council to launch an ambitious effort to encourage development in Third World countries. Blake preferred simpler language. He called it a program for "the poor world, the people who don't have any money." To determine how best to assist in development service, the World Council sponsored a consultation at Montreux, Switzerland in 1970 that identified basic objectives such as justice, self-reliance, and economic growth. In wide-ranging discussions, participants sought ways to increase technical assistance, government aid, voluntary service, and church support of projects designed to remove inequalities which had made parts of the world affluent at the expense of others. As one of the conference speakers, Blake described his understanding of development in realistic terms.

> The word "development" as used by the World Council of Churches never means simply a utopian, unrealistic dream of materialistic fulfillment. It refers rather to possible processes whereby the people of the whole world together may establish economic structures of sufficient justice and equality so that men may have a truly human life. We do not suppose that the under-developed nations should simply strive to copy the technological advances of the rich nations. Unless the life and goals of the "rich" nations are as radically changed in the process of world development as is the life of the "poor" nations, the end of the process will clearly become more like hell on earth than like a heavenly utopia. . . . A community of men using the scientific knowledge and engineering techniques now available but oriented towards a life that is good in a moral and spiritual sense is the concept towards which Christian development programmes must always aim.[15]

Following the Montreux Conference, the Executive Committee of the Central Committee established the Commission on the Churches' Participation in Development (CCPD) in order to provide the World Council with an instrument of overall strategy and concerted effort on development issues. The CCPD undertook a number of specific studies designed to discover how well the prevailing economic systems were meeting the real needs of poor people in their quest for self-reliance. The study findings, which called for some radical changes in the patterns of international trade, were published at the time of the Third United Nations Conference on Trade and Development (UNCTAD) in Santiago, Chile, and contributed significantly to the ongoing debate. Another study, "Poverty 2000," projected the magnitude of poverty by the end of this century. Based on selected studies in countries such as Egypt, Tunisia, Ivory Coast, Ghana, Uganda, Madagascar, Tanzania, and Zambia, the study predicted dire consequences based on the continuation of present trends.[16]

The CCPD also administered the Ecumenical Development Fund, which had been recommended by the Montreux Consultation. This was based on an appeal to churches to set aside 2 percent of their regular income for development purposes. Initially only a few member churches made significant contributions to the fund. In the period between 1972 and 1974, however, the Ecumenical Development Fund secured a total of about $7.5 million, the major share of which went to projects in Ethiopia, Cameroon, Indonesia, and the Caribbean.[17]

In addition to creating new agencies such as the PCR and the CCPD, the World Council of Churches under Blake's leadership played an increasingly significant role in the international quest for peace. When Blake assumed office in 1966, one of his first actions was to call for an interchurch study of the problem of peace that would stress the "world community of peoples." Although Blake personally never adopted traditional pacifist theology, he did believe that war was an immoral tool of foreign policy, especially in a nuclear age when total destruction was a possibility. In particular, Blake concurred with the strong stand taken by the World Council of Churches against United States involvement in Vietnam, and as an international church leader defied public sentiment in America by supporting antiwar protestors.[18]

Blake's most symbolic identification with the peace movement came in 1967 when he decided that he must return to his own country to deliver a major address critical of President Johnson's escalation policy in Vietnam. Blake spoke in Norwalk, Connecticut, the town adjacent to his New Canaan home, at a meeting sponsored by the Council of Churches of Greater Bridgeport and other religious groups. His words at this meeting were carried on the front pages of newspapers throughout the country. In his speech Blake warned that United States action in Vietnam had all the elements of high tragedy. "Unable to distinguish friend from foe, caught in a dilemma which makes any decision increasingly difficult," he said, "the United States seems to be stumbling on towards final disaster." He urged the United States to stop bombing immediately and "to agree with our allies in Asia and Europe that we will accept any peace that they will develop and agree to with us." Calling upon Americans to "heed the warnings of the

173

whole world before it is too late," Blake said that the picture of a world power like the United States mobilizing to bring a small, long-suffering Asian nation to capitulation "means clearly that the more we win the more we lose, and each American soldier dead or wounded is a useless sacrifice."[19]

These comments were unpopular in 1967, especially from a person of Blake's stature. As a result of this speech, Blake became "unacceptable" in the White House as a religious representative.[20] However, throughout the remainder of the conflict in Vietnam, Blake continued to oppose United States efforts to heighten the war and made repeated appeals to world leaders to use their influence to initiate peace negotiations. In 1972 Blake's public outrage at President Nixon's decision to bomb dikes in North Vietnam involved him in a controversy with Father John McLaughlin, the president's official religious adviser. Blake's persistent opposition to American foreign policy also resulted in having his name placed on President Nixon's so-called "enemies list," which was revealed during John Dean's testimony in the Watergate hearings in 1973. Blake shrugged off opposition about his personal stance on the war in Vietnam and regretted only that he had not perceived the problems sooner and acted more quickly.[21]

Blake's efforts for world peace and justice were not limited solely to the war in Vietnam. He repeatedly took stands for peace and reconciliation among peoples and frequently challenged specific governmental policies that he deemed counter to this goal. In 1970, for example, Blake sent an open letter to the British Council of Churches condemning the proposed sale of arms by Britain to South Africa as "clearly unacceptable to Christian moral conviction" and as having "the symbolic effect of aligning Britain with the racist and repressive regimes of Southern Africa."[22] In the same year Blake sent an open letter to U Thant, secretary-general of the United Nations, citing "the increasing deterioration of the cause of human rights" and calling attention to the "stream of documented pleas for justice and redress" that had come to the World Council of Churches. Without presuming to prescribe all the answers to world problems, Blake raised some sharp and penetrating questions for United Nations consideration.

174

Can you, Mr. Secretary-General, take an initiative through
the UN Commission on Human Rights or otherwise to resist
this apparently increasing tendency on the part of governments to act politically against their own citizens in the
name of law and order? Is it possible that the great powers
would agree to restrain their own tendencies to support regimes with whom they are sympathetic when these regimes
violate the standards of civil and religious liberty to which the
member nations of the United Nations are committed? Is it
possible that the great powers themselves will examine their
own practices in this regard?[23]

Blake utilized the international prestige of his office to promote
in troubled spots throughout the world lines of communication
that helped the World Council of Churches to function more effectively as an agency of reconciliation and social amelioration. In the
spring of 1969, for example, he undertook a personal visitation of
Lebanon, Jordan, Egypt, and Israel for conversations with political and religious leaders. Subsequently Blake reported his findings
to the State Department and was granted a rare interview with
President Nixon. Blake complimented the administration for progress in establishing peace in the Middle East and once again gave
the president his "Vietnam pitch."[24] The following year Blake met
with representatives of the Palestine Liberation Organization in
Geneva and made the first official visit of a World Council secretary to the Republic of Ireland where he attended the opening of
the Irish School of Ecumenics in Dublin. In 1971 Blake visited
Salvador Allende in Chile "to symbolize the interest of Christian
Churches of the world in the socio-political experiment going on in
Chile."[25]

During Blake's six years as general secretary, the World Council
of Churches stressed the vertical (theological) as well as the hori-
zontal (social) aspects of ecumenical endeavors. Blake's personal
philosophy, expressed at the Faith and Order Commission meeting at Louvain in 1971, characterized the World Council as a
whole. "We have agreed," Blake said, "that action without sufficient theological reflection leads to frustration and that academic
theology which does not give light and stimulus for action leads to

175

futility."[26] Even during a period when enthusiasm for organic church union waned because of questions about the relevancy of institutional structures, the World Council of Churches made significant progress in ecumenical conversation. In 1967 the Faith and Order Commission convened a Consultation on Church Union negotiations in Geneva to exchange information on the status of pending church union programs and proposals. Three years later at Limuru in Kenya a similar conversation stressed the importance of fostering unions as interim steps toward the achievement of a more comprehensive union.[27]

In 1970 a Joint Committee of the Lutheran World Federation and the World Alliance of Reformed Churches at a meeting sponsored by the Faith and Life Commission of the World Council agreed that previous "doctrinal condemnations" by both traditions had been rendered obsolete by recent theological developments. The groups also proposed that a concordat should be established between the two confessions so that full pulpit and altar fellowship could be achieved. A number of other similar events indicated that Faith and Order had not been relegated to low priority because of increasing emphasis on social program and secular involvement.[28]

Beyond structured Faith and Order activities, the Blake era will perhaps best be remembered for the increasing participation of the Roman Catholic church in ecumenical structures. Blake labored to nourish relationships with Catholicism as it began to implement the theological breakthroughs of Vatican Council II. Between 1966 and 1972 Blake and Bishop (later Cardinal) Willebrands worked together in leading the efforts of the Joint Working Group of the World Council of Churches. They served as co-chairmen from 1966 to 1969. Willebrands appreciated Blake's patient, determined grappling with doctrinal and organizational problems on the Joint Working Group and described Blake as "essentially fairminded, and tenacious in a way that called for one's respect because it grew out of his deepest convictions." In this context, Willebrands said, "he could be firm, he could speak with anger, in a way that one felt was appropriate because it did not seem a personal thing but sprang from his unshakable belief in the rightness of the cause of the ecumenical movement."[29]

Blake also worked closely with the Joint Roman Catholic–World

Council of Churches Committee on Society, Development and Peace (SODEPAX), which had been approved by the Uppsala Assembly as a cooperative ecumenical venture. SODEPAX sponsored major international consultations at Cartigny, Switzerland (1969), Driebergen, Holland (1970), and Baden, Austria (1970) to discuss the theology of development and peace in the world community. Many smaller seminars were also held on local and regional projects for development and education for civic action. After its first three-year period, however, the staff and program of SODEPAX was reduced and its mandate redefined to serve primarily as a liaison between the Pontifical Commission on Justice and Peace and the World Council's newly formed Commission on the Churches' Participation in Development.[30]

A most spectacular example of the progress in Protestant–Catholic rapprochement came in June 1969 when Pope Paul VI visited the World Council of Churches offices in Geneva, Switzerland. The pope had accepted an invitation to address a conference celebrating the fiftieth anniversary of the International Labour Office in Geneva. At the suggestion of Cardinal Willebrands and by the invitation of Blake, the pope added the World Council to his itinerary. It was the first visit of a Roman pope to Geneva in more than four hundred years and marked the first time since the Reformation that a pope had prayed publicly in a worship service that he himself did not conduct. For the head of the Roman Catholic church to take such a precedent-shattering step was of great ecumenical significance, especially when the question of Catholic membership in the World Council of Churches had been so prominently featured at the Uppsala Assembly.[31]

On June 10, 1969 Blake welcomed Pope Paul VI to the ecumenical headquarters of the World Council of Churches. Blake described the progress of the ecumenical movement and cited the pope's visit as proclaiming both to the church and to the world "that the ecumenical movement flows on ever wider, ever deeper towards the unity and renewal of Christ's Church as He wills it." Blake also utilized a word of the Orthodox theologian Basil the Great, *sympnoia*, being together in one spirit, as an apt term to characterize the new direction of Protestant–Catholic–Orthodox relationships. While acknowledging that many differences and divisions barred the way to full unity, Blake expressed hope that through "mutual encouragement and mutual correction" both Protestant and Catholic could find new ways of living under the Lordship of Christ.[32]

In response, the pope called the meeting a "prophetic moment" and described the World Council of Churches as "a marvelous movement of Christians who had been scattered and who were seeking to reconstitute their unity." In guarded language Paul VI also put on the agenda for discussion and study the question of Roman Catholic membership in the World Council. "In fraternal frankness," he declared, "we do not consider that the question of membership of the Catholic Church in the World Council of Churches is so mature that a positive answer could or should be given. . . . It requires profound study and commits us to a way that honesty recognizes could be long and difficult." Nevertheless, the pope concluded on a positive note that Catholicism would continue the search "filled with hope and pastoral realism, for the unity willed by Christ."[33]

At various points in his address the pope paused, folded his hands across his chest, and then spoke in a voice heavily charged with emotion. Those present sensed how much he was moved by the religious significance of the occasion. Although the pope maintained his composure throughout a series of public appearances, including a boisterous motorboat crossing of Lake Geneva and a solemn ecumenical worship service, he privately revealed the extent of his deep personal feelings about the hopes and frustrations of Christian unity. In Blake's office, with Cardinal Willebrands and M. M. Thomas present, the pope uncharacteristically began to speak excitedly in French. As Blake recalled, the substance of what the pontiff said was: "I am like a man who has been in the desert without food and drink for days, and suddenly before me is spread a whole banquet of food and wine, and I find I cannot drink or eat."[34]

The pope evoked some controversy in his brief address at the World Council headquarters by making a claim to universal leadership and jurisdiction by use of the phrase: "Our name is Peter." Some in the audience felt that such language was a prime example of the great obstacles to Christian unity. Blake, however, saw no problem with the pontiff's open statement of a deeply held conviction.

> I am very glad Pope Paul made his position clear and did not feel the necessity to disguise it with diplomatic glosses. In this he showed that he understood better than some others that the ecumenical movement requires honesty and truth from all if it is not to degenerate into a movement of mere politeness and tolerance. One does not leave his convictions behind when he enters the door of the Ecumenical Centre. If Pope Paul is not free to state his convictions, neither is any one of us, Evangelical or Orthodox, free to contest them—always, I hope, in the same spirit of fraternal love with which the Pope made his claim. For I remind you that in the same paragraph in which he said to us and to the world, "Our name is Peter," he also said, "And the name Paul which We have assumed sufficiently points out the orientation which We have wanted to give Our Apostolic ministry."[35]

Blake's hopes that the momentum of the pope's visit would carry over into conversations about Roman Catholic membership in the World Council have not been realized. After several years of study and discussion by the Joint Working Group, it became increasingly evident that, for the time being at least, the Roman Catholic church was not prepared to commit itself to membership. In the preface to a report issued in 1972, signed by Cardinal Willebrands and Blake, the two leaders stated bluntly that membership was "not expected in the near future."[36] Although this decision was a personal disappointment to Blake, he was heartened by increasing signs of cooperation with the Roman Catholic church, and he viewed these events as positive steps toward the ultimate reunion of Christ's church.

Blake also gave sustained support to the improvement of dialogue with people of other faiths and ideologies. The Uppsala Assembly had affirmed that encounters with people of other faiths or no faith at all must ultimately lead to dialogue. At Addis Ababa in 1971 the Central Committee adopted policy statements and guidelines for achieving such dialogue. Building on previously existing programs relating Christianity and Judaism, the World

Council invited Muslim dialogue in 1969 on both local and international levels. In 1972 a week-long Christian–Muslim conversation took place in Lebanon with participants ranging from an Indonesian cabinet minister to a sheik from Tanzania, as well as persons from Algeria, Nigeria, India, Pakistan, Bangladesh, and most of the Arab countries. Roman Catholic, Greek Orthodox, Coptic, and Protestant Christians, many of the latter from Third World countries, also participated. In March of 1970, at the Ajaltoun Consultation, people of four different faiths—Hindu, Buddhist, Christian, and Muslim—came together for the first time under World Council auspices. Although it was more difficult to find partners for secular dialogue, conversations between Christians and Marxists were held on a number of occasions.[37]

Blake considered this expansion of dialogue to be one of the most exciting developments to occur during his term as general secretary of the World Council of Churches. Throughout his association with the World Council, Blake had opposed the viewpoint that dialogue was either a substitute for believing the gospel or simply a disguised form of evangelism. "Now, it can't be both," Blake argued. "If you say, 'We belong to Jesus Christ,' and don't say, 'Jesus Christ belongs to us,' then you have a chance to talk to people. But you can't talk if you think you have a monopoly on God and truth."[38] Blake's personal commitment to this wider ecumenism had an effect on the development of World Council programming in efforts to communicate with people of varying worldviews.

In a number of other ways the World Council showed signs of growth and renewal during the period of Blake's leadership. Between 1967 and 1972, for example, nearly fifty churches became full members of the World Council and about a dozen joined as associate members. Significantly, many of these churches were young, small, conservative, evangelical denominations from developing countries. Among the full members were the Methodist Church of Kenya, the Evangelical Lutheran Church in Southern Africa, the Evangelical Pentecostal Church "Brazil for Christ," the Church of Christ on Earth by the Prophet Simon Kimbangu, the Moravian Church in Jamaica, the Church of the Province of Burma, the Church of the Province of Tanzania, the

Church of Nias, Indonesia, and the Evangelical Methodist Church in the Philippines. Included in the smaller associate member status were the African Protestant Church, the Methodist Church in Cuba, the Presbytery of Liberia, the Evangelical Methodist Church in Bolivia, and the Methodist Church of Peru. The addition of these and other churches contributed significantly to the inclusiveness of the World Council in the period preceding and following the Uppsala assembly.[39]

Even though Blake preferred to work with existing administrative structures rather than expending time and energy creating new ones, he did help bring to completion a long, tedious process of structural reorganization of the World Council that had been initiated in 1963. The structure of the World Council had evolved rather casually since its founding in 1948, and most members agreed that some ordering and updating had to be done. The difficulty, however, came in trying to obtain a consensus among staff and Central Committee members as to what changes should be made. For a time it appeared that an annual "progress report" on restructuring would become a fixture on the Central Committee's agenda.

Working closely with a committee chaired by Bishop James K. Matthews of the United Methodist Church in the United States, Blake helped to shape a structure of Program Units (rather than the traditional Divisions) which had both a theological and practical rationale and combined familiar groupings and new nomenclature. When Blake tested out his proposed solution to the structural problems at a private dinner meeting with Visser 't Hooft, the former general secretary commented: "I admire your nerve, but it's the best arrangement I have seen."[40] The Central Committee approved the three Program Units of Faith and Witness, Justice and Service, and Education and Communication in 1971, and dismissed the structure committee with thanks for a job well done.[41]

Blake utilized his organizational skills to create an atmosphere of unity and cohesiveness among staff members whose morale had suffered during the interim between Visser 't Hooft's announced retirement and the election of his successor. One of Blake's first actions was to meet with members of his executive staff in small groups and give them ample opportunity to air their complaints and frustrations. After studying working conditions of the three hundred employees at the ecumenical center, Blake recommended substantial wage increases and approved revised work rules after consultation with staff members themselves. Blake's accessibility, concern for the personal well-being of his staff, and ability to make administrative decisions quickly and fairly gained him respect and support at the Geneva headquarters.[42]

Blake also worked with measurable success to make the World Council staff representative. In particular, Blake tried to increase the number of Orthodox, Asians, Africans, Latin Americans, and other Third World citizens to positions of leadership. Nevertheless, he refused to recommend anyone to a staff position whom he considered incapable of performing the assigned task. "There is nothing worse you can do for people," Blake said, "than to put them into a job that they cannot do, especially if they are from a minority group."[43] A perusal of the appointments listed in the *Minutes and Reports* of the Central Committee between 1967 and 1972 indicates that Blake brought together experts from all over the world to implement the expanding programs and activities of the World Council of Churches.[44]

Although one needs to study the complete list in order to chronicle the history of staff appointments, a few representative names will reflect the quality and diversity of Blake's recommendations: Mrs. René Karefa-Smart helped to launch the race program and served on a voluntary basis as research secretary in the Development on Co-operation of Men and Women in Church, Family and Society; Dr. William Kennedy functioned as administrative officer in the new Office of Education; Mr. Leopoldo Juan Niilus led the CCIA; Professor Paulo Freire served as special consultant to the Office of Education; Dr. Kodwo Ankrah became African secretary in the Service to Refugees; Mr. Sunny Kuruvilla, a young layman from the MarThoma Church in India, became an associate administrative secretary; and Canon Burgess Carr, an Anglican priest from the Church of Liberia, served as co-secretary for Africa. Key Orthodox appointments included Archpriest Vitaly Borovoy as a member of the Secretariat of the Commission on Faith and Order and Father George Tsetsis to important responsibilities in Greece and the Middle East. Blake is quick to admit, however, that he had only begun to "de-westernize" the World Council staff, but he left the staff stronger and more unified than when he began.[45]

As a westerner himself, Blake found it difficult to adjust to different mindsets and philosophical orientations of nonwestern staff members. One staff member recalled a conference led by a Vietnamese Buddhist to advise the World Council on developments in Vietnam. The Vietnamese chairman began the meeting by describing point five of a five-point proposal. Blake, anxious to know the starting point, interjected, "Let's start with point one." "No," said the chairman, "we will begin with point five and move to point one." Blake acquiesced and waited impatiently through the long presentation and began to relax only when the speaker reached point one. Much to Blake's consternation, however, the Vietnamese chairman then proceeded to reexplicate his points, concluding with point five. This time, however, he ended with a different point five. Perplexed by the nonsyllogistic, Oriental logic, Blake ended the meeting by saying: "It sounds fine to me even though I don't understand it all. I trust your judgment."[46]

Staff members testified favorably about Blake's willingness to delegate authority and to support responsible decisions made at lower levels. At the time of the Munich Olympic tragedy in 1972, for example, Blake was in the United States when staff members wanted to publish an open letter critical of the German police. Although the letter could have had considerable ecumenical impact on the German churches in the World Council, Blake had only one question when reached by telephone in the United States: "Are you sure of your facts? If so, go ahead."[47] On another occasion, Dr. Albert Van den Heuvel, director of the Department of Communication, had been quoted in some European newspapers as having made uncomplimentary statements about the military government in Greece. Since the remarks indirectly involved the status of the Orthodox Church in Greece, on his return to Geneva, the communication director was instructed to report to Blake immediately. Blake looked up at him and said, "Albert, did you say that?" After an affirmative nod from the nervous staffer, Blake said: "I think you should not make such statements more than twice a year." He said nothing else about the incident.[48]

Although Blake's vigor and energy showed no signs of diminishing, he had decided at the time of his ratification as general secretary by the Uppsala Assembly to announce his plan to retire in good time before the next assembly. Nothing happened to make him change that decision. In July 1970 Blake told the Executive Committee of the Central Committee that he wanted to retire as soon as possible after November 1971. Although he promised to remain long enough to make a smooth transition of leadership possible, Blake hoped that a new general secretary could be elected at the latest by the summer of 1972. On August 16, 1972, at its meeting in Utrecht, the Central Committee unanimously elected Dr. Philip Potter, a native of the West Indies and director of World Mission and Evangelism for the World Council, to succeed Blake.[49]

In his final report as general secretary, Blake described some important events, opportunities, and responsibilities that lay before the World Council of Churches. Blake stressed as one important responsibility the need to deal with tensions existing between various secular and religious movements and church structures.

> During the years of my responsibility as General Secretary, I have attempted with all my energies to make this sharp polarization creative rather than destructive. As a former "hierarch" in a member church, I have tried to use the fruits of that experience to persuade the official church leaders of the World Council to support through the Council those movements of which they were afraid, and which sometimes seemed to them to be shaking the very foundations of their ecclesiastical structures. In this broken world we who lead the churches need less, I judge, to fear heresy, schism, and anarchy than to look to our own actions so that, as much as in us lies, the structures and fellowship of our churches may embrace and include all who, however strange to us their ways, call upon and serve the Lord Jesus.[50]

Blake concluded his remarks to the Central Committee on a positive note.

Let my last word be based on Christian faith and hope. I believe now as I was learning to believe at the beginning of my ministry forty years ago this past April, that Jesus Christ is Lord, and that the ecumenical way is the way of obedience to Him. At the end of my service to the World Council, I am as hopeful and as thankful as I was when I began.[51]

When Blake took office in 1966, the World Council was in a "state of suspended puzzlement" as it groped for a new sense of mission in the midst of theological, political, and social change. That the World Council moved forward with new personnel and with programs designed to deal directly with the major issues of the day indicates this quality of Blake's leadership and his administrative ability. Blake was not merely an interim leader. He served as a link between one era of ecumenical history that was rapidly disappearing and another period that was taking shape. Blake's combination of experience and willingness to experiment gave the World Council both a sense of continuity with the past and an atmosphere amicable to change. There is an old German saying for pastors: "Whatever you do in your office—remember your predecessor and your successor." Judged by that standard, Eugene Carson Blake was a good pastor.

EPILOGUE

There is no future for a sectarian church whether it is Protestant, Roman Catholic, or Orthodox—no future—period!

When Eugene Carson Blake retired in 1972, he told Cornish Rogers of *The Christian Century* that his only future projects were to reduce and to stop smoking. Rogers was skeptical that an activist like Blake could ever drop completely out of public life. "As I drove toward home," Rogers concluded, "I thought to myself: in retirement, he'll be doing a great deal more than losing weight and breaking the cigarette habit."[1]

Rogers reasoned correctly. In 1973 Blake permitted the Presbytery of San Gabriel, California to submit his name as a candidate for moderator of the General Assembly of the United Presbyterian Church in the U.S.A. In a five-way race Blake came in fifth, and Clinton M. Marsh, a Black Presbyterian minister from the Presbytery of Omaha, became the new moderator. It was one of the rare times in Eugene Carson Blake's career that he miscalculated an ecclesiastical election. Blake had been out of the country for nearly seven years and had lost touch with the inner workings of his denomination. Younger commissioners did not know him well, and, at sixty-six, Blake no longer symbolized the cutting edge of theological inquiry and social involvement.

Following his defeat Blake displayed no bitterness or resentment. He accepted an appointment from his good friend Clinton Marsh as chairman of the powerful Bills and Overtures Committee, skillfully handling a number of very difficult bills and overtures on the assembly floor. When he concluded his last presentation, Blake received a standing ovation from appreciative commissioners. Although one national religious journal suggested that Blake's defeat was not so much a rejection of the man as of the era he personified, the facts do not bear out this assessment. For example, the General Assembly voted to rejoin COCU, after having dropped out at a previous assembly. In this action, Blake's positions on ecumenism and social involvement were endorsed by the majority of assembly commissioners. J. Martin Bailey, editor of *A.D. Magazine*, claimed: "The causes for which Eugene Carson Blake had labored so effectively were not lost. They had come of age."[2]

Blake continues to make his services available to the church. He has served as a member of COCU's special commission to study the theological basis of church union and is presently chairman of a Church and Society Task Force dealing with peacemaking and American foreign policy. He is also in demand as a preacher and lecturer.

A major interest in his retirement years, however, has been his association with a Christian citizens' group called Bread for the World, an agency that attempts to keep elected officials informed about issues that vitally affect hungry people throughout the world. As president of Bread for the World, Blake thought that he had at last accepted a noncontroversial position. "I soon found out," he said, "that everything worthwhile is controversial." Blake's outspoken views on the possibility of dealing directly with the problems of world hunger has brought him into conflict with people who think that feeding the starving masses will only make more starve later. Blake remains adamant, however, that Bread for the World is moving in the right direction and continues to merit his full support.[3]

There have been some changes in Blake's personal life. After her long illness, his wife Valina died in 1973. Blake subsequently married Jean Ware Hoyt of Stamford, Connecticut, a long-time family friend who had been a community leader, a member of the denomination's General Council as well as of a number of special committees of the General Assembly, the synod, the presbytery, and a member of the Session of the Stamford Presbyterian Church. They share many personality traits: activism, quick-mindedness, openness, expressiveness. They travel together and frequently entertain guests in their comfortable home on the shores of Long Island Sound.

At seventy-one Eugene Carson Blake is still vigorous and physically active. When he leans forward to express a conviction about some humanitarian or theological issue (the two are usually the same), there is no mistaking the charisma and intensity that characterized his entire career. In reply to an interview-ending question, "Does the ecumenical movement have a future?" Blake responded with unhesitating confidence: "I would put it this way. There is *no future* for a sectarian church whether it is Protestant, Roman Catholic, or Orthodox—*no future—period!*"

NOTES

Preface

1. Edward G. Boland, "Toward Church Unity and a New Image: An Interview with Eugene Carson Blake," *Pastoral Life* (September 1967), p. 469.

2. Francis X. Gannon, *Biographical Dictionary of the Left* (Belmont, Massachusetts and Los Angeles, California, 1968), vol. I, p. 20.

3. *Christianity Today*, January 21, 1966, p. 432.

4. William Hall, interview with author, May 16, 1977.

5. Eugene Carson Blake, interview with author, July 20, 1976, p. 47. All subsequent references to interviews with Dr. Blake will be indicated by ECB, the date of the interview, and the page number of the typed transcript if one is available. Tapes of the interviews are in the archives of the Presbyterian Historical Society, 425 Lombard Street, Philadelphia, Pennsylvania.

6. Eugene Carson Blake, "Prophetic Preaching Today," typescript (January 25, 1954), pp. 13–14.

7. Eugene Carson Blake to editor, *Christianity and Crisis*, July 9, 1952, p. 1.

8. ECB, July 20, 1976, p. 48.

9. Eugene Carson Blake, "The Ecumenical Movement Flows on—ever wider, ever deeper," typescript (November 21, 1969), p. 4–5.

10. Eugene Carson Blake, "Memorandum," typescript (April 1, 1968), p. 1.

11. Albert Van den Heuvel to R. Douglas Brackenridge, April 20, 1976.

12. Frank Heinze, interview with author, March 1, 1977.

189

13. Ibid. Heinze attributed these words to another Presbyterian executive.

14. Henry L. McCorkle, "The Church's Four-Letter Man," *Presbyterian Life*, December 11, 1954, p. 8.

15. Eugene Carson Blake to Mrs. Arthur Probst, April 11, 1966.

16. William C. Schram, interview with author, April 13, 1977, and Frank Heinze, interview with author, March 1, 1977.

17. Eugene Carson Blake, "The Moral Responsibility of the Church in a Secular Society," typescript (June 1960), p. 8.

I: Child of a Christian Home

1. Eugene Carson Blake, "What It Means to Be a Christian," printed sermon (June 21, 1942), p. 4. Blake had one older brother, Howard Carson Blake, and one older sister, Rhea Carson Blake, an adopted child. Rhea was Lulu Carson's niece, the daughter of Lulu's brother, Cassius Carson, a widower.

2. Winthrop Hudson, *Religion in America*, 2d ed. (New York, 1973), pp. 315–17.

3. *The Literary Digest*, November 17, 1906, p. 720; *The World's Work*, November 1906, p. 8147, and December 1906, p. 8283; and the New York *Times*, November 9, 1906, p. 2.

4. ECB, March 3, 1976.

5. Ibid., and Howard Carson Blake, interview with author, February 23, 1976. Hereafter referred to as HCB. Other information about the early history of the Blake family is contained in a letter from Mary Alice Willcockson to Eugene Carson Blake, March 22, 1969. Ms. Willcockson belonged to the Carson family and had made an extensive genealogical study based on a careful search of family records and public documents.

6. St. Louis *County Watchman*, August 3, 1882; ECB, March 3, 1976; and HCB, February 23, 1976.

7. ECB, March 3, 1976, and HCB, February 23, 1976.

8. Ibid.

9. Ibid.

10. ECB, March 3, 1976.

11. HCB, February 23, 1976, and ECB, March 3, 1976.

12. Orville P. Blake, "Spiritual Finance versus Financial Spirituality, An Address Delivered at the Annual Meeting of the Synod of Missouri of the Presbyterian Church in the U.S.A.," October 12, 1916. A copy of this address is in a family scrapbook belonging to O. P. Blake and now in the possession of Howard Carson Blake. Hereafter referred to as Blake Family Scrapbook.

13. ECB, March 3, 1976. Many memorabilia from O. P. Blake's political activities can be found in the Blake Family Scrapbook.

14. Ibid.

15. Ibid.

16. Ibid.

17. ECB, March 3, 1976.

18. Eugene Carson Blake, "Address to the General Assembly of the Presbyterian Church in the United States," typescript (June 6, 1968), pp. 2–3.

19. Eugene Carson Blake, "The Education of a Christian," printed sermon (October 31, 1937), p. 4.

20. ECB, March 3, 1976. See also *Presbyterian Life*, January 8, 1949, pp. 18–20.

21. ECB, March 3, 1976, and HCB, February 23, 1976.

22. ECB, March 3, 1976.

23. HCB, February 23, 1976, and ECB, March 3, 1976.

24. ECB, March 3, 1976.

25. West Presbyterian Church was formally organized in 1888 in the Cabanne district of St. Louis, serving an area west of Union Avenue and south of Page Boulevard, a section that is today predominantly Black. Its first building was dedicated in 1891. By 1920 the congregation had over a thousand members and was considered to be one of the most prominent Presbyterian churches in St. Louis. Despite prosperous years during and following World War II, West Church faced the inevitable problems of inner-city churches. In 1958 the congregation voted to remain in the Cabanne district and to "work aggressively to evangelize its neighborhood." Integration brought

new members and opened new fields of community service. Today West Presbyterian Church serves a largely Black constituency in a Black community. Information based on "Souvenir Program of the 75th Anniversary Celebration of the West Presbyterian Church, October 30 to November 28, 1963," n.p.

26. Blake Family Scrapbook. There is no date on the letters but the handwriting suggests that Eugene Carson Blake was about six or seven years old.

27. ECB, March 3, 1976.

28. Rhea Carson Blake Harvey, interview with author, July 28, 1976.

29. ECB, March 3, 1976.

II: Student with Religious Priorities

1. See Hudson, *Religion in America*, pp. 360–62.

2. Ibid., pp. 363–70.

3. ECB, March 3, 1976.

4. Ibid.

5. Thornton Wilder, *The Angel That Troubled the Waters* (New York, 1928), p. xv. An excellent summary of Wilder's literary work in Leonard Unger, ed., *American Writers: A Collection of Literary Biographies* (New York, 1974), Vol. IV, pp. 355–77.

6. ECB, March 3, 1976, and Thornton Wilder, *Heaven's My Destination* (New York, 1935).

7. Wilder, *The Angel That Troubled the Waters*, p. xv.

8. Dean G. Peerman and Martin E. Marty, eds., *A Handbook of Christian Theologians* (Cleveland and New York, 1965), pp. 233–55.

9. Leslie Glenn to R. Douglas Brackenridge, April 12, 1976.

10. ECB, March 3, 1976.

11. Ibid.

12. Ibid.

13. Ibid.

14. Ibid.

15. Ibid.

16. Eugene Carson Blake, "Albany Business College Football Dinner Address," typescript (October 30, 1936), n.p.

17. ECB, March 3, 1976.

18. Ibid.

19. Ibid.

20. Ibid.

21. Eugene Carson Blake, "Wanted: Christian Scholars," *The Christian Scholar*, December 1956, p. 265.

22. ECB, March 3, 1976.

23. Ibid.

24. John M. Roots, "An Apostle to Youth," *The Atlantic Monthly*, December 1928, pp. 807–17.

25. James W. Laurie to James A. Laurie, Jr., July 2, 1928.

26. ECB, March 3, 1976.

27. Ibid.

28. Ibid. and HCB, February 23, 1976.

29. ECB, March 3, 1976, and HCB, February 23, 1976. For thirty-two years Howard Carson Blake devoted his energies to the Oxford Group, or Moral Rearmament as it was later called. He left that work in June 1960 to become pastor of a Presbyterian, U.S. congregation in Weslaco, Texas. His brother, Eugene Carson Blake, preached the installation sermon on March 2, 1962. In January 1966 Howard Blake resigned from the Weslaco post to become the executive officer of South Texas Presbytery. In 1970 he joined the Celebration of Evangelism movement and in 1973–74 he worked with the H. E. Butt Foundation in Texas. Since then he has been working on a program entitled, "The Laity—A New Direction." Blake was honorably retired from the Presbyterian ministry on November 1, 1972.

30. Eugene Carson Blake, "A Letter from the Stated Clerk to Members of the United Presbyterian Church in the United States of America," *Presbyterian Life*, June 1, 1966, p. 6., and ECB, March 3, 1976.

31. ECB, March 3, 1976.

32. Ibid.

33. Ibid.

34. Ibid.

35. E. D. Lucas to editor of *Presbyterian Life*, November 2, 1954.

36. Ibid.

37. Ibid.

38. ECB, March 3, 1976.

39. Ibid. The Blakes were married for forty-four years. They had no children. In the late 1940s Valina Blake suffered a stroke from which she never fully recovered. She died in 1973.

40. Ibid. For a description of the Princeton controversy, see Lefferts A. Loetscher, *The Broadening Church: A Study of Theological Issues in the Presbyterian Church Since 1869* (Philadelphia, 1954), pp. 125–55.

41. R. Park Johnson to R. Douglas Brackenridge, May 10, 1976.

42. ECB, July 20, 1976, pp. 194–95.

43. *The Dictionary of National Biography* (London, 1949), pp. 581–82. Mackintosh's three most influential books were *The Doctrine and Person of Jesus Christ* (1912), *The Christian Experience of Forgiveness* (1927), and *Types of Modern Theology, Schleiermacher to Barth* (1937).

44. Eugene Carson Blake, "The Idea of God Underlying the *Westminster Confession*: Is it Christlike?" typescript (November 6, 1929), p. 4.

45. Ibid.

46. Eugene Carson Blake, "A Letter from the Stated Clerk to Members of the United Presbyterian Church in the United States of America," *Presbyterian Life*, June 1, 1966, p. 6.

47. Eugene Carson Blake, "The Bearing of Dogmatics and Preaching on Each Other," typescript (October 1929), p. 4.

48. ECB, March 3, 1976.

49. Eugene Carson Blake, "A Discussion of the Two Natures of Christ," typescript (March 9, 1931), p. 3.

50. A note from Charles Hodge to Eugene Carson Blake on class paper, March 9, 1931.

51. Eugene Carson Blake, "Wanted: Christian Scholars," p. 262.

52. ECB, March 3, 1976. For a colorful account of Wheeler see "Minis-

ters' Coach: Professor Donald Wheeler of Princeton Theological Seminary," *Presbyterian Life*, March 4, 1950, pp. 28–30.

53. ECB, March 3, 1976.

54. Ibid.

55. Ibid.

III: Minister in the Parish

1. Eugene Carson Blake, "A Church Both Evangelical and Ecumenical," *Princeton Seminary Bulletin*, October 1973, p. 20. For a background of this period see Hudson, *Religion in America*, pp. 357–90.

2. Sydney E. Ahlstrom, *A Religious History of the American People* (New Haven and London, 1972), p. 203.

3. William Brower and Henry Miller, *The Collegiate Reformed Protestant Dutch Church of the City of New York* (New York, 1928), p. 103.

4. ECB, March 3, 1976.

5. Ibid.

6. Ibid.

7. Ibid.

8. Victor Paltsits, *The Beginnings of Presbyterianism in Albany* (Albany, 1909), pp. 21–28, and *185th Anniversary of First Presbyterian Church of Albany, New York* (Albany, 1948), pp. 3–4.

9. ECB, March 3, 1976, and First Presbyterian Church of Albany, group interview with author, October 14, 1976. Hereafter referred to as Albany Group Interview.

10. Albany Group Interview, October 14, 1976.

11. ECB, March 3, 1976, and Session Minutes of the First Presbyterian Church, Albany, New York, May 29, 1938. Blake also persuaded the Pasadena Presbyterian Church to abolish its pew rental system. See Session Minutes of the Pasadena Presbyterian Church, January 9 and February 3, 1941.

12. Albany Group Interview, October 14, 1976, and Truman D. Cameron to R. Douglas Brackenridge, April 10, 1976.

13. Albany Group Interview, October 14, 1976, and Roger H. Johnson to Eugene Carson Blake, July 3, 1951.

14. ECB, March 3, 1976.

15. John C. Bennett to Eugene Carson Blake, May 20, 1938.

16. Eugene Carson Blake, "Reinhold Niebuhr and the Preacher," typescript (June 1943), pp. 4–5.

17. ECB, March 3, 1976.

18. Blake, "Reinhold Niebuhr and the Preacher," p. 6.

19. Ibid., p. 9.

20. Ibid., p. 12.

21. ECB, March 3, 1976.

22. Ibid.

23. Pasadena Presbyterian Church news release, typescript (December 1940), and Pasadena *Star-News*, December 11, 1940.

24. J. S. Macdonnell, et al., *The Story of Pasadena Presbyterian Church* (Pasadena, 1966), pp. 3–10.

25. Arthur Cooper, "Fifty Foremost Presbyterian Parishes," *The Presbyterian Tribune* (November 1949), pp. 23–24. The statistics and information about Pasadena Presbyterian Church are taken from Annual Reports of the Pasadena Presbyterian Church, 1941–50.

26. *The Clarion*, May 30, 1942, p. 1. See also Pasadena Presbyterian Church group interview with author, September 27, 1976. Hereafter referred to as PPC Group Interivew.

27. PPC Group Interview, September 27, 1976.

28. Ibid., September 28, 1976.

29. Ibid., and Dorothy and Gilbert Babcock, interview with author, September 27, 1976.

30. PPC Group Interview, September 27 and 28, 1976.

31. *The Clarion*, October 9, 1948, p. 3. See also *Presbyterian Life*, November 13, 1948, p. 16.

32. PPC Group Interview, September 28, 1976.

33. Howard Swan, interview with author, September 28, 1976.

34. PPC Group Interview, September 28, 1976.

35. Pasadena *Star-News*, December 10, 1949; Howard Swan, interview with author, September 28, 1976; and *Presbyterian Life*, September 3, 1949, p. 29.

36. PPC Group Interview, September 28, 1976.

37. Eugene Carson Blake, "The Embarrassment of the Ministry," typescript (June 20, 1948), p. 5.

38. For a discussion of Blake's preaching on racial attitudes, see chapter V.

39. Eugene Carson Blake, "The Vice of Loyalty," typescript (May 10, 1936), p. 5. See also Pasadena *Star-News*, February 27, 1948.

40. Robert H. Heinze, interview with author, May 27, 1976.

41. Eugene Carson Blake, "God and Collective Bargaining," typescript (September 3, 1944), p. 4.

42. These generalizations about Blake's preaching are based on the author's reading of manuscript sermons in the archives of the Presbyterian Historical Society, Philadelphia, Pennsylvania.

43. Donald MacLeod, ed., *Here Is My Method: The Art of Sermon Construction* (Los Angeles, 1952), p. 25.

44. Eugene Carson Blake, "How Comes the Spirit of God?" typescript (May 12, 1940), p. 6.

45. Eugene Carson Blake, "The Scheme of Salvation," typescript (March 11, 1951), p. 4.

46. ECB, March 3, 1976.

47. E. A. Hackett, "California Challenge," *Presbyterian Life* (July 3, 1948), pp. 21–22.

48. ECB, July 19, 1976, and Glenn W. Moore to R. Douglas Brackenridge, July 5, 1976. Blake has frequently mentioned his debt to Holden and Moore. On the flyleaf of a gift book to Moore, Blake wrote: "To Glenn W. Moore, who taught me a great deal about Presbyterian law and its importance."

49. Minutes of Los Angeles Presbytery of the Presbyterian Church in the United States of America, June 25, 1948, p. 882. Hereafter referred to as Los Angeles Presbytery Minutes.

50. Los Angeles Presbytery Minutes, September 14, 1949, p. 994. See also ECB, July 19, 1976.

51. The General Assembly supported the action of Los Angeles Presbytery. See *Minutes of the General Assembly of the Presbyterian Church in the U.S.A.*, 1955, Part I, pp. 169–74.

52. Eugene Carson Blake to Ganse Little, June 9, 1964.

53. ECB, July 19, 1976.

54. *The Clarion*, November 18 and March 25, 1944, p. 1, and January 27, 1951, p. 1. During this period Blake's name appeared frequently in the pages of *Presbyterian Life*, the denominational magazine.

55. ECB, July 20, 1976.

56. Eugene Carson Blake, "The Ecumenical Task of a General Secretary," in Robert L. Friedly, ed., *Four Faces of Christian Ministry* (St. Louis, 1973), pp. 43–45.

57. Paul C. Payne, interview with author, October 5, 1976. For a description of the Faith and Life Curriculum see *Presbyterian Life*, October 16, 1948, pp. 8–9.

58. Eugene Carson Blake, "Nominating Speech for Jesse Baird," typescript (May 27, 1948), p. 3.

59. See accounts in Newark *Evening News*, May 22 and June 2, 1948.

60. Eugene Carson Blake, "To Live Is to Change," typescript (November 13, 1949), p. 4.

IV: Servant of the General Assembly

1. Frank H. Heinze, "Eugene Carson Blake: The Call to Geneva," *Presbyterian Life*, March 1, 1966, p. 7.

2. For a concise background of this period, see Hudson, *Religion in America*, pp. 382–391.

3. *Presbyterian Life*, September 30, 1950, pp. 12–13; October 14, 1950, p. 18; and November 11, 1950, p. 17.

4. *Presbyterian Life*, March 17, 1951, p. 14. See also R. Douglas Brackenridge, *Beckoning Frontiers: A Biography of James Woodin Laurie* (San Antonio, 1976), pp. 104–5.

5. *Presbyterian Life*, June 23, 1951, p. 9.

6. *The Clarion*, June 9, 1951, p. 4.

7. *Presbyterian Life*, June 23, 1951, p. 10.

8. ECB, June 20, 1976, p. 36, and *Presbyterian Life*, June 23, 1951, pp. 11–12.

9. I have no specific documentation for this idea but various church

leaders whom I have interviewed agree that this might have been a factor in Blake's election.

10. A letter to the editor of *Presbyterian Life* expressed what many Presbyterians thought about the title "stated clerk." "When is the General Assembly of the Presbyterian Church in the U.S.A. going to select a title worthy of the dignity of the most important administrative position in the Church, in place of the colorless, commonplace, and undignified title of Stated Clerk?" *Presbyterian Life*, July 7, 1951, p. 4.

11. *Presbyterian Life*, February 1955, p. 20. For a perceptive study of the historical background of the office of stated clerk, see Bruce David Forbes, "William Henry Roberts: Resistance to Change and Bureaucratic Adaptation," *Journal of Presbyterian History*, Winter 1976, pp. 405–21.

12. ECB, July 20, 1976, p. 67.

13. ECB, July 20, 1976, pp. 38–39.

14. Ibid., pp. 36–37.

15. Ibid.

16. In response to a letter from John Mackay, president of Princeton Theological Seminary, questioning a statement issued in Blake's name on the subject of integration, Blake said: "It seems to me that our authority for this kind of statement rested upon our wisdom in the timeliness of it and in the freedom that every Presbyterian minister has to speak his mind in the pulpit or out of it. I do not believe the officers of the Assembly give up this essential Presbyterian freedom. Of course it is true that if we misuse this right or misjudge the temper or belief of the Church we are subject to censure. But so is every preacher when he preaches every Sunday by his presbytery." Eugene Carson Blake to John A. Mackay, December 30, 1958.

17. Eugene Carson Blake to Harry S Truman, October 21, 1951.

18. *Monday Morning*, December 17, 1951, p. 13.

19. David A. Shannon, *Twentieth Century America* (Chicago, 1963), pp. 508–68.

20. Eugene Carson Blake, "Freedom and Authority in Church and State," *Presbyterian Life*, October 27, 1951, p. 10.

21. Ibid.

22. Ibid.

23. Ibid., p. 38.

24. Ibid.

25. Ibid.

26. *Presbyterian Life*, February 1954, p. 28. See also Samuel McCrea Cavert, *The American Churches in the Ecumenical Movement 1900–1968* (New York, 1968), pp. 215–18.

27. *Presbyterian Life*, February 1954, p. 29.

28. *Presbyterian Life*, November 14, 1953, p. 10. For a detailed account, see Stephen K. Parmalee, "A Letter to Presbyterians during the McCarthy Era" (B.D. thesis, Union Theological Seminary, New York, 1962).

29. *Presbyterian Life*, November 14, 1953, p. 10.

30. Ibid.

31. Ibid., pp. 10–11.

32. Ibid., p. 11.

33. *Presbyterian Life*, February 1954, p. 29. Prior to the "Letter to Presbyterians," Methodist Bishop G. Bromley Oxnam had testified before the Committee on Un-American Activities to refute charges made against him. This was a personal rather than a corporate repudiation of McCarthyism. See Cavert, *The American Churches in the Ecumenical Movement 1900–1968*, pp. 216–17.

34. *Presbyterian Life*, June 12, 1954, p. 13.

35. Summary of his testimony is given in *Presbyterian Life* (October 15, 1955), pp. 25–26. Blake also later advocated that churches voluntarily contribute up to 10 percent of the estimated real estate tax on their properties in order to share the public's tax burdens. See Eugene Carson Blake, "Tax Exemption and the Churches," *Christianity Today*, August 3, 1959, pp. 6–8.

36. Ibid., p. 25.

37. *The Christian Century*, October 12, 1955, p. 1164.

38. *Presbyterian Life*, October 15, 1955, p. 25.

39. *Time*, December 13, 1954, p. 69, and *Presbyterian Life*, September 15, 1964, p. 25.

40. *The Christian Century,* May 4, 1960, p. 533.

41. *Presbyterian Life,* June 1, 1960, p. 18.

42. See Martin Marty, *The New Shape of American Religion* (New York, 1959).

43. Eugene Carson Blake, "Is the Religious Boom a Spiritual Bust?" *Look,* September 20, 1955, pp. 27–31.

44. Edward F. Owen, Jr., "Interchurch Men Meet," *The Christian Century,* October 3, 1956, p. 1126.

45. Ibid., p. 1126.

46. *Presbyterian Life,* January 19, 1952, p. 23, and Eugene Carson Blake, "Barbed-Wire Prayer Meetings," *Presbyterian Life,* February 2, 1952, pp. 26–27.

47. *Newsweek,* March 28, 1955, p. 27.

48. Otto Finkbeiner, interview with author, October 11, 1976.

49. ECB, July 20, 1976, pp. 47–50. For list of publications, see bibliography.

50. Samuel W. Shane, interview with author, May 21, 1976.

51. Hans Knight, "Eugene Carson Blake—Christian Soldier," *The Philadelphia Sunday Bulletin Magazine,* February 21, 1965, p. 17.

52. Otto Finkbeiner, interview with author, October 11, 1976.

53. Voluminous correspondence relating to General Assembly planning in Blake's papers, Record Group 3, Presbyterian Historical Society, Philadelphia, Pennsylvania.

54. William C. Schram, interview with author, April 13, 1977.

55. This conclusion is based on a number of interviews. See also Shaun Herron, "Who ever heard of a Stated Clerk who gave a free hand to the Holy Ghost at an Assembly?" *The British Weekly,* June 14, 1956, p. 7.

56. A movement led by the Reverend Edward W. Stimson in 1965 to censure Blake for his "tendency to usurp power and manipulate the Church in the directions of his theological and ecumenical purposes" was resoundingly put down by the General Assembly in that same year. See *Christianity Today,* April 9, 1965, pp. 17–23, and *Presbyterian Life,* June 15, 1965, p. 7. The assembly praised Blake "for the sound exercise of his ministry."

57. ECB, July 20, 1976, pp. 81–83.

58. ECB, May 2, 1977.

59. Cited in Elizabeth H. Verdesi, *In But Still Out: Women in the Church* (Philadelphia, 1976), p. 133. Blake is commended for his role in assisting women in their move for ordination. See pp. 114–35.

60. Eugene Carson Blake to Margaret Shannon, n.d.

61. Eugene Carson Blake, "The Scriptures and the Ministry," typescript (November 24, 1957), p. 1. Wilmina Rowland Smith also gives Blake credit for helping women to organize the Women's Task Force and the Committee on Women in the Church in the early 1960s. Wilmina Rowland Smith, interview with author, May 6, 1977.

62. ECB, July 20, 1976, p. 90.

63. Edward A. Dowey, Jr., *A Commentary on the Confession of 1967 and an Introduction to the Book of Confessions* (Philadelphia, 1968), p. 7.

64. *The Presbyterian Outlook*, September 27, 1976, p. 7. For a critical evaluation of the Confession of 1967 and its deleterious effect on the United Presbyterian Church, see John R. Fry, *The Trivialization of the United Presbyterian Church* (Philadelphia, 1975).

65. Paul C. Payne, interview with author, October 5, 1976.

66. William R. Laws to R. Douglas Brackenridge, March 24, 1976.

V: Spokesman for Civil Rights

1. Harvey G. Cox, "The 'New Breed' in American Churches: Sources of Social Activism in American Religion," *Daedalus*, Winter 1967, p. 139.

2. ECB, July 19, 1976, p. 21.

3. Stephen C. Rose, "Eugene Carson Blake: A Welcome-Home Interview," *The Christian Century*, October 18, 1972, p. 1037.

4. Eugene Carson Blake, "Who Is on the Lord's Side?" typescript (June 20, 1943), p. 5.

5. Eugene Carson Blake, "Christianity and Racial Animosity," typescript (February 10, 1946), p. 6.

6. *Presbyterian Life*, April 16, 1949, p. 13.

7. Ibid., p. 15.

8. Los Angeles Presbytery Minutes, November 14, 1947.

9. Ibid., January 13, 1948. See also *Presbyterian Life*, February 14, 1948, p. 13.

10. Los Angeles Presbytery Minutes, November 4, 1947.

11. Eugene Carson Blake, "The History of a Very Small Step in Christian Social Action," typescript (January 10, 1948), p. 1.

12. ECB, July 19, 1976, p. 26.

13. Gayle Gibbs, "An Interview with Dr. Eugene Carson Blake," *Pasadena Junior League News*, April 10, 1948, pp. 9–12.

14. ECB, July 19, 1976, pp. 19–21.

15. Ibid., p. 20.

16. Ibid., pp. 19–21.

17. Ibid., pp. 21–22.

18. Ibid., p. 22.

19. Ibid., p. 22.

20. Gibbs, "An Interview with Dr. Eugene Carson Blake," p. 12.

21. ECB, July 19, 1976, p. 3.

22. Los Angeles Presbytery Minutes, March 10, 1942.

23. ECB, July 19, 1976, p. 3.

24. Eugene Carson Blake to Robert E. Coates, Jr., August 30, 1955.

25. For a succinct survey of civil rights history see *Race Relations in the U.S.A. 1954–1968—Keesing's Research Report* (New York, 1970).

26. *Presbyterian Life*, April 28, 1956, p. 19.

27. *Minutes of the General Assembly of the Presbyterian Church in the U.S.A.*, 1956, Part I, pp. 226–30.

28. H. B. Sissel, "Segregation in Sumter, South Carolina," *Presbyterian Life*, January 5, 1957, pp. 6–7.

29. Ibid., p. 7. See also ECB, July 20, 1976 and Paul C. Payne, interview with author, October 5, 1976.

30. *Monday Morning*, June 4, 1957, p. 4.

31. ECB, July 20, 1976 and Eugene Carson Blake to William R. Laws, February 2, 1971.

32. *Presbyterian Life*, January 7, 1956, p. 24.

33. Eugene Carson Blake and Theophilus M. Taylor, "Our Role in the Integration Crisis," *Presbyterian Life*, October 1, 1958, p. 23.

34. Ibid., p. 23.

35. The Chicago *Tribune*, September 11, 1958; *News and Views*, October 1958; and *The Presbyterian Outlook*, September 29, 1958, p. 10.

36. Anonymous to Eugene Carson Blake, September 11, 1958.

37. Otto Finkbeiner, interview with author, October 11, 1976.

38. Robert H. Heinze, interview with author, May 27, 1976.

39. Otto Finkbeiner, interview with author, October 11, 1976.

40. *Minutes of the General Assembly of the Presbyterian Church in the U.S.A.*, 1946, Part I, pp. 211–12.

41. Gayraud Wilmore, Jr., "The New Commission on Race: What Exactly Was Launched?" *Presbyterian Life*, November 15, 1963, pp. 25–26.

42. The New York *Times*, August 4, 1963, p. 57.

43. *Time*, May 17, 1963, pp. 23–27.

44. ECB, July 20, 1976.

45. *Minutes of the General Assembly of the United Presbyterian Church in the U.S.A.*, 1963, Part I, pp. 141–42.

46. Robert H. Heinze, "Eugene Carson Blake among 283 Arrested in Baltimore," *Presbyterian Life*, August 1, 1963, pp. 25–26.

47. ECB, July 19, 1976, p. 171.

48. ECB, February 28, 1977, p. 32.

49. Heinze, op. cit., p. 24.

50. ECB, July 20, 1976, p. 172.

51. Heinze, op. cit., p. 26.

52. *Time*, July 12, 1963, pp. 17–18, and ECB, July 20, 1976, p. 173.

53. Robert Heinze, interview with author, May 27, 1976.

54. *Time*, July 12, 1963, p. 17, and the New York *Times*, July 5, 1963, M, p. 1.

55. Ibid.

56. All of the letters are preserved in Blake's papers in the Presbyterian

Historical Society, Philadelphia, Pennsylvania, Record Group 3, Boxes 14–16.

57. Anonymous to Eugene Carson Blake, July 12 and 17, 1963.

58. Jay M. Logan to Eugene Carson Blake, July 11, 1963.

59. *Presbyterian Life*, August 15, 1963, p. 4.

60. Elwyn Smith to Eugene Carson Blake, July 14, 1963.

61. John Brooke to Eugene Carson Blake, October 13, 1963.

62. George McKeag, interview with author, May 17, 1976.

63. *Presbyterian Life*, August 1, 1963, p. 27. Blake's problem was compounded by the way his statement was quoted in the New York *Times:* "I don't question that the law is constitutional, but I question whether the law is right." July 5, 1963, p. 36M. Blake claims that he was misquoted and that the version in *Presbyterian Life* is accurate.

64. Eugene Carson Blake, "Law and Order and Christian Duty," typescript (September 15, 1963), p. 3, and *Monday Morning*, August 1963, pp. 12–14.

65. Blake, "Law and Order and Christian Duty," p. 3.

66. Ibid., p. 4. For a critique of Blake's position see the Cincinnati *Enquirer*, February 27, 1966, pp. 1–2.

67. Eugene Carson Blake, "Should the Code of Ethics in Public Life be Absolute or Relative?" *The Annals of the American Academy of Political and Social Science*, January 1966, p. 9.

68. Eugene Carson Blake to Ben Strong, April 22, 1964.

69. ECB, July 20, 1976.

70. *Minutes of the General Assembly of the United Presbyterian Church in the U.S.A.*, 1964, Part I, p. 44.

71. *Presbyterian Life*, June 15, 1964, pp. 19–20.

72. *Minutes of the General Assembly of the United Presbyterian Church in the U.S.A.*, 1964, Part I, p. 331.

73. *Presbyterian Life*, June 15, 1964, pp. 6–7, and *The Christian Century*, June 17, 1964, p. 813.

74. ECB, July 19, 1976.

75. *The March on Washington for Jobs and Freedom: Speeches by the Leaders*

(New York, 1963), n.p. See an account of the march in the New York *Times*, August 29, 1963, p. 1.

76. Eugene Carson Blake, "Testimony at a Hearing of Sub-committee #5 of the House of Representatives Committee on the Judiciary," typescript (July 24, 1963), pp. 1250–91.

77. Louis Cassels, "A Minister Who's Not Afraid to Fight," *Look*, May 31, 1966, p. 81.

78. Jacob K. Javits to Eugene Carson Blake, June 15, 1964.

79. *Presbyterian Life*, December 15, 1963, pp. 30–31.

80. *Presbyterian Life*, June 15, 1964, pp. 6–7, and *The Christian Century*, June 17, 1964, pp. 812–13.

81. Martin Luther King, Jr. to Eugene Carson Blake, January 13, 1964.

82. Stephen C. Rose, "Eugene Carson Blake: A Welcome-Home Interview," *The Christian Century*, October 18, 1972, p. 1038.

83. Gordon E. Jackson to R. Douglas Brackenridge, September 14, 1976.

VI: Ecumenist of Growing Influence

1. Ruth Rouse and Stephen Neill, eds., *A History of the Ecumenical Movement 1517–1948* (Philadelphia, 1967), pp. 405–37.

2. Harold Fey, ed., *A History of the Ecumenical Movement 1948–1968* (Philadelphia, 1970), pp. 1–27.

3. ECB, February 28, 1977.

4. Ibid. The senior pastor was Norman Vincent Peale.

5. Eugene Carson Blake, "Is It Still a Movement?" typescript (April 28, 1971), pp. 10–11.

6. Eugene Carson Blake, "Preparatory Lecture," typescript (November 5, 1937), p. 2.

7. Eugene Carson Blake, "The Building of Faith," typescript (December 5, 1937), p. 4.

8. ECB, July 19, 1976, p. 115.

9. *The Federal Council Bulletin*, January 1947, pp. 5–6.

10. Gordon E. Jackson to R. Douglas Brackenridge, September 14,

1976. Jackson went on to become a distinguished professor at Pittsburgh Theological Seminary.

11. Fey, *A History of the Ecumenical Movement 1948–1968*, p. 33.

12. ECB, July 20, 1976, p. 95.

13. Eugene Carson Blake, "Amsterdam Report," typescript (September 12, 1948), p. 1.

14. Ibid.

15. *Presbyterian Life*, September 18, 1948, p. 10, and *The Christian Century*, October 6, 1948, p. 1040.

16. Blake, "Amsterdam Report," p. 3.

17. Although Blake regularly attended World Alliance meetings and served on the Administrative Committee of the Alliance's North American Area Council, he always considered confessional bodies to be secondary to the World Council of Churches. Blake's personal views on the World Alliance are expressed in ECB, July 20, 1976, pp. 101–4. For an excellent summary of the World Alliance and Blake's role in its history, see Marcel Pradervand, *A Century of Service: A History of the World Alliance of Reformed Churches 1875–1975* (Grand Rapids, 1975).

18. Blake, "Amsterdam Report," p. 4.

19. ECB, July 20, 1976, p. 96, and Pasadena *Star-News*, February 5, 1949.

20. *National Council Outlook*, January, 1951, p. 11.

21. Virginia Irwin, "St. Louis-Born National Churchman," St. Louis *Post-Dispatch*, August 17, 1955, p. 15.

22. Paul Calvin Payne, interview with author, October 5, 1976.

23. Robert H. Heinze, interview with author, May 27, 1976.

24. Albert Crews to Eugene Carson Blake, October 22, 1953.

25. *Presbyterian Life*, March 1, 1956, p. 36.

26. ECB, July 19, 1976, p. 108.

27. Ibid., p. 109.

28. Eugene Carson Blake, "Poverty Is Embarrassing," typescript (December 27, 1964), and *Presbyterian Life*, April 1, 1971, pp. 12–13.

29. *Christianity Today*, February 4, 1966, p. 50.

30. Eugene Carson Blake to Dean Rusk, July 2, 1965.

31. Eugene Carson Blake to Lyndon B. Johnson, September 25, 1965.

32. *Christianity Today*, March 4, 1966, p. 590, and Eugene Carson Blake, "Press Release," typescript (December 1, 1966).

33. *Time*, July 9, 1973, p. 19.

34. Accounts of Blake's tours can be found in *The Christian Century*, February 16, 1955, pp. 207–8, and *National Council Outlook*, January 1957, pp. 3 and 22.

35. "American Churchmen Visit the Soviet Union" (World Council of Churches booklet, 1957), p. 3.

36. Ibid.

37. Ibid., p. 4.

38. Eugene Carson Blake, "Conversations in Moscow," *Presbyterian Life*, April 28, 1956, pp. 6–10.

39. ECB, July 20, 1976, p. 152.

40. Eugene Carson Blake, "A Churchman's Plan for Dealing with Russia," *U.S. News and World Report*, January 4, 1957, p. 113.

41. Ibid.

42. Blake and McIntire were at one time members of the same presbytery and knew each other from their seminary days. For a full account of McIntire's ministry, see James Morris, *The Preachers* (New York, 1973), pp. 189–234, and Erling Jorstad, *The Politics of Doomsday* (Nashville and New York, 1970), pp. 26–37.

43. Eugene Carson Blake to Carl McIntire, December 28, 1962. Blake's letter was reproduced in the *Christian Beacon*, January 10, 1953, p. 5 along with McIntire's response.

44. Eugene Carson Blake, "The Truth about the National Council of Churches," typescript (March 19, 1961), pp. 10–11. See also *Presbyterian Life*, April 15, 1961, p. 24.

45. Eugene Carson Blake, "Lund: City of Questions," *Presbyterian Life*, September 20, 1952, pp. 21–22.

46. Nelson Chapel, interview with author, September 25, 1976. Chapel was the general secretary of the World Council of Christian Education and a delegate to the Evanston Assembly. Blake was also responsible for organizing the campaign to raise money to build a new

World Council headquarters in Geneva, Switzerland. ECB, July 20, 1976, pp. 204–5.

47. Fey, *A History of the Ecumenical Movement 1948–1968*, pp. 221–31.

48. ECB, July 19, 1976, p. 206.

49. ECB, March 3, 1976.

50. Eugene Carson Blake, *The Church in the Next Decade* (New York, 1966), p. 137.

51. ECB, July 20, 1976, pp. 205–7.

52. Ibid., p. 130.

53. Blake, "Lund: City of Questions," p. 21.

54. Eugene Carson Blake, "New Trends in the Ecumenical Movement," typescript (December 18, 1968), p. 4.

55. Blake, *The Church in the Next Decade*, p. 24.

56. Eugene Carson Blake, "The New Ecumenical Reformation," *Christianity and Crisis*, January 23, 1956, pp. 12–14.

57. ECB, July 19, 1976, pp. 70–73.

58. *Monday Morning*, May 12, 1958, p. 10. See also John Coventry Smith, "World Mission of Our Church," *Monday Morning*, December 5, 1960, pp. 3–6.

59. *The Christian Century*, November 2, 1955, p. 1261.

VII: Architect of Church Union

1. *The Christian Century*, January 31, 1962, p. 128. Blake had already made the cover of *Newsweek*, March 28, 1955, but the feature article was about the surge of religious interest in the 1950s rather than about Blake himself.

2. James A. Pike to Eugene Carson Blake, September 14, 1961.

3. Eugene Carson Blake to James A. Pike, October 3, 1961.

4. ECB, July 20, 1976, p. 133.

5. Eugene Carson Blake, "Toward the Reunion of Christ's Church," *Presbyterian Life*, January 1, 1961, p. 9. The Proposal was also published separately by the Office of the General Assembly of the

United Presbyterian Church and by *The Christian Century*, December 21, 1960, pp. 1508–11 and various other publications. The pagination here is from *Presbyterian Life* and referred to as Blake Proposal.

6. ECB, July 20, 1976, p. 132.

7. Eugene Carson Blake to James A. Pike, October 14, 1960.

8. Ibid.

9. Eugene Carson Blake to James A. Pike, November 9, 1960.

10. ECB, July 20, 1976, p. 137.

11. An exception to this general rule is Paul A. Crow, Jr., "Ecumenism and the Consultation on Church Union," *Journal of Ecumenical Studies*, Fall 1967, p. 584.

12. Blake Proposal, p. 12.

13. *Time*, December 19, 1969, p. 64.

14. Ibid.

15. Blake Proposal, p. 38. See also Pradervand, *A Century of Service*, pp. 210–11.

16. Blake Proposal, p. 38.

17. Ibid.

18. ECB, February 28, 1977, p. 30. As far back as 1954 Blake stated that the Presbyterian church could have bishops "so long as basic Presbyterian principles are protected." *Presbyterian Life*, June 12, 1954, p. 37. Ever since his sermon in 1960, Blake has repeatedly tried to lift the discussion of episcopacy out of the limited context of western Christianity. He has had little success, however, in getting his critics to take a worldwide perspective, including Orthodoxy and the younger Asian, African, and Latin American churches. His most recent analysis of the problem is in a review of *Ecumenical Testimony: The Concern for Christian Unity within the Reformed and Presbyterian Churches* (Philadelphia, 1974) by John T. McNeill and James Hastings Nichols, published in the *Journal of Presbyterian History*, Summer 1976, pp. 278–80.

19. Blake Proposal, p. 39.

20. Ibid.

21. In later discussions the Consultation on Church Union was able to

reach agreement on the nature and function of sacraments with relatively little controversy. See Crow, "Ecumenism and the Consultation on Church Union," pp. 589–91.

22. Blake Proposal, p. 39.

23. This principle again reflects Blake's understanding of Orthodox theology.

24. Blake Proposal, p. 39.

25. Ibid.

26. Ibid., p. 40.

27. Ibid.

28. Ibid., p. 41.

29. Ibid.

30. Ibid.

31. *Time*, December 19, 1960, p. 64; *Newsweek*, December 19, 1960, pp. 50–51; and *Life*, December 19, 1960, p. 24.

32. *Presbyterian Life*, April 1, 1961, p. 32.

33. Ibid., January 15, 1961, p. 28.

34. Ibid., February 1, 1961, p. 28.

35. Ibid., April 1, 1961, p. 32.

36. *The Christian Century*, February 15, 1961, pp. 195–96.

37. *Christianity Today*, December 19, 1960, p. 26.

38. See the excellent analysis of Martin Marty, "The Orders of Reunion," *The Christian Century*, December 28, 1960, pp. 1528–29.

39. *Time*, December 19, 1960, p. 64.

40. ECB, July 20, 1976, p. 149.

41. Ibid., p. 151.

42. *Minutes of the General Assembly of the United Presbyterian Church in the U.S.A.*, 1961, Part I, pp. 19–22.

43. *The Christian Century*, June 7, 1961, pp. 702–3.

44. *Presbyterian Life*, June 15, 1961, p. 9. Presbyterian opposition to the Blake Proposal was led by the Reverend Edward W. Stimson of Omaha, Nebraska. His views are set forth in "What Unity Should We Seek?" *Presbyterian Life*, May 1, 1961, pp. 6, 37–39.

45. Crow, "Ecumenism and the Consultation on Church Union," p. 586.

46. Louis Cassels, "Architect of Protestant Unity," typescript (April 19, 1965), p. 19.

47. Crow, "Ecumenism and the Consultation on Church Union," p. 592.

48. Robert McAfee Brown, "The Blake Proposal: Some Pros and Cons," *Presbyterian Life*, May 1, 1961, pp. 40–42.

49. Blake, *The Church in the Next Decade*, p. 130.

50. ECB, July 20, 1976, p. 48.

51. Eugene Carson Blake, "The Union Proposal Two Years Later," *The Christian Century*, March 27, 1963, pp. 394–98, and *The Church in the Next Decade*, pp. 117–31.

52. Eugene Carson Blake, "Second Thoughts on Church Union," typescript (January 24, 1965), p. 5.

53. Crow, "Ecumenism and the Consultation on Church Union," p. 595. See also *Christianity Today*, April 29, 1960, pp. 46–47.

54. *Digest of the Proceedings of the Fifth Meeting of the Consultation on Church Union*, Dallas, May 2–5, 1966, pp. 32–33.

55. Priscilla Chaplin, interview with author, September 26, 1976.

56. ECB, July 20, 1976, p. 147. Blake reportedly indicated during a press conference in 1970 that he had "about lost all interest" in COCU, saying that organizational concerns had overrun the original intent of "spiritual renewal." Blake later denied any disaffection with COCU. See *Christianity Today*, March 13, 1970, p. 41.

57. Church papers and religious periodicals from this period are filled with examples of cooperation and dialogue stemming from Blake's proposal and COCU.

58. Cavert, *Church Cooperation and Unity in America 1900–70*, p. 342.

VIII: General Secretary of the World Council of Churches

1. *Presbyterian Life*, March 1, 1966, p. 7.

2. W. A. Visser 't Hooft, *Memoirs* (London, 1973), pp. 358–59.

3. *Christianity Today*, March 18, 1966, p. 637.

4. John Coventry Smith, interview with author, May 21, 1976. See also, *The Christian Century*, February 3, 1965, pp. 131–32.

5. John Coventry Smith, interview with author, May 21, 1976.

6. Eugene Carson Blake to John Sadiq, August 28, 1965.

7. ECB, July 19, 1976, pp. 213–15.

8. *The Christian Century*, January 19, 1966, p. 69.

9. *Christianity Today*, February 1966, p. 44.

10. These telegrams and other correspondence relative to Blake's election as general secretary are in the Blake Papers, Record Group 3, the Presbyterian Historical Society, Philadelphia, Pennsylvania.

11. ECB, July 19, 1976, pp. 216–17. Blake also had to face a troublesome relationship with Franklin Clark Fry, who resigned as chairman of the Central Committee, a position he had held since 1954, when Blake was elected general secretary. Fry said that it would be "abnormal" and "undesirable" to have Americans in two top positions in the World Council. His resignation was not accepted. However, it was well known that Blake and Fry had clashed on a number of policy matters over the years. See *Christianity Today*, March 4, 1966, p. 46. Fry died shortly after Blake became general secretary, so the impact of this relationship on Blake's service as general secretary is not of great significance for this biography. In terms of a history of the World Council of Churches, the interplay of Blake and Fry as strong leaders on the Central and Executive Committees deserves attention.

12. *Minutes and Reports of the Central Committee of the World Council of Churches*, August 15–26, 1967, pp. 100–104.

13. Norman Goodall, ed., *The Uppsala Report 1968: Official Report of the Fourth Assembly of the World Council of Churches* (Geneva, 1968), p. xv. Hereafter referred to as Goodall, *Uppsala Report*.

14. Cited in Robert McAfee Brown, "Uppsala: An Informal Report," *The Journal of Ecumenical Studies*, Fall 1968, p. 644. Hereafter referred to as Brown, "Informal Report."

15. Brown, "Informal Report," pp. 635–36.

16. Alan Geyer, "Old and New at Uppsala," *The Christian Century*, August 21, 1968, p. 1032. The findings of Section III and other

parts of the Uppsala recommendations were based to a large degree on the conclusions of the Geneva Conference. See Goodall, *Uppsala Report*, p. 240.

17. *The Christian Century*, August 10, 1966, p. 979.

18. *Presbyterian Life*, September 1, 1966, p. 26. Follow-up conferences on similar themes were held at Zargorsk, Russia (March 1968), and Beirut, Lebanon (April 1968). Roman Catholics shared in the planning and presentations of these meetings. See Brown, "Informal Report," pp. 636–40.

19. *Presbyterian Life*, September 1, 1966, pp. 26–27.

20. ECB, June 28, 1977.

21. Eugene Carson Blake, "Religion: Revolutionary or Reactionary?" typescript (October 5, 1967), p. 12.

22. Godall, *Uppsala Report*, pp. 11–18.

23. Ibid., p. 17. See also, J. Robert Nelson, "The Holy Spirit and the Catholicity of the Church," *The Christian Century*, August 21, 1968, pp. 1038–41.

24. Geyer, "Old and New at Uppsala," p. 1031.

25. Ibid., pp. 1031–35.

26. Brown, "Informal Report," pp. 647–48. It must also be recognized, however, that during Blake's secretariat a gradual transition of leadership was taking place. A generation of ecumenical pioneers were passing from the scene through death or retirement. For example, Roswell P. Barnes, Martin Niemöller, Frederick Nolde, and Kenneth Grubb retired. J. H. Oldham, Hendrik Kraemer, Leslie Cooke, Philippe Maury, Otto Dibelius, Korula Jacob, Dai Kitagawa, and Franklin Clark Fry all died during this interim. See Norman Goodall, *Ecumenical Progress: A Decade of Change in the Ecumenical Movement 1961–71* (London, 1972), pp. 2–4. Hereafter referred to as Goodall, *Ecumenical Progress*.

27. Máire Pompe, "Uppsala 1968," *Convergence*, September 1968, p. 14.

28. Brown, "Informal Report," p. 648.

29. Geyer, "Old and New at Uppsala," p. 1034.

30. Interview, David Gill with author, June 24, 1976. This was the consensus of other staff members as well.

214

Notes

31. Goodall, *Uppsala Report*, p. 290.

32. ECB, June 28, 1977.

33. Brown, "Informal Report," p. 659.

34. For a complete list of churches represented see Goodall, *Uppsala Report*, pp. 407–44.

35. Brown, "Informal Report," p. 645.

36. Goodall, *Uppsala Report*, pp. 323–30. See also Brown, "Informal 'Report," pp. 645–46.

37. Goodall, *Uppsala Report*, pp. 179–80. For a fuller discussion see J. Robert Nelson, "Relations with Roman Catholicism at Uppsala," *The Journal of Ecumenical Studies*, Fall 1968, pp. 669–75.

38. Goodall, *Uppsala Report*, pp. 292–303. See also, Helene Iswolsky, "Uppsala and Orthodox Involvement," *The Journal of Ecumenical Studies*, Fall 1968, pp. 661–68.

39. Fey, *A History of the Ecumenical Movement 1948–68*, p. 413. See also, Brown, "Informal Report," pp. 642–44.

40. Goodall, *Uppsala Report*, pp. 45–56.

41. Homer A. Jack, "World Economic and Social Development," *The Christian Century*, August 21, 1968, p. 1048.

42. Fey, *A History of the Ecumenical Movement 1948–68*, p. 428.

43. ECB, June 28, 1977.

44. Ibid.

45. Goodall, *Uppsala Report*, p. 130, and *The Christian Century*, August 21, 1968, p. 1033.

46. Goodall, *Uppsala Report*, p. 242.

47. Ibid., pp. 242–45.

48. Ibid., p. 192.

49. Geyer, "Old and New at Uppsala," p. 1036. See also, Goodall, *Uppsala Report*, pp. 197–99, and Fey, *A History of the Ecumenical Movement 1948–68*, pp. 438–39.

50. Goodall, *Uppsala Report*, p. 287.

51. Ibid., p. 291.

52. Fey, *A History of the Ecumenical Movement 1948–68*, p. 415.

53. Geyer, "Old and New at Uppsala," p. 1037.

54. *The Christian Century*, August 21, 1968, p. 1063.

55. Brown, "Informal Report," p. 660.

IX: Leader of Continuity and Change

1. Goodall, *Uppsala Report*, p. 292.

2. David Gill, interview with author, June 24, 1976.

3. *The Christian Century*, June 25, 1969, p. 862, and ECB, July 19, 1976, pp. 229–31.

4. *The Christian Century*, June 25, 1969, p. 863.

5. *Minutes and Reports of the Central Committee of the World Council of Churches*, August 12–22, 1969, p. 35.

6. Ibid., pp. 35–39, and ECB, July 19, 1976, pp. 231–32.

7. *Minutes and Reports of the Central Committee of the World Council of Churches*, August 12–22, 1969, pp. 272–73, 277.

8. Goodall, *Ecumenical Progress*, p. 56.

9. This correspondence is in the Blake Papers at the World Council Library, Geneva, Switzerland.

10. *The Christian Century*, January 6, 1971, p. 17.

11. Eugene Carson Blake, "Toward a World Community of Man," typescript (March 28, 1972), pp. 10–14. See also David Johnson, ed., *Uppsala to Nairobi: Report of the Central Committee to the Fifth Assembly of the World Council of Churches* (New York and London, 1975), p. 156. Hereafter referred to as Johnson, *Uppsala to Nairobi*.

12. Johnson, *Uppsala to Nairobi*, pp. 152–62.

13. Eugene Carson Blake, "Light and Wisdom from an Unexpected Source," typescript (January 4, 1976), p. 4.

14. ECB, June 28, 1977.

15. Goodall, *Ecumenical Progress*, p. 50.

16. Johnson, *Uppsala to Nairobi*, pp. 142–44.

17. Ibid., pp. 147–48.

18. *The Christian Century*, December 14, 1966, p. 1530.

19. The New York *Times*, April 26, 1967, pp. 1 and 10, and *The Christian Century*, May 17, 1967, p. 643.

20. ECB, July 19, 1976, p. 277.

21. ECB, July 21, 1976, p. 277; *The Christian Century*, October 18, 1972, p. 1034; and *Time*, July 9, 1973, p. 19.

22. *The British Weekly*, August 6, 1970, pp. 1, 12.

23. *The Christian Century*, May 13, 1970, p. 588.

24. *The Christian Century*, February 19, 1969, p. 245, and ECB, July 21, 1976, p. 279.

25. *The Christian Century*, October 28, 1970, pp. 1279–80, and August 11, 1971, p. 946.

26. *The Christian Century*, September 12, 1971, p. 1016.

27. Goodall, *Ecumenical Progress*, p. 61.

28. Ibid., pp. 62–64. See also Johnson, *Uppsala to Nairobi*, pp. 69–91.

29. John Cardinal Willebrands to R. Douglas Brackenridge, December 22, 1976.

30. Johnson, *Uppsala to Nairobi*, p. 37, and *Minutes and Reports of the Central Committee of the World Council of Churches*, January 10–21, 1971, pp. 230–31.

31. ECB, July 19, 1976, pp. 249–53, and Visser 't Hooft, *Memoirs*, pp. 338–39.

32. Eugene Carson Blake, "Address to His Holiness Pope Paul VI on the Occasion of His Visit to the Headquarters of the World Council of Churches," typescript (June 10, 1969), pp. 1–3.

33. *The Christian Century*, July 9, 1969, p. 931.

34. Ibid., and ECB, July 19, 1976, pp. 251–52.

35. *Minutes and Reports of the Central Committee of the World Council of Churches*, August 12–22, 1969, p. 142.

36. Johnson, *Uppsala to Nairobi*, pp. 37–38. See also *The Ecumenical Review*, July 1972, pp. 247–88.

37. *Minutes and Reports of the Central Committee of the World Council of Churches*, January 10–21, 1971, pp. 130–35; Johnson, *Uppsala to Nairobi*, pp. 101–3; and *The Christian Century*, October 14, 1972, p. 1044.

38. ECB, July 19, 1976, p. 235.

39. Johnson, *Uppsala to Nairobi*, pp. 24–33.

40. ECB, June 28, 1977.

41. *Minutes and Reports of the Central Committee of the World Council of Churches*, January 10–21, 1971, pp. 25–28, 136–98.

42. David Gill, interview with author, June 24, 1976.

43. ECB, July 19, 1976, p. 227.

44. Lists of appointments can be found in the *Minutes of Reports of the Central Committee* for the years 1967–72.

45. ECB, July 19, 1976, pp. 220–21.

46. Duane Paul Epps, interview with author, June 24, 1976.

47. Ibid.

48. Albert Van den Heuvel to R. Douglas Brackenridge, August 21, 1976.

49. Johnson, *Uppsala to Nairobi*, p. 45. See also William H. Gentz, *The World of Philip Potter* (New York, 1974).

50. *Minutes and Reports of the Central Committee of the World Council of Churches*, August 13–23, 1972, p. 139.

51. Ibid., p. 140.

Epilogue

1. Cornish Rogers, "Black on Blake," *The Christian Century*, October 18, 1972, p. 1034.

2. *A.D. Magazine*, Presbyterian Life edition, July 1973, p. 29.

3. ECB, June 28, 1977. See also Arthur Simon, *Bread for the World* (New York, 1975).

SELECT BIBLIOGRAPHY

Eugene Carson Blake's personal papers dated prior to 1972 are in two depositories: the Presbyterian Historical Society in Philadelphia, Pennsylvania and the Archives of the World Council of Churches in Geneva, Switzerland. Correspondence and papers from 1972 to the present and miscellaneous family photographs and documents are in Blake's possession but eventually will become part of the collection at the Presbyterian Historical Society.

The materials in the Presbyterian Historical Society archives include papers and letters dating back to Blake's career at Princeton University, the University of Edinburgh, and Princeton Theological Seminary (c. 1924–31), his pastorates in Albany, New York (1935–40) and Pasadena, California (1940–51), and his tenure as stated clerk of the United Presbyterian Church, USA (1951–66). Personal correspondence for the period 1935–51 is not in the collection, and Dr. Blake has no knowledge of its location or existence. Beginning with Blake's term as stated clerk, the collection is extensive and well organized. Contained primarily in Record Groups 3 (30 boxes), 95 (24 boxes), and 121 (16 boxes) are Blake's personal and official correspondence, committee reports and working papers, travel diaries, biographical materials, newspaper clippings, and National and World Council of Churches documents. In addition there is a collection of tape recordings, motion pictures, and photographs.

In the library of the World Council of Churches, Geneva, Switzerland, Blake's papers are located in the restricted archival collection under the general heading "General Secretariat 1966–72." Included in this material are correspondence (divided into "American" and "Other"), speeches, staff working papers, committee reports, and miscellaneous mimeographed and published monographs and articles. Several boxes of papers are marked "confidential" and deal with staff matters and international negotiations. At the time when I consulted Blake's papers in Geneva (1976), they had not yet been formally organized or identified by any numbering or letter system. There are many duplicate reports and publications. The library staff intends to organize the material in order to make it more readily accessible to scholarly study and investigation.

In this select bibliography, I have not included privately printed or mimeographed sermons and addresses, forewords or prefaces to books, communiqués and announcements in *Monday Morning*, short devotional articles and prayers in National and World Council of Churches publications and *Presbyterian Life*, or book reviews in popular and scholarly periodicals. Virtually all of these items can be found in the Blake Papers in Philadelphia and Geneva. Instead I have tried to include a fair representation of Blake's writing in published form both in the United States and abroad. My general references, especially in regard to the ecumenical movement and the Presbyterian church, reflect the books and articles most useful to me in the preparation of this book and in no way describe the vast amount of material available on these subjects.

All the recorded interviews with Dr. Blake and various friends and associates and all other incidental letters and papers collected during my research process will be sent to the Presbyterian Historical Society. These materials will be indexed in the card catalogue of the Presbyterian Historical Society. Any use of the recorded interviews and/or transcripts for research or citation must be cleared through the Manager of the Presbyterian Historical Society.

General References

BOOKS

Ahlstrom, Sydney E. *A Religious History of the American People.* New Haven and London: Yale University Press, 1972.

Selected Bibliography

Brown, Robert Mc. *The Ecumenical Revolution.* New York: Doubleday and Company, 1967.

————, and Scott, David H. *The Challenge to Reunion.* New York: McGraw-Hill, 1963.

Cavert, Samuel McCrea. *The American Churches in the Ecumenical Movement 1900–1968.* New York: Association Press, 1970.

————. *Church Cooperation and Unity in America 1900–1970.* New York: Association Press, 1970.

Fey, Harold E., ed. *The Ecumenical Advance: A History of the Ecumenical Movement 1948–1968.* Philadelphia: The Westminster Press, 1970.

Fry, John R. *The Trivialization of the United Presbyterian Church.* Philadelphia: The Westminster Press, 1975.

Gaines, David P. *The World Council of Churches: A Study of Its Background and History.* Peterborough, New Hampshire: Richard R. Smith, 1964.

Goodall, Norman. *The Ecumenical Movement,* 2d ed. London: Oxford University Press, 1966.

————. *Ecumenical Progress: A Decade of Change in the Ecumenical Movement.* London: Oxford University Press, 1972.

Hudson, Winthrop. *Religion in America,* 2d ed. New York: Charles Scribner's Sons, 1973.

Johnson, David, ed. *Uppsala to Nairobi: Report of the Central Committee to the Fifth Assembly of the World Council of Churches.* New York and London: Friendship Press and SPCK, 1975.

Loetscher, Lefferts A. *The Broadening Church: A Study of Theological Issues in the Presbyterian Church since 1869.* Philadelphia: The Westminster Press, 1954.

Mackay, John A. *The Presbyterian Way of Life.* Englewood Cliffs, New Jersey: Prentice-Hall Inc., 1960.

Maertens, Marlene. *The Challenge to the Church: The Niemoeller—Blake Conversations.* Philadelphia: The Westminster Press, 1965.

————. *Eugene Carson Blake: Der zweite Generalsekretar des Okumenischen Rates.* Berlin: Lettner-Verlag, 1966.

McNeill, John T., and Nichols, James H. *Ecumenical Testimony: The Concern for Christian Unity within the Reformed and Presbyterian Churches.* Philadelphia: The Westminster Press, 1974.

221

Pradervand, Marcel. *A Century of Service: A History of the World Alliance of Reformed Churches 1875–1975*. Grand Rapids, Michigan: Wm. B. Eerdmans Publishing Company, 1975.

Rouse, Ruth, and Neill, Stephen, eds. *A History of the Ecumenical Movement 1517–1948*. Philadelphia: The Westminster Press, 1967.

Visser 't Hooft, Willem A. *Has the Ecumenical Movement a Future?* Atlanta: John Knox Press, 1976.

———. *Memoirs*. London and Philadelphia: SCM Press and Westminster Press, 1973.

PERIODICALS AND NEWSPAPERS

A.D. Magazine, 1974–76 passim.

Boland, Edward G. "Toward Church Unity and a New Image: An Interview with Eugene Carson Blake." *Pastoral Life* 25 (September 1967): 465–71.

Brown, Robert Mc. "The Blake Proposal: Some Pros and Cons." *Presbyterian Life* 14 (May 1, 1961): 7, 40–42.

———. "Uppsala: An Informal Report." *The Journal of Ecumenical Studies* 5 (Fall 1968): 633–60.

Cassels, Louis. "A Minister Who's Not Afraid to Fight." *Look* 30 (May 31, 1966): 79–82.

The Christian Beacon, 1953–66 passim.

The Christian Century, 1940–76 passim.

Christianity and Crisis, 1950–66 passim.

Christianity Today, 1956–76 passim.

Cox, Harvey G. "The 'New Breed' in American Churches: Sources of Social Activism in American Religion." *Daedalus* 96 (Winter 1967): 135–49.

Crow, Paul A., Jr. "Ecumenism and the Consultation on Church Union." *Journal of Ecumenical Studies* 4 (Fall 1967): 581–602.

Driver, Christopher. "Ecumenical Steer-Buster." The Manchester *Guardian*, February 10, 1967, p. 9.

Selected Bibliography

"Eugene Carson Blake: Zealous Advocate of Church Cooperation." *National Council Outlook* 4 (January 1955): 11, 22.

The Federal Council Bulletin, 1947–50 passim.

Forbes, Bruce David. "William Henry Roberts: Resistance to Change and Bureaucratic Adaption." *Journal of Presbyterian History* 54 (Winter 1976): 405–21.

Freese, Arthur S. "I Believe: An Interview with Eugene Carson Blake." *Modern Maturity* 19 (June–July 1976): 67–69.

Geyer, Alan. "Old and New at Uppsala." *The Christian Century* 85 (August 21, 1968): 1031–37.

Heinze, Frank H. "Eugene Carson Blake: The Call to Geneva." *Presbyterian Life* 19 (March 1, 1966): 7–9, 41.

Heinze, Robert H. "Eugene Carson Blake among 283 Arrested in Baltimore." *Presbyterian Life* 16 (August 1, 1963): 24–27.

The Interchurch News, 1966–72 passim.

Irwin, Virginia. "St. Louis-Born National Churchman." St. Louis *Post-Dispatch*, August 17, 1955, p. 4.

Knight, Hans. "Eugene Carson Blake—Christian Soldier." Philadelphia *Sunday Bulletin Magazine*, February 21, 1965, pp. 16–18.

Low, Ruth. "The Rev. Dr. Eugene C. Blake of New Canaan: Apostle of Ecumenicity." Bridgeport, Connecticut *Sunday Post*, April 10, 1966, p. 4.

McCorkle, Henry L. "The Church's Four-Letter Man." *Presbyterian Life* 7 (December 11, 1954): 7–9.

Monday Morning: A Magazine for Presbyterian Ministers, 1950–66 passim.

National Council Outlook, 1951–66 passim.

The New York *Times*, 1951–56 passim.

Presbyterian Life, 1950–66 passim.

The Presbyterian Outlook, 1950–70 passim.

The Presbyterian Survey, 1955–66 passim.

"Resurgent Protestantism." *Newsweek* 51 (March 28, 1955): 58–59.

Rogers, Cornish. "Black on Blake." *The Christian Century* 89 (October 18, 1972): 1033–34.

Rose, Stephen C. "Eugene Carson Blake: A Welcome-home Interview." *The Christian Century* 89 (October 18, 1972): 1036–39.

Schalk, Adolph. "Eugene Carson Blake: An Administrator with a Casual Approach." *National Catholic Reporter* 3 (March 22, 1967): 1.

Start, Clarissa. "From St. Louis to a Top World Church Post." St. Louis *Post-Dispatch*, February 23, 1966, p. 12.

Thompson, Betty. "Eugene Carson Blake: The End of an Era." *The Christian Century* 89 (September 6, 1972): 864.

"To End a Scandal." *Time* 77 (May 26, 1961): 62–68.

Official Ecclesiastical Records

Minutes and Reports of the Central Committee of the World Council of Churches 1962–72. Geneva: World Council of Churches.

Minutes of the General Assembly of the Presbyterian Church in the United States of America 1940–57.

Minutes of the General Assembly of the United Presbyterian Church in the United States of America 1958–76.

Minutes of the General Council of the Presbyterian Church in the United States of America 1951–57.

Minutes of the General Council of the United Presbyterian Church in the United States of America 1958–66.

Minutes of the Presbytery of Los Angeles of the Presbyterian Church in the United States of America 1940–51.

Minutes of the Session of the First Presbyterian Church of Albany, New York of the Presbyterian Church in the United States of America 1935–40.

Minutes of the Session of the Pasadena Presbyterian Church of Pasadena, California of the Presbyterian Church in the United States of America 1940–51.

The Uppsala Report 1968: Official Report of the Fourth Assembly of the World Council of Churches Uppsala July 4–20, 1968. Geneva: World Council of Churches, 1968.

Selected Bibliography

Personal Communications*

INTERVIEWS

Albany, Group Interview, October 14, 1976.

Babcock, Dorothy and Gilbert, September 27, 1976.

Barraclough, Henry, May 21, 1976.

Blake, Eugene Carson, October 7, 1975; March 3, July 19 and 20, and October 9, 1976; February 28, May 2, and June 28, 1977.

Blake, Howard C., February 23, 1976.

Blake, Rhea Carson Harvey, July 28, 1976.

Brash, Alan, June 23, 1976.

Chapel, Nelson, September 25, 1976.

Chaplin, Priscilla, September 26, 1976.

Elson, Edward L. R., May 31, 1977.

Epps, Paul Dwayne, June 22, 1976.

Finkbeiner, Otto, October 11, 1976.

Gill, David, June 24, 1976.

Harrison, Everett F., September 27, 1976.

Heinze, Frank, March 1, 1977.

Heinze, Robert, May 27, 1976.

McCord, James I., October 8, 1976.

McKeag, George, May 17, 1976.

Neigh, Kenneth, October 10, 1976.

Northam, Frank, June 24, 1976.

Pasadena, Group Interviews, September 27 and 28, 1976.

Payne, Paul, October 5, 1976.

Schram, William C., April 13, 1977.

Scott, Marshal L., July 5, 1976.

Shane, Samuel W., May 21, 1976.

Smith, John Coventry, May 21, 1976.

Smith, Wilmina Rowland, May 6, 1977.

Swan, Howard, September 28, 1976.

Thompson, William P., October 11, 1976.

LETTERS AND TAPES

Blake, Howard C., March 8, 1976.

Bokeleale, Itofo B., January 24, 1977.

---

* All interviews are on tape and have been deposited in the Presbyterian Historical Society archives, Philadelphia, Pennsylvania. All letters and tapes are addressed to the author and have been placed in the same depository.

Brown, Robert McAfee, November 29, 1976.
Cameron, Truman D., April 10, 1976.
Fleming, Jean, September 26, 1976.
Glenn, Leslie, April 12, 1976.
Hunt, Mabel, November 18, 1976.
Jackson, Gordon E., September 14, 1976.
Johnson, R. Park, May 10, 1976.
Laws, William R., Jr., March 24, 1976.
Lloyd, Ralph W., September 2, 1976.
Mehl, Roger, October 14, 1976.
Moore, Glenn W., July 5, 1976.
Payne, Paul, July 24, 1976.
Potter, Philip, October 6, 1976.
Scott, Marshal, March 29, 1976.
Stair, Lois H., July 1, 1976.
Taylor, Theophilus M., January 7, 1977.
Tiffany, Douglas, October 6, 1976.
Van den Heuvel, Albert, April 20, 1976.
Willebrands, John Cardinal, December 22, 1976.
Wright, Paul S., April 25, 1976.

Publications by Eugene Carson Blake

BOOKS

Christian Faith: Bulwark of Freedom. Houston: Elsevier Press, Inc., 1956.

The Church in the Next Decade. New York and London: Macmillan Company, 1966.

He Is Lord of All. Philadelphia: The Westminster Press, 1958.

Presbyterian Law for the Local Church (edited by Blake). Philadelphia: Office of the General Assembly, 1953, 1956, 1957, 1959, 1960.

Presbyterian Law for the Presbytery (with Richard B. Shaw). Philadelphia: Office of the General Assembly, 1958, 1959, 1960, 1961, 1962, 1964, 1965, 1966.

ARTICLES

"Address on the Occasion of the Conference of the International Labour Organisation." *The Ecumenical Review* 18 (June 1969): 268.

Selected Bibliography

"Address to Pope Paul VI on His Visit to the World Council of Churches." *The Ecumenical Review* 18 (June 1969): 265.

"The American Churches and Ecumenical Mission." In *The Ecumenical Era in Church and Society. A Symposium in Honor of John A. Mackay*, edited by Edward Jurji. New York: Macmillan, 1959, pp. 75–91.

"The American Dream: Two Hundred Years After." *The Princeton Seminary Bulletin* 68 (Winter 1976): 16–23.

"Anxiety, Frustration and Subconscious Hatred." *Pittsburgh Perspective* 2 (June 1961): 11–16.

"The Basis of Christian Fellowship." In *The Nature of the Unity We Seek*, edited by Paul Minear. St. Louis: Bethany Press, 1958, pp. 136–42.

"The Character of Religious Authority in Protestantism." *The Journal of Religious Thought* 5 (Autumn–Winter 1948): 15–24.

"Christian Culture Requires a Two Way Conversation." In *Christian Perspective in Contemporary Culture*, edited by Frank S. Baker, New York: Twayne Publishers, 1962, pp. 15–26.

"A Church Both Evangelical and Ecumenical." *The Princeton Seminary Bulletin* 65 (October 1973): 19–24.

"A Churchman's Plan for Dealing with Russia." *U.S. News and World Report* 42 (January 4, 1957): 112–14.

"Covenant Old and New." *The Reformed and Presbyterian World* 31 (September–December 1970): 157–62.

"Do-Gooders? Let's Accept the Label." *Presbyterian Life* 10 (October 5, 1957): 6–7.

"The Ecumenical Movement." In *Contemporary Christian Trends: Perspectives on the Present*, edited by William M. Pinson. Waco, Texas: Word Books, 1972, pp. 106–22.

"The Ecumenical Movement and What to Do about It." *Digest of the Proceedings of the Fifth Meeting of the Consultation on Church Union* 5 (Spring 1966): 33–35.

"The Ecumenical Task of a General Secretary." In *Four Faces of Christian Ministry: Essays in Honor of A. Dale Fiers*, edited by Robert L. Friedly, St. Louis: Bethany Press, 1973, pp. 43–52.

"Freedom and Authority in Church and State." *Presbyterian Life* 4 (October 27, 1951): 8–10, 38.

"General Secretary's Louvain Address, August, 1971." *The Ecumenical Review* 24 (January 1972): 26–29.

"God and American Education." *Journal of the New York State School Boards* 18 (December 1954): 37–42.

"Ground Rules for Theological Debate." *Monday Morning* 30 (April 26, 1965): 3–5.

"The Horizons of Knowledge and Religious Faith." *Cross Currents* 19 (1968/1969): 441–51.

"How Our Church Relates Itself and Its Program to That of Other Christian Churches in the Light of Its Own Confessional Position." *The Princeton Seminary Bulletin* 54 (July 1960): 23–25.

"How the Church Contributes to the Transformation of Society." *The Ecumenical Review* 18 (July 1966): 461–63.

"How the World Council Serves the Churches." *Monday Morning* 25 (April 4, 1960): 9–11.

"Human Rights in Uruguay" (with G. Bromley Oxnam). *The Ecumenical Review* 25 (January 1973): 112–13.

"Identity, Power and Community." *The Ecumenical Review* 23 (April 1971): 105–17.

"Is the Religious Boom a Spiritual Bust?" *Look* 19 (September 20, 1955): 27–31.

"A Letter from the Stated Clerk to Members of the United Presbyterian Church in the United States of America." *Presbyterian Life* 19 (June 1, 1966): 5–8.

"Letter on the Vietnam War." *The Ecumenical Review* 24 (July 1972): 351–52.

"Looking for God's Miracles." *The Lamp* 66 (July 1968): 5–11.

"Lund: City of Questions." *Presbyterian Life* 5 (September 20, 1952): 21.

"Militant Christianity: Defense and Offense." *The Princeton Seminary Bulletin* 59 (June 1966): 4–11.

"The Ministry and Church Union." *McCormick Quarterly* 17 (March 1964): 30–34.

"Mission and Unity—Slogan or Program? A Searching Appraisal of the Challenge to Unite Presbyterian Churches in America." *Presbyterian Life* 8 (January 24, 1955): 14–15, 38.

"More Than Mere Independence." *Presbyterian Life* 17 (February 15, 1964): 7–9.

"The New Ecumenical Reformation." *Christianity and Crisis* 15 (January 23, 1956): 187–89.

"No Wall Is as High as Heaven." *Presbyterian Outlook* 138 (July 2, 1956): 7–9.

"Open Letter on Human Rights." *The Ecumenical Review* 24 (July 1972): 347–50.

"The Presbyterian Church." In *Congregational Christian Journal Advance* 145 (November 16, 1957): 14–15.

"The Progress, Promise and Problems of the Ecumenical Movement." *Studies* 60 (Spring 1971): 23–32.

"Prophet and Priest, but Not a King." *The Princeton Seminary Bulletin* 56 (October 1962): 27–31.

"Proposed Methodist Mergers: Should Six Become One?" *Classmate* 72 (October 1964): 20–21.

"Reconciling Church." *Expository Times* 81 (August 1970): 330–33.

"The Religious Issue in This Campaign: A Protestant View." *The Reader's Digest* 77 (September 1960): 68–70.

"Report of the General Secretary." *The Ecumenical Review* 24 (October 1972): 411–21.

"Report on Africa." *Monday Morning* 25 (January 11, 1960): 3–5.

"Report on Japan and Korea." *The Christian Century* 72 (February 16, 1955): 207–8.

"Rights of State and Church." *The Churchman* 169 (October 15, 1955): 7.

"Russia Revisited." *Presbyterian Life* 15 (November 1, 1962): 8–12, 38–39.

"The Servant, Not the Master." *National Council Outlook* 4 (October 1955): 5.

"Seven Questions about COCU: Excerpts from Statement by World Council of Churches' General Secretary." *The Christian Century* 87 (February 15, 1970): 242–43.

"Should the Code of Ethics in Public Life Be Absolute or Relative?" *The Annals of the American Academy of Political and Social Science* 363 (January 1966): 4–11.

"Some Personal Observations on COEMAR." *Monday Morning* 23 (July 1958): 10–11.

"Special Communication on Baltimore Arrest." *Monday Morning* 28 (August 1963): 12–14, and (November 4, 1963): 12–13.

"Speech in Honor of John C. Bennett." *Christianity and Crisis* 31 (May 3, 1971): 78–79.

"The State of the National Council of Churches." *Triennial Report of the National Council of Churches of Christ in the U. S. A.* (1957): 7–9.

"The Strategy of the Churches." *The Christian Century* 72 (March 23, 1955): 364–67.

"Tax Exemption and the Churches." *Christianity Today* 3 (August 3, 1959): 6–8.

"That Controversial Ecumenical Movement." *The Lawrentian* 29 (Summer 1965): 14–15.

"Three Guides for Decision." *Crossroads* 6 (October–December 1955): 3–4.

"To Avoid Arrogance and Idolatry." *The Presbyterian Outlook* 158 (September 27, 1976): 7.

"Toward the Reunion of Christ's Church." *The Christian Century* 77 (December 21, 1960): 1508–11. Also in *Presbyterian Life* 14 (January 1, 1961): 8–9, 38–41.

"The Trustees' Responsibility for a Learned Ministry." *Theological Education* 4 (Winter 1968): 662–63.

"The Twenty-Fifth Hour." *Convergence* 5 (1968): 6–8.

"Two Years Later." In *The Challenge to Reunion*, by Robert Mc. Brown and David H. Scott. New York: McGraw-Hill, 1963, pp. 258–70.

"Uncertain Sounds." *Christianity and Crisis* 15 (June 27, 1955): 83–85.

"The Union Proposal Two Years Later." *The Christian Century* 80 (May 27, 1963): 394–98.

"A United Church: Evangelical, Catholic, and Reformed." *Thought* 41 (Spring 1966): 52–60.

"Uppsala and Afterwards." In *The Ecumenical Advance: A History of the Ecumenical Movement 1948–1968*, edited by Harold E. Fey. Philadelphia: The Westminster Press, 1970, pp. 411–46.

"Visser 't Hooft: A Tribute." *The Christian Century* 83 (November 30, 1966): 1467–69.

"Wanted: Christian Scholars." *The Christian Scholar* 39 (December 1956): 260–65.

"Ways the Church Can Transform Society." *Face to Face* 4 (February 1970): 31–32.

"Why Does the National Council of Churches Sponsor a Conference on Religion and Public Education?" *Religious Education* 51 (July–August 1956): 259–65.

SERMONS

"The Bulwarks of Peace." In *Best Sermons Protestant Edition 1966–1968*, edited by George P. Butler. New York: Trident Press, 1968, pp. 242–46.

"The Church and the Western World: Its Belief." In *Best Sermons Protestant Edition 1951–1952*, edited by George P. Butler. New York: Macmillan, 1952, pp. 150–56.

"The Crack in the Bell." In *Best Sermons Protestant Edition 1946*, edited by George P. Butler. New York: Harper, 1946, pp. 185–90.

"Faith Is a Two-Edged Sword." *National Council Outlook* 5 (October 1956): 19.

"Good Faith." In *Representative American Speeches 1957–1958*, edited by A. Craig Baird. New York: H. W. Wilson Company, 1958, pp. 168–73.

"Jesus Christ, Lord of All Life." In *Herald of the Evangel*, edited by Edwin T. Dahlberg. St. Louis: Bethany Press, 1965, pp. 29–43. Also in *Presbyterian Life* 18 (January 1, 1965): 11–15, 32.

"Law and Order and Christian Duty." In *The Pulpit Speaks on Race*, edited by Alfred T. Davies. Nashville: Abingdon Press, 1965, pp. 107–18.

"A Living Response to Christ and His Gospel." *National Council Outlook* 4 (March 1955): 3.

"The Mark of Maturity." *Presbyterian Outlook* 133 (April 16, 1951): 5–6.

"Now Is the Time for Living." *Lawrentian* 38 (July 1974): 7–10.

"Prayer and Morality." *Theology Today* 29 (July 1972): 133–37.

"The Strangest Place." In *Here Is My Method: The Art of Sermon Construction*, edited by Donald MacLeod. Los Angeles: Fleming H. Revell Company, 1952, pp. 25–36.

"The Sum Is More." In *Preaching on Pentecost and Christian Unity*, edited by Alton M. Motter. Philadelphia: Fortress Press, 1965, pp. 18–25.

"That Man at My Gate." In *Best Sermons Protestant Edition 1962*, edited by George P. Butler. Princeton: Von Nostrand, 1962, pp. 237–42.

"War and Resurrection." In *Best Sermons Protestant Edition 1944*, edited by George P. Butler. Chicago: Ziff-Davis Publishers, 1944, pp. 202–7.

"Where the Trumpet Call?" *Presbyterian Survey* 59 (November 1955): 15–16, 59.

"A Young Man Came to Our Town." *Presbyterian Life* 2 (April 16, 1949): 13–15.

INDEX

233